MY
ANGRY SON

MY
ANGRY
SOMETIMES

SON

LOVE IS NOT ENOUGH

by

BARBARA BARTOCCI

With a foreword by JOHN BARTOCCI

DONALD I. FINE, INC.
New York

Library of Congress Catalogue Card Number: 84-073515
ISBN: 0-917657-16-0
Manufactured in the United States of America
10   9   8   7   6   5   4   3   2   1

This book is printed on acid free paper. The paper in this book meets the guidelines for permanence and durability of the Committee on Production Guidelines for Book Longevity of the Council on Library Resources.

With the exception of my name, those of my children, and of my husband and late husband, the names of all characters appearing in this book have been changed in the interest of privacy. Similarly, the occupations of the family members referred to in the family therapy sessions at the home have also been changed.

ove and affection to

as managing editor of Readers Digest,
e to write our story...

, who made such a difference in our lives...

And most of all, to

Bill, who has been not only a loving husband and father,
but an excellent editor whose judgment and keen eye helped
this story be the best it could be.

FOREWORD
BY JOHN BARTOCCI

WHEN MY father was killed in the Vietnam War, it nearly destroyed my family. For years afterwards, we lived in constant turmoil. Our house became a battleground for angry, noisy arguments that sometimes lasted for hours. This intensified after my mother remarried. We used our tongues like daggers, especially my mother and I, to stab at each other, degrade each other. We hacked away until there was almost nothing left and then we would break into tears, sorry for the hurt we had inflicted, because deep down, we knew we loved each other very much.

Most of the problems stemmed directly from me. I had never gotten over the death of my father, never dealt with the grief, and neither I nor my parents realized this. I was angry at my father for abandoning us, for making our lives so much tougher. I took this anger and lashed out at everyone around me, making life miserable for as many people as I could.

When I was thirteen, my parents sent me to live in a home for emotionally disturbed boys. At the time, I hated them for it. I felt as if I was being kicked out of the family and I swore I would never forgive them for it. Today, I am thankful that they had the courage to get help; not just for me, but for my entire family. We had hurt each other too deeply to make it on our own. We needed help.

I know now that it was not easy for my mother, as a single working parent, to raise a family. My mother felt she failed us. Yet today, all three of her children are happy, well-adjusted young adults, capable of taking care of themselves and with the skills and emotional balance to become successful.

Admittedly, we did not have an easy childhood. After my mother's remarriage, life seemed to get even tougher, because our stepdad was more demanding and expected my mother, in turn, to be more demanding of us. Unlike our mother, our stepdad held us accountable for our behavior and actions. I realize now that a successful parent is not someone who provides a carefree environment for a child, but someone who cares enough to raise that child to be a self-sustaining adult—no matter what the cost. That's what my stepdad tried to do.

It was hell for me to adjust to all the restraints of a boys' home. I felt like a freak, kicked out of the family and labeled "unfit." A part of me still feels a sense of loss at being denied three years with my family. However, I realize that if we had tried to continue on our own, as we were doing, we would surely have ended in disaster. My biggest fear at the time was that the stress of living in our turbulent household might lead me to some irrational act such as suicide. Occasionally, I wondered what it would be like to just do away with myself. I never got to the stage of actually planning suicide, but there were boys at the Boys' Home who did.

Unfortunately, suicide has become an answer for many children and teenagers today. That's why it is important for parents to communicate with their children. Parents need to find out what is really going on in a child's mind, so that they can get help if it is needed. This is hard to do when a lot of fighting is going on in the home.

It was impossible for me to communicate with my parents because we spent so much time arguing and hurting each other. A child has to find someone to talk to, though. I don't mean everyone has to find an expensive psychiatrist— an adult friend or a counselor at school can help. But when problems *are* severe, psychiatric help is the best bet.

There are many influences that destroy family relationships: drugs and alcohol, divorce and remarriage, death. I experienced them all.

By age thirteen, every kid in America will have an opportunity to smoke marijuana or try other drugs. I tasted marijuana when I was twelve, before I'd even tried cigarettes. Of course, it wasn't long before I smoked those, too. The worst part about marijuana and other drugs is the deception. Children start living a lie. After I started smoking pot, I became defensive around my parents. I treated normal conversations as if they were interrogations. I built up a wall to block out my parents. I would have outbursts of anger during which I would accuse them of prying—anything to protect the lie.

Whenever you have a relationship where one side is continually lying to the other, you're going to have problems. It's impossible to lie consistently to the people you live with. Eventually, the truth will come out, and then there is no trust left. Relationships can't work without trust.

Divorce strains family relationships, too. No child can handle a divorce without help, although today, with divorce such a common occurrence, it's rare for a child not to be able to talk to at least one friend who shares the problem. Parents can make it easier by making, together, those decisions that affect the child's life.

Death is even more significant than divorce. I was seven when my father died. By age eleven, I had a temper like a wildcat. I was placed in outpatient therapy, but by then I had built up too strong a wall. I needed discipline and around-the-clock supervision. It was easy for me to ignore my weekly visits with the psychologist, but I could not ignore the Boys' Home.

Remarriage can be even harder for a child to deal with than death or divorce. Step-parents make a child feel threatened. Suddenly, a stranger is living with the family. I used to think my stepdad was trying to steal my mother's love from me. It was harder still, after I entered the Boys' Home, to know that a stranger was living with my family when I wasn't allowed to. Next to my father's death, my mother's remarriage to Bill had the most impact on my life.

I have had some experience with all the major traumas that can occur in a child's life, but there are many families that live in painful chaos even without divorce or death or drugs. Stressful family conditions are common, even among the rich. I saw this at the Boys' Home.

There was a time when I was ashamed of my family because we had so many problems. I felt as if we were the only family in all of suburbia experiencing such difficulties. I was afraid of what my friends might think if they saw our family arguments, so I didn't invite many friends to my home.

My mother felt ashamed, too. She felt ashamed of herself and her inability to raise children. She felt ashamed of me. She was angry at me for making her job as a parent so hard. She was afraid people would see how messed up our family was and see her as a failure.

Well, now we have written this book. It is a book about our lives and the problems we shared. I wrote the sections about my life in the boys' home and my mother incorporated the sections into the story as she lived it.

We're not ashamed today. Our family is strong, bonded by love and understanding. We are all good friends and enjoy each other's company. I would be missing out on a lot of love if my parents—my mother and my stepdad— had not had the courage to suffer all the embarrassment and pain that it took to get help. The money they spent was an investment in my future.

It is my hope that parents will find this book a source of inspiration and courage. There were times when all hope seemed lost, but we pulled through. Maybe by sharing some of our experiences, other families will keep working towards building a loving relationship. It can happen. We were fortunate to get good help. Not everyone can find such help, but if you can—believe me, it's worth it.

CHAPTER ONE

HE BEGAN to scream as soon as we turned the corner of the graveled road and the red brick buildings came into sight.

"I won't go! I won't! You can't make me! I'll run away! I'll kill myself! I swear, I'll kill myself!" Four-letter words spewed from his mouth, and he twisted and turned on the car seat until I feared he might yank open the door and jump.

We finally reached the entrance. My husband braked hard and sounded his horn. We had called before leaving home, so they knew we were on our way.

Two burly young men, both in their early twenties, hurried out of the building's front door toward our car. A screen door banged behind them.

Bart was still screaming, but now tears spilled, streaking his cheeks. He grabbed my hands, clinging to me piteously.

"No, Mom, please! Don't sent me here! I'll be good. I promise! I'll be good! I'll change. Please, Mom, no..."

The young men had the car's back door open and were pulling Bart out as he screamed for me again. "No, Mom, no..." He was dragged, still kicking and screaming, up the walk and into the building.

A tall, gray-haired woman in her early sixties stepped from the porch to our car. Mrs. Tabor. We had met her when we signed the papers.

"It's all right," she said. "Remember, you're bringing him here because this is where he needs to be. Go home now."

But as she retreated inside the building, I could still hear my son screaming. The sound left me feeling nauseated inside.

What were we doing here? I wondered wildly.

How could I be leaving my son—my son!—in a home for severely disturbed teenage boys?

"...neurotic character disorder...destructive family relationships..." the psychiatrist had said. Words. Meaningless words.

What I remembered was the remark of a doctor we knew. "Emotional disturbance... mental illness... what's the difference?" he shrugged.

And the remarks of my husband's business colleague... "You're sending your kid to a boys' home? Listen, friend, haven't you heard of those four old-fashioned letters: L-O-V-E? Try a little of that, instead of dumping your kid in some home."

Oh, God. Was he right? Why wasn't our love enough?

The screams faded.

We were left alone, my husband and I, standing in the grassy park-like area that surrounded the Boys' Home. It looked like a school more than an institution. A red brick dorm stood to one side, a gymnasium was just visible through the trees, the swimming pool was alive with the splashes and shouts of swimmers on this hot July day. No one had looked up at the screams. Were they so used to them? I wondered.

"Count on your son being here at least a year and a half," warned Dr. George Kruepper, the admitting psychiatrist, in his Oklahoma twang.

In fact, the year and a half would stretch far longer, but mercifully we didn't know that then. I stood on the grass by the open door of our car, the hot prickles of July sweat alive on my arms and the summer sounds of insects and a lawn mower's drone heavy in my ears, and it was all I could do to think of eighteen months.

What had brought us to this point, I couldn't help thinking again. How had it happened?

"Barbara," said Bill, "it's time to go." His voice was gentle. I climbed into the car, and, with a spin of tires against gravel, we left the Boys' Home—and my son—behind.

Both of us were silent on the drive home—a drive we would come to know well in the long months and years ahead. The Home was just twenty minutes from our house, but in the land-rich Midwest, that put it out in the country, adjacent to a small farm town.

We sped down the freeway, back to suburbia. On the way, we passed the local Catholic church. I suddenly had a wild desire to laugh. What was a nice Catholic girl like me doing in a situation like this?

Already my life and the lives of my children had departed from the happy-ever-after middle-class script I had once expected. Yet reality still left me surprised, angry, and filled with guilt. The responsibility was mine to raise my children right. And I hadn't succeeded. I was a failure.

"Your son, Bart, is thirteen years old chronologically," Dr. Kruepper explained to me, puffing on his pipe, "but emotionally, he's stuck at age seven. A very angry seven. And he'll stay that age all his life if you don't get help."

Seven.

Bart was seven when his father died.

"We're home," Bill said, swinging the car into the garage. I didn't move to get out, just sat there, staring ahead. "Are you coming inside?"

"In a minute."

It had been winter, not summer, the day Bart's father told us goodbye, but it was a California winter's day, with the January sun warm and mellow above the pastel expanse of San Diego.

Barty sat on the edge of our king-size bed, watching as his Daddy adjusted his pilot's wings and brushed lint off the sleeve of his gold-striped lieutenant commander's uniform.

Outside our Labrador retriever, Val, barked in morning concert with the dog next door and I could hear the shouts of the neighbors' kids as they headed toward school. How ordinary it all sounded!

Allison, with the gawkiness of an eight-year-old, leaned against the bedroom doorjamb. Andy sat on the floor next to John's suitcase, inspecting with his usual intensity the socks and underwear and crisply starched white shirts.

"So. Is it time to leave?" I asked.

"Almost."

John turned from the mirror and sat down on the bed. Barty's eyes, the same clear blue as his father's, examined his father's face carefully. He reached up one hand, the fingers still little-boy dimpled, and gently touched John's chin.

John glanced over at me. His eyes held a shiny brightness that made me swallow, hard. Then he blinked and gave Barty's small shoulders a squeeze.

"You'll be a big boy of seven by the time I get back."

"I'm a big boy now."

"Me, too," piped Andy. Indignantly, he jumped up and slid between his father's knees. "I'm big. I'm four."

"You're both big boys. Big enough to be good brothers for my princess..." His arms opened wide and Allison, looking almost shy, came towards him from the doorway. "I want all of you to promise to be good for Mommy."

"We will," Barty promised. His hand moved up to pat his father's cheek. "But I wish you wouldn't go."

John crushed them to him, his three precious children. The heavy lump in my chest grew larger. Each child got a kiss. Then he pushed himself up and reached for his white Navy hat. A quick adjustment before the mirror and— always his very last act—he picked up our silver-framed wedding picture and placed it on top of his shirts. The suitcase zipper racketed loudly in the quiet bedroom.

In our wedding photo, John wore a rakish grin and starched summer dress whites. His Naval Academy class-mates, on either side of us, made a canopy over our heads with their silver dress swords. How jubilant I felt as we walked between them that June morning in 1958. How grown up! What difference did it make that I was only nineteen?

"Where will you live?" asked one of the wedding guests.

"Pensacola," I replied. "John is training to be a naval aviator. A carrier jet pilot." Merely saying the words sent a romantic shiver through me. *Imagine being married to a jet pilot!*

"Oh yes," I said to another guest. "We plan to have at least four children. Maybe more." The thought of lots of children didn't scare me. All the womens' magazines provided ample reinforcement for the loving delights of a large family. Besides, John and I were both Catholic.

Our reception neared its end. "I'll go change," I whispered to John. But as I started to leave, my father approached. His arm went around me.

"I'm going to miss this little girl." His voice deepened in mock sternness. "You take good care of her, you hear me?"

"Yessir!"

I reached up and kissed my father's cheek. "Part of me will always be your little girl."

"She says I remind her of you," added John.

"Is that so?" my father said. But I could tell he was pleased. I tossed kisses at them both and ran upstairs.

My college roommate helped me change. "I'll miss you," said Shar.

I hugged her. "I'll miss you, too. But I'm so happy. I feel like a fairy-tale princess who's married the crown prince."

"And plans to live happily ever after?"

"Of course!"

I ran downstairs, tossed my bouquet so Shar would catch it; then together, laughing and waving, John and I roared off in his new Corvette. I leaned back against the leather seats, letting the wind catch my hair. The diamond and gold miniature of John's Naval Academy ring was a welcome weight on my left hand.

"I'm so happy," I whispered. And I felt, then, that I would always be.

Pensacola in June meant muggy heat, cockroaches that crackled when stepped on, and a tiny apartment whose rented plastic furniture stuck to our legs whenever we sat down. We couldn't afford air conditioning.

But Pensacola also meant white sandy beaches on the weekends, coolers of beer and lots of laughter with the other student pilots and their wives. One of John's Annapolis classmates lived next door. Tod and Janet, John and I often went out together.

While the men practiced taking off and landing in bright yellow T-28 trainer planes, we wives compared notes on wedding gifts and traded recipes and discussed how to be good Navy Wives. We never discussed careers of our own. Our careers, we felt, lay in supporting husbands. I was determined to be the best Navy Wife ever.

John was on an early morning flight schedule. This meant we rose at four a.m., the darkness wrapped around us like a soggy blanket. While John pulled on his orange flight suit, I fried eggs and bacon. Sometimes I went back to bed when he left. Other times I stayed up and read.

One morning, around eight, while I was reading, sirens went off at the air base. They had a peculiar wail, different from the civilian police and fire sirens. I dropped my book, pulled on my robe, and ran outside to our tiny front stoop. Janet, next door, came running out, too. In a few minutes we saw it: a thin spume of black smoke rising in the early morning air.

When the navy chaplain's car pulled up, we recognized it instantly. He stepped out, a tall, slender man in khakis that had already wilted in the heat. He stood by his car door for a moment, consulting a small slip of paper. Then he wiped his face with a large white handkerchief, and started up the walk.

A great stillness fell within me. I couldn't look at Janet. The two of us stood and waited. The chaplain reached the small patch of dried brown grass that edged our apartments. He looked at me. My breath stopped. Then he walked up the two small steps to Janet's stoop.

I had never experienced death before. Not the death of a young man twenty-two years old who had sat at our kitchen table, drinking beer.

I clutched John to me that night. Our bodies were sweaty and slipped against each other, but all that mattered was holding him close. "Don't you die," I whispered fiercely in the Florida darkness. "Promise me you won't?"

He didn't reply.

"Promise!" I said again, and tears mingled with sweat.

Now the tears were John's. I could taste them. "I promise."

Then we cried together, because our friend had died and we were sad and young and scared.

But life was stronger than death, and life seemed to be everywhere we looked. I looked at my rounded belly in the mirror. John came up behind me, placed his hands over mine. "You sure there's a baby in there?" he said, his voice teasing.

"That's what the doctor says."

"Baby boy Bartocci."

"It could be a girl."

"Doesn't matter. We'll love it. Him. Her."

I rubbed the smooth skin of my belly, feeling in awe of this baby growing inside me. We had been married four months. I was nineteen and a half. Yet I didn't feel too young. Around me, the other navy wives were blossoming, too. I felt as if I had joined a special club.

A couple named Miller already had a baby. Jim was a naval air cadet, and he and Janie had been married longer than the rest of us. They brought their baby boy with them to our casual beer-and-pretzel parties, and the wives who were not pregnant looked on enviously.

John and I soon traded in the Corvette for a blue Ford station wagon, and one month after our first wedding anniversary, I gave birth to Allison. From the minute the doctor plopped her on my belly, eight pounds of squalling infant, I adored her. "Every mother should have a daughter," my mother had once told a friend within my hearing. Now I understood what she meant.

Allison was such a good baby, greeting our nervous ministrations with smiling aplomb. We took her out with us at night, and she slept with no fuss in makeshift beds in the homes of our friends. When we journeyed across country to John's first squadron assignment in California, she traveled happily, never objecting to the taste of strange water or the constant shift in surroundings. From the first, Allison showed the capacity to handle change.

In San Diego, we bought a house in a neighborhood of other young married couples. The squeals of children and clank of tricycles made noisy beginnings to our mornings. On Friday nights, the aroma from charcoal fires filled the air. Most of the other husbands were civilians who car pooled into downtown San Diego for jobs in banks and insurance offices. I still didn't know many wives who worked. Most of us in the neighborhood spent our mornings like the women in television commercials, waxing kitchen floors and cleaning house. In the afternoons we gardened or joined one another on someone's patio to watch our kids play.

A few months after we moved in I said to John, "Let's have another baby."

"So soon?"

"If we have our children eighteen months apart, they'll grow up as friends."

John Bartocci II (we gave him his grandfather's middle name) was born in May, twenty-two months after Allison. He was a round, dimpled baby with blue eyes and downy hair the color of spun sunlight. So that he wouldn't be dubbed "Little John" we called him Bart, John's Naval Academy nickname.

Allison, with her sturdy, practical nature, took the new intruder in stride. When I let her hold him and give him his bottle, she touched him gently, without jealousy.

John adored his new son. "You're my Barty-Boy," he'd say, scooping him into his arms.

Barty was as happy as his sister had been. I remember the sweet, milky scent of him as I buried my nose in his belly, nuzzling him until he chuckled with delight.

Together we were a happy family. I didn't feel housebound. My life was what I wanted it to be, what I expected. Twice a week, when my turn came for the car, I traded

18

babysitting with a neighbor and ran errands and bought groceries. I also took a class at our local college. At night, after the children were in bed, John and I watched television, and on weekends someone in the squadron usually threw a party or we would join a group of friends at the officers' club. It wasn't that much different from Pensacola, and again we settled into a contented lifestyle, just as I'd expected it would be.

Occasionally, on the news, we heard Vietnam mentioned.

"Where is Vietnam?" I asked.

"Oh," John said casually, "next to Thailand, I think." It had no connection with our lives.

But in 1964, the Gulf of Tonkin made the news. We were now living in Monterey, California, where John earned a graduate degree at the naval postgraduate school, and where Andrew became our Monterey baby, born two years after Barty.

John now sat riveted to the television set as news commentators discussed what the Tonkin Gulf incident meant for American involvement in Vietnam.

"It means we're in the game for sure!" he said. "And here I am," he added, in frustration, "stuck on the sidelines, going to school."

"Hey," I protested, "Is this the same man who said, just last Sunday, how wonderful it is to have three years of shore duty with our family?"

John reached down and plucked Andrew from his infant seat. Andrew, long and skinny compared to Barty's dimpled roundness, reached up and grabbed his daddy's nose. John laughed and wiggled his nose until Andrew laughed, too. It was their favorite game. Barty, who was playing on the rug with his Tonka truck, jumped up and ran over to stand beside his daddy's chair.

"Me, too, Daddy. Me, too."

John grinned and reached out one arm to circle his two-and-a-half-year-old son. We had commented, privately, how intense Barty's needs seemed to be for a show of love. Especially where his father was concerned.

19

"He follows you around like a little puppy dog," I'd once commented. I thought it was endearing. And it gave me some relief. Three children below the age of four were a handful. My blithe wedding talk of "four children—or more" was beginning to seem unrealistic. John and I had never practiced birth control—only the Catholic "rhythm method"—but lately, I had heard that some priests were looking the other way when women went on the pill. I thought I might check into it. I loved our children deeply, but they had so many needs! Thank God, I thought, that John was such a loving, involved father.

He looked at me now with a shamefaced grin. "You're right. I *am* glad to have this time with the kids. Flying in the war—if it turns into a war—will come soon enough."

Allison emerged from the bedroom hallway, her face framed in a neat "Dutch girl" cut. Her friend, Kim, wandered out behind her. Allison and Kim played Barbie doll by the hour, although if Kim wasn't available, Allison played just as contentedly by herself.

"Daddy," she said, "Will you sing us the Old Witches' song?"

The news was over; John turned off the TV. "Sure, kids. Let me get my guitar." John was a good natural tenor and he liked singing for the kids. The neighborhood children called him "Uncle John" and on weekends, like a pied piper in blue jeans, I'd see him circled by a group of kids on our patio, strumming and singing and making them laugh.

He was also the family disciplinarian. Whenever the kids got too obstreperous, I'd warn, "Settle down, or I'll have your Daddy give you 'The Word.'" "The Word" had become our family shorthand. At first John would say sternly, "Okay, kids, The Word is: no more noise or you go to your rooms!" Eventually, all he had to do was point a finger and say, "Okay, kids, you've heard 'The Word'!" Whatever was going on would magically stop. *If* The Word came from their Daddy.

John sang on our camping trips too, and we camped a

lot while we lived in Monterey, bouncing our way over rutted dirt roads into the back country of the High Sierras. John showed infinite patience, taking Allison and Barty with him to fish in the cold mountain streams while Andrew and I shared the camp ground. I was becoming worried about Andrew. By now, he was past two and still not talking! There was certainly nothing slow about him physically. He never sat still. But why didn't he talk?

"Barbara, it's a good thing you don't worry about me the way you worry about that boy," John said with a grin. "I'd never dare fly."

"How do you know I don't worry?"

"Because you promised me you wouldn't."

"Well, remember what you promised me. Back in Pensacola."

The grin left his face and we fell silent.

We both knew what lay on the horizon.

It seemed like no time before our three years in Monterey ended and John got his new orders. San Diego . . . and flying combat over Vietnam.

It was time for us to drive to the ship. John finished zipping his suitcase over our wedding picture, and Barty reached for the handle. "Let me help you, Daddy. Let me help."

The bag weighed almost as much as he did. John smiled. "Tell you what, son, you carry this—" he handed Barty a folder of papers—"these are more important. Okay?" Barty beamed and strutted off. Allison slid her hand quietly into her father's and walked beside him to the car. Andrew hung back by the bed until I reminded him to stop dawdling and come along.

We were silent on the drive to the harbor. So much had been said—and not said. We were a career navy family so I never questioned whether John should go to Vietnam. But fear curdled inside me.

Barty sat very close to his father. His face had grown

almost panicky when I told him to hop in the back seat with his brother and sister. Now he sat up front, between us, one hand holding tight to his Daddy's arm.

I recalled the afternoon—last summer, had it been? — when John and I sat outside on our patio, watching Barty play with a friend. The two boys had argued about something and the neighbor boy left in a huff. Barty watched him go, a forlorn, bereft expression on his face.

"You know," John said slowly, "I don't know what it is about Barty, but I think he'll have a tougher time growing up. He's very sensitive." He paused. "I have a special feeling about Barty, Barbara. I love all three, you know that, but I feel a—a special closeness to Barty."

"I'm glad." And I was glad, as I had been in Monterey, when we first noticed Barty's intense need for attention from John.

I was spending my time, lately, worrying about Andrew. His slowness to speak had finally been diagnosed as a speech impediment. We were getting help for that. But now his nursery school teacher had recommended additional tests. In a tentative voice, she had even suggested "an electro-encephalogram." Why, I worried, did she think we should measure Andrew's brain-wave pattern?

With that on my mind, it was a relief to let John worry about Barty; to let Barty be "his Daddy's boy."

And now that John was leaving? I shook my head and looked quickly out the window, burying the thought.

The aircraft carrier came into view, reminding me that he was really leaving. He held each of us tightly as we bravely said goodbye.

CHAPTER TWO

31 Jan.   Dearest Barb, It was sad watching you and the children drive out of sight as the carrier pulled out of the harbor. Our three years of shore duty were so wonderful. The children's characters have really taken shape. I know them so much better now, and that makes leaving so much more difficult.

4 Feb.   My darling John, I miss you! Seven long months till homecoming. I've enrolled in two college classes. The University assigned me Junior status. Allison says she's going to paint you a picture you can hang on your wall because those steel gray walls of the ship are "yucky."

19 Feb.   My birthday, Barb. Does thirty-three sound old? It used to, and I think it still does. When I went down to the Ready Room, I found a large birthday cake and when I went up to man my aircraft, I found "Happy Birthday" written on the fuselage. We've got a good crew. I like them, and they know it.

Tomorrow is your birthday, but you don't age. You're as attractive as you were when you were seventeen years old—only now, more exciting. As I write these words, I'm thinking of you and how you act, sound, feel, smell. I'm so in love with you, Barb.

19 Feb.   My darling John, Hope you like the enclosed. The kids decided they should each create their own birthday card for Daddy.

25 Feb.	The time has come, Barb. Tomorrow we'll be on the line and I'm on the flight schedule. I feel like it was before an exam and I'm not prepared. Nervous as a cat. You can't imagine our schedule. My days start at 5:30 a.m. and go to 6 p.m. without a break. We then must share Condition I Air Defense (CAP) all night. (You sit in your aircraft ready to go. Two-hour watches per pilot.) Then we start again the next morning—for twenty-eight days straight or until we leave the line. I admit I'm scared of the thought of getting shot at.
27 Feb.	Well, Barb, my first combat hop involved climbing through the clouds and heading for a target, only to find it was too far away. The problem then became one of landing back aboard in horrible weather. Windy, low ceilings. A tragic loss today of one of our helicopters and crew. I played guitar with those pilots only last week.
7 Mar.	Darling John, We heard about the helo pilots. One of the new wives got real teary-eyed at the squadron wives' potluck supper. It suddenly hit her that all this war news on t.v. is real. And our guys are there.
8 Mar.	Dearest Barb, you can't imagine what lousy weather we've been flying in. The men are fatigued and walking around in a daze. I'm glad the children like my letters to them. I think it's better if they have a tangible communication from Daddy rather than just a word passed via you. I can just picture Andrew saying you "lost Daddy." Poor little guy. He can't know why the normal order of things is disturbed. I'm not sure I know, myself.
10 Mar.	I'm back from a strike, Barb. It was a success. We (four planes) were the fighter cover and had to orbit inland to fend off MiGs if they came.

24

No MiGs, but the 12 minutes we spent over North Vietnam seemed like 12 years.

12 Mar.   John, Darling, all goes well, except the water heater popped a hole. Damn. We don't need that expense. The kids and I are spending the weekend with my folks. I got an A on my English Lit midterm. Fly carefully, my love.

16 Mar.   I'm sitting in the cockpit of an aircraft at 1:20 a.m. Condition I CAP. It't a lovely evening. The sea is calm and the only sound is the low whir of the gyros in my cockpit. Just now, I saw a falling star. It seems almost out of the question that I could go flying at a moment's notice.

I'm rambling on, Barb. Sort of mentally chatting with you. I can't think of anything substantial or joyous without thinking of you. I can't think of a most exquisite love without thinking of you.

24 Mar.   Dearest Barb, By the time you get this letter you will undoubtedly have heard of the loss of Lt. j.g. Don S. yesterday. Possibly he took an enemy hit.

3 Apr.   John, darling, we heard about Don. How peculiar to walk across campus after such news and see all the anti-war demonstrators. You and the other pilots are risking your lives yet your countrymen are angry at you. It makes it harder for us at home. Barty and I did our "homework" together yesterday. He says he is practicing so he can "read Daddy a story when Daddy comes home from the war."

24 Apr.   The dangers of this business hit home again, Barb. They bagged another of our squadron pilots. A parachute was seen so he is probably alive. I'm scheduled for a strike tomorrow. I shudder to think of capture. Please pray that I'll have the presence of mind to do my job properly and with honor.

1 May	Darling John, the squadron wives have rallied around Marlene. She is clinging to the hope that Jim is alive.
6 May	Waiting to go on a big strike the past two days but weather has prohibited. After the pressures of this air war, I know what a treasure the serenity of my family is. I long to feel the children's arms around me, Barb; to play the role of the lion with his cubs. Tears come to my eyes when I think how I want to be with my children, playing with them, explaining things to them, trying to give them some of myself. And then to think of you, my greatest asset. You've flooded my life with goodness. You are the source of all that's dear to me.
14 May	Dearest Barb, we're now steaming full speed toward Yankee Station (line combat) two days early. Could this be escalation? Stay tuned.
19 May	Another bad day for us, Barb. The opposition was the worst ever, they say. Two pilots are reported missing. A good chance they were captured. I hope so. As one man put it, "You can't come back from the dead but you might make it out of a prison camp."
23 May	It's Barty's birthday, John. You know how he loves parties! Allison took string and we made a "spider web" maze for the kids out in the back yard. Lots of cake and ice cream. Barty blew out all his candles. When I asked him what he wished for, he said "for Daddy to come home safe." My wish too, my darling. And my prayer.
25 May	Dearest Barb, I went to Mass this morning. We brief for the big strike at noon. Before the strike, my darling, it's important for me to tell you again how much I love you. Without you, my life would be shallow and empty.

... I am happy to be continuing this letter. The strike was a success and we got everyone back, |

which is the most important thing. I have done difficult things in my life but that has got to be the roughest. I had to fly right over downtown Hanoi. They shot everything in the book at us, and I'll bet I perspired five gallons of water.

1 June   Darling John, it's nerve-wracking here, too. As one of the squadron wives said at bridge last night, "Everytime I go to the grocery store, I think, 'While I'm buying cereal for the kids, my husband could be getting shot down.'" Tends to keep the anxiety level high.

What seems strangest to me is when I look out our kitchen window and watch the neighbor husbands drive off to their nice, safe civilian jobs and I think, it's as if John and I inhabit a whole different world from Ron and Harriet, next door.

I like to picture us sitting around a campfire again, high in the Sierras. By the way, speaking of pictures, hope you like the enclosed.

8 June   Today was glorious, Barb. Received the wonderful photograph of you and the children. I can't tell you not to worry or be afraid. All I can say is, I hope it's God's will that I return to you in August as scheduled. There's nothing I want more than to go on the camping trip that Barty keeps talking about.

10 Jun.   Thanks for your letter with Barty's tooth in it, Barb! I wish I could hear Barty laugh right now. He has such an infectious laugh. I love him so. Tell Allison that I love my little girl very much. And Andrew, too.

12 Jun.   I am sad to report that Dave W. was lost at sea early this morning. Search is still in progress. He took off at 2:30 a.m. and that was the last contact. In the face of war, one tends to forget the hazards of flying off a carrier.

Hope you're saying some prayers. My emotions are a mix of fear, pride, self-pity, sadness,

27

anger. I wonder if I have courage—and if I do, what is it all worth? Of course, we must maintain our outward appearance of fearless composure.

13 Jun. Dear Barty: How are you, son? I sure enjoyed the tape recording you, Mommy, Allison and Andrew made. And I enjoyed your joke, too...

Dear Allison: I like getting letters from you. Help your mother and be a good big sister to your brothers. Love, "Daddy-O."

14 Jun. My Darling John, How incredible that we are celebrating ten years of marriage. You are still my knight in shining armor! My prince! I can't imagine life without you. Two more months until we're together again. Oh, my darling, I am getting impatient!

14 Jun. Barb, Happy Anniversary, Without you, my darling, I'd be like an autumn leaf—dry and lifeless. With you loving me, spring is always in the offing.

30 Jun. It's a quiet Sunday, Barb. Only two big air strikes. A new pilot came aboard yesterday—an ensign. Poor kid was in the Ready Room when we got back from the Hanoi raid. Must have been something to see all these pilots come in soaked in their own perspiration, hair askew, with dry mouths, adrenalin still up and breathing heavy. That's a hell of a way to meet the squadron!

I'm looking at the beautiful pictures you sent me of the children. I see such *hope* in their eyes. I want so much to hold them in my arms. I want to be there to influence my children, to bring out their good qualities. What greater success can a father ask?

4 Jul Dearest Barb, Awards were given out today and I got my first Air Medal. The award that would please me most is a trip back home. The ship expects to arrive in San Diego in August. That

means our big camping trip can go forward in September.

10 Jul   John Darling, I received the tape of you singing Happy Birthday to Allison and Andrew. They'll love it! Andrew says his best birthday present will be camping with his Daddy. We're getting excited, as August draws near. The squadron wives have all gone on diets!

25 Jul   Three more days, Barb, until we leave the line.

29 Jul   Darling Barb, I can't believe this had happened. This morning at 0700, I was thinking happy thoughts. Combat flying was over at last. The pilots congratulated each other for conducting ourselves honorably and with excellence. At 1100, we got word of a fire on the aircraft carrier *Forrestal*. We steamed full speed to give assistance. Smoke was billowing out of her stern section, and the charred remnants of some aircraft were visible on the flight deck. At least twenty people killed and a lot more injured.

How does it affect us? We're extended on the line for an indefinite period. Hold the good thought, my darling, that we still make our camping trip in September.

CHAPTER THREE

"WHAT'S ODD," my father said. "I don't recognize that car." Through the gathering dusk, we all peered at the white Buick that sat parked in my parents' driveway.

A few months after John's departure, my parents had retired to California. They bought a house up the coast, about an hour's drive from San Diego.

29

The kids and I had driven up for Labor Day weekend. We had gone out to eat an early supper.

My father opened the gate that led to the patio and swimming pool. Two shadowy forms stood up. I recognized my navy friends, Bob Stewart and his wife, Irene.

Abruptly, the world slowed. I experienced a vivid awareness of each small motion—Bob's mouth opening wide, his hand reaching out, Irene's arm sliding around my shoulders, my mother's horrified stare, my father's slight stumble as he took in the news. I heard myself scream, but it wasn't me, it was somebody else, for John and I were going camping. John couldn't die. Not my John. No! Not my John!

Only years later did Allison confide what it had been like for the children that night. "No one would tell us anything," she said, and in her voice, I heard little-girl hurt and accusation. "Mom [the name they gave their grandmother] hustled us off to bed. She turned off the lights and closed the door and we lay there and we knew something awful had happened but we didn't know what and we were so scared, Mommy, we were so scared.

"I said to Barty, 'I think Daddy died,' and he jumped out of his bed and ran over and started hitting me until I screamed, but quietly, because somehow, I knew we weren't supposed to disturb anyone, and he whispered to me, as if he knew, too, we had to be quiet, 'My Daddy's not dead.' I heard Andrew make a funny gasping noise, like he couldn't breathe, and I didn't know what to do, Mommy. I lay awake most of the night, and it was like waiting for Christmas morning, only not Christmas, but something awful... something very awful..."

We drove to San Diego the next day. Navy friends and neighbors gathered around. John's parents arrived from New York. The navy chaplain came.

"We're so sorry, Barbara. John's plane crashed as he tried to bring it aboard the carrier. It was a night mission. His body was lost at sea."

"My boy, my precious boy," cried John's mother. She wept and rocked and when she learned there was no body,

30

her voice rose in a keening wail. Her grief was so intense that it would lead to her death six months later.

The children were small shadows, hovering in corners as the adults scurried about. I had forms and papers to sign. There was the memorial service to plan. I was obsessed with the need to make sure people felt John's presence in the chapel even though we had no body, no casket. I spent hours writing the eulogy, which I took from his letters. The planning, the practical matters gave a certain ease, a momentary narcotic for the pain.

Someone, I thought, was surely taking care of the children.

No one noticed when Barty slipped outside after the memorial service. Our house was filled with guests—neighbors and navy friends, some of them fellow pilots who had flown in from the east coast. No one seemed in a hurry to leave, and I kept urging people to stay, dreading the reality that would face me when the house, at last, grew empty and still.

Allison and Andrew drifted like pale-faced guests through the smoke-filled crowded living room. Listening. Absorbing.

Barty wandered outside, alone. Hot Santa Ana winds had blown in from the desert and the September sun made sparkles on the sidewalk that hurt Barty's eyes. He squinted them shut, then opened them fast, playing a mindless little game with himself.

His aimless stroll brought him to Donny Hayward's house. Donny was ten, a skinny, scab-kneed boy who always seemed to need a haircut.

He met Barty at the edge of his yard, his voice a jeer.

"Your father died in that crummy war! *My* father says it served him right!"

Barty stopped. For a moment, he couldn't move. His chest heaved. The hot sun glimmered on the two boys. Then Barty exploded into motion. His arms and fists flailing, his eyes squeezed shut, he began to pummel Donny. His words burst out in short, agonized gasps.

"My—father—is—not—dead!"

Donny stepped backward, then jabbed hard at Barty's nose. Blood spurted. His right fist connected with the side of Barty's head. Barty gasped and stumbled backward, falling to the ground. The older boy kicked him in the belly. Barty scuttled away, crabwise, to the edge of the sidewalk. Blood and tears smeared his face and shirt. He struggled to his feet and ran, haltingly, toward home.

When he stumbled into the house, his grandmother—John's mother—saw him first. "Barty!" she cried, "Fighting on the day of your father's services? Shame on you!"

"B-but—"

"Go clean yourself up. Right now! Hurry—before your mother sees you."

Barty limped down the hall. Allison saw him. Years later, she told me she never forgot the sad, bewildered look of pain in Barty's eyes.

The next few months I lived in a haze. I had pre-registered, in June, for the fall semester at San Diego State University. Now there was a real urgency to completing my degree. As a widow, I would need it. Even though I was eligible for navy benefits, in the long haul I would have to go to work. I decided to hold to my fall schedule.

"Good idea," said my friend, Polly. Polly was working on her degree, too. Her husband, another pilot, had been killed two years earlier. "The busier you are, the better." I reasoned that it was good advice from someone who had been through it before...

I had always stayed busy, and I had lived alone while John was at sea. But now, how different everything seemed! Before, I had the navy support system—weekend potluck suppers and bridge games with the other wives. Letters home. And most of all, the knowledge that my loneliness would end.

Now...loneliness stretched as an endless horizon. I was unprepared emotionally. Like women I later met who had divorced, I grew up believing in the happily-ever-after end-

32

ing. It had not occurred to me—despite the reality I saw about me!—that John might actually die in the war; that life doesn't always play by rules we consider "fair."

As I walked across the rolling green hills of San Diego State, stepping around picketers who were demonstrating against the war, aching from the physical *weight* of my grief, I found myself wondering, in startled surprise: is this the way it is? Is this the way life *really* is?

Outwardly, I seemed to be in control. People complimented me for the way I was holding up and getting my life back in order. First, I enrolled in fifteen units of classes. Next I hired a Mexican live-in housekeeper from nearby Tijuana. I wanted to make sure the children would never be left alone. (I didn't think about the fact that my Mexican lady didn't speak English.)

I was very concerned about the children.

"You know what I keep remembering?" I said to Polly as we sat on her patio, two weeks after John's memorial service.

She looked at me questioningly, but for a moment I couldn't go on. Tears formed in my eyes. It often happened that way. Suddenly—in the midst of driving or walking or reading or washing dishes—the tears would come, would catch me by surprise and fall, insistently, of their own accord.

"Take your time," Polly said softly.

I nodded and finally managed to finish. "What I remember is *me* in sixth grade. In my bedroom, listening to music on my white plastic radio. And for some reason, I started to imagine what it would be like if my parents died. And pretty soon, I was crying. I almost got hysterical.

"It was the worst thing I could imagine ever happening to me—to any child—I mean, after all these years, I can still see myself, Polly, lying on my bed, crying and crying, and now—" I was crying again, for real "—it *has* happened. To *my* children. And I can't bear it. How can I make it up to them?"

"You can't," she said. "No one can make up for the loss

of their father. You just have to go on, that's all. All of you."

Go on? Yes. I went on, determined that I must—that I could—compensate my children for John's death. I didn't care what Polly said. My children had lost a child's greatest treasure. It was my responsiblity to make it up to them.

With Maria in the house, the children were well taken care of, I felt, while I was at school. Maria cooked and cleaned with easy efficiency, and like most Mexicans, did not expect her gringo charges to pick up after themselves. Although faces changed several times over the next three years, Maria, then Rosina, then Marmelita each took efficient charge of the household.

On weekends, when my housekeepers returned to Tijuana, I took the children on "family outings." That first autumn we explored museums, visited skating rinks, and spread our towels on nearly every beach in San Diego.

"I'll bet I take my children more places than most two-parent families," I told Polly. It was a matter of pride with me to say that. My children, I vowed, would not suffer because they had no father; as if Sunday at the museum could ever make up for the loss of a parent.

There was another aspect to our outings I didn't see at the time. When their father was alive, ours was a family that had fun together. Love was carried on wings of laughter. But John had been the catalyst. Now, I had no laughter left in me. I took the children places, but more like a chaperone than a participant. At the ice skating rink, I sat on the sidelines and studied while the kids skated. At the beaches, while they splashed in the surf, I sat on my towel and read. Or stared, blindly, at the rolling ocean, yearning for John and all that I had lost.

I was there ... yet I wasn't there.

When Allison thinks back to that time, she remembers how often I shut my bedroom door and left the children to eat dinner alone, in a puddle of dim light from the TV set, or in the housekeeper's Spanish-speaking company.

I was present in our home ... yet I wasn't.

I would shut my bedroom door and lie across my bed, grieving. I felt like a rudderless boat, about to capsize from the waves that engulfed me. Huge gray waves of sadness. Fear. Loneliness. As I flung myself across the bed, a whisper would drift through my mind over and over again.

"Love me. Please, somebody, love me..."

I missed John so much. But I missed, too, the simple comforts of marriage. Silly little things like the way John and I would touch toes when we slept. His habit of humming while he shaved. And I missed the sense of "belonging" that had been mine as a navy wife.

As I struggled to make up to the children for the loss of their father, I was also beginning a long, lonely struggle to discover who *I* was. Not daughter of... or wife of... or even mother of... but me. Barbara. Who was I if I was no longer "Mrs. John Bartocci"? What energy it required to attempt to answer that question!

Andrew is the child I remember most during that period.

Although John and I had promised not to hide things from each other while he was at sea, I had never written him about those awful six weeks while I waited to see Dr. Rosenberg.

Responding to the nursery school teacher's earlier concern, I took Andrew to our pediatrician. "I think Andrew is hyperactive," she said, introducing me to a term that was new in the late sixties. "And maybe more than that," she added, giving me the name of a child psychologist.

After spending two hours with Andrew, Dr. Allen called me into his office.

"Mrs. Bartocci," he said slowly, "I have bad news. I believe Andrew is an autistic child."

"Autistic?" I had never heard the word. First hyperactive, now autistic?

That very evening, I went to the library to learn all I could about autism. What I read horrified me. "Autism," I read, "is incurable. Autistic children live in their own world. They are frequently beautiful but possess no sense of reality. Often, they won't speak. They engage in repetitive activities that have little or no meaning. They live in inner worlds of their own making."

And there was more . . . a lot more. It numbed me. Some of what I read seemed to fit Andrew. He'd always been content to play by himself. I saw, in my mind, a scene at the beach: Allison and Barty, running along the sand together; Andrew, as usual, tagging along behind, in a dreamy world of his own. I had thought he was just a self-sufficient, imaginative child. But now, in horror, I saw his behavior in a new light.

The next afternoon was Andrew's regular appointment with his speech therapist. Barely able to say it, I whispered, "Miss Kimble, I've just learned Andrew is autistic."

Judy Kimble resembled in elf with shaggy bangs and a narrow, high cheekboned face. Andrew adored her.

I didn't have to explain autism to her. She *knew.* And she grew indignant. "I don't believe it," she said. "I've been around Andrew twice a week for six months. He's intelligent, creative . . . hyperactive, maybe. But *not* autistic. Please, get a second opinion." She suggested Dr. Ron Rosenberg.

Dr. Rosenberg could not see us for six weeks. Six agonizing weeks when I noted Andrew's every action in a journal, as Rosenberg's office nurse requested.

I watched him draw pictures. The same subject matter over and over. Airplanes. Surely a symptom! Fear gripped me. But when, at last, we met with Dr. Rosenberg and Andrew was tested again, the neurologist reported: "Andrew's basic intelligence is fine but his verbal and motor skills are developing at an uneven rate. He's what we call a learning disabled child. But autistic? Not in the least."

Learning disabled; another new term. But not autistic! I began to cry from relief and joy.

Still, the problems were serious. In addition to speech therapy, I now drove Andrew to a private school for learning disabled children. Monthly, we visited Dr. Rosenberg. And, twice a day, I gave Andrew doses of Ritalin to control his hyperactivity.

Today, we know more about learning disabilities and the hyperactive child. But then it was all very new. I was afraid for Andrew—afraid of the problems he might face in being "different"; I ached for his vulnerabilities. And I was determined to protect him.

Slender and fine-boned, with a shock of yellow hair that fell in bangs across his forehead, Andrew also seemed to grieve most for his father.

His kindergarten teacher, Mrs. Alexander, stopped me one day after class. "I asked Andrew why he doesn't smile anymore. Do you know what he told me?" Numbly, I shook my head. Her voice caught. "He said, 'I tried on a smile. But when I looked in the mirror, it didn't fit.'"

Tears glistened in both our eyes.

Abruptly, after John died, Andrew stopped playing outdoors or seeing other children. Instead, he sat for hours with his red toy telephone, holding long conversations with an imaginary "ship's captain."

"I talked to the captain," he would tell me, "and he says it's okay. Our daddy didn't drown. He'll come home, soon."

But the weeks went by and Daddy didn't come home. One day, Andrew threw himself into my arms, sobbing.

"He's not coming home, is he? He's under the water with the fishes, forever and ever, isn't he?"

I could only hold him until he cried himself out.

Allison, too, cried. And more times than I can remember she lay awake long past midnight.

I discovered this one night, late, when I needed something from her room. Quietly, I tiptoed in. My hip bumped her dresser. A drawer rattled. In the darkness, I heard a small sigh.

"It's okay, Mommy. I'm awake."

I reached for the lamp on her dresser. Her room, blue and white, with her gingham bedspread fallen to the floor, sprang into soft focus. On shelves above her bed, her collection of dolls seemed to peer at me—dolls from around the world, mostly brought to her as gifts from her Daddy.

"How come you're still awake, honey?"

"It's hard to fall asleep since Daddy died. I think about things."

I sat down beside her on the bed, and ran my fingers lightly through her hair, still cut in the Dutch girl bob. It seemed to fit so well this sturdy, precise little girl of mine.

"What do you think about?"

"Oh . . . about Daddy and all the fun we had. Remember when he showed me how to clean a fish? And how silly he looked in your wig?"

I laughed, remembering. During our last year in Monterey, John had offered to take the kids trick or treating—but not before he dressed himself up in my wig and an old evening gown, so he could strut to each neighbor's front door with his children while they giggled hysterically at their funny Daddy.

"Your daddy was silly, sometimes. A nice kind of silly."

"You know what I wonder?"

"What, honey?"

"I wonder why God needed Daddy when I need him so much more."

"Oh, Allison!" Tears, sudden and deep, spilled out, and I clasped my daughter in my arms, rocking the two of us back and forth, although whether to comfort her or to comfort me, I don't really know.

Basically, though, hers was a practical nature. She was able to cope and go on.

Barty was the one who didn't seem to grieve at all. If anything, he stayed outdoors rough-housing with the neighborhood boys even more than usual. I felt annoyed—angry, even—because he didn't seem to care. He, his father's special child—and I'd never seen him shed a tear.

One day I came home from school to find Barty and his friend, Jimmy, playing with one of John's model airplanes. Several scale models of the airplanes he flew had been given to him over the years. Most pilots had similar collections.

Barty zoomed the airplane over his head, making noises. Suddenly, with a rumbly "v-rooom-pow!" he made the airplane dive. It crashed into the family room couch. He laughed hysterically.

I stood in the doorway. A cold tingle ran through me, followed by a flash of burning heat that rose through my fingers, into my cheeks.

"How dare you laugh!" I shouted at him. "Your father died in a plane crash! Don't you care? Don't you care that your father is *dead*?"

The laughter stopped, like water turned off. The boys stared at me, at my upraised arm, at the wild look in my eyes. Jimmy seemed uncertain, embarrassed, but oh, the stricken look on Barty's face! His eyes grew enormous, the pupils black and dilated, and his mouth worked, as if he wanted to speak, but nothing came out. Suddenly, as suddenly as it came, my anger left.

"Barty," I whispered, "I'm sorry."

But he didn't seem to hear. He simply stood by the couch, one hand still touching the fallen jet airplane. Jimmy sidled past me and ran out our front door towards home. I took a step toward Barty. Quickly, he dropped the airplane, pushed past me, and ran out after Jimmy.

I stood alone in the family room. Maybe it was true. Maybe he *didn't* care!

I didn't realize then that grief can be buried. Or how destructive such buried grief can be. It was years before I was able to see a connection between Bart's intense, unexpressed grief and his angry acting-out behavior. I didn't know it, but of all my three children, Barty was the child in greatest peril.

CHAPTER FOUR

BECAUSE WE stayed in the same house in the same neighborhood, the children's daily lives differed very little from the pattern we had followed during their father's months at sea. Although I didn't know it, this encouraged Barty's fantasy: that his father wasn't really dead. He was lost on an island somewhere and one day, he would return.

John's belongings arrived from the ship. When I unpacked his wooden cruise chest, when I buried my face in shirts that still bore the special scent of him, when I pulled out the box that held his wedding ring (he never wore it while flying, in case of enemy capture) and saw the ribbon-tied packets of letters from me—then, the enormity of my loss and its *permanence* swept over me again. I wept, with tears that came from some hollow, hurting place I had never known before. Yet it became one more milestone I had passed.

After Christmas, one of my history professors invited me to a student-faculty party at his house. In my nervousness, I showed up fifteen minutes early and sat, terrified, in my car, glancing at my watch every few seconds. For ten years I had functioned as half a couple. Now I was about to embark in the unfamiliar sea of singleness among people I didn't know. What if no one talked to me? What if I wasn't dressed right? What if I made a fool of myself with some awful conversational gaffe?

The evening went fine. A graduate student asked me out. I wasn't ready to date yet, but I went home with a new awareness of myself as a single woman.

Between semesters, my mother baby-sat while Polly and I went skiing. Polly had skied for years; I was a beginner.

But, as I wobbled down the beginners' slope and joked with other member of my ski class, I took another step toward a new autonomy.

At least I *thought* I did.

Later that spring, Polly suggested camping. Our kids were about the same ages and we had all the gear.

"I don't know..." I said, hesitantly. "I'm not sure I can set up the tent. John always did the hard stuff."

"Oh, pooh. You can do it. I'll show you how."

She convinced me. Excitedly, the kids helped load our tent, our cookstove, our sleeping bags. We took off in our station wagon behind Polly in hers, heading for the Colorado River.

"I can put up the tent, Mommy," Barty said manfully. "I remember what Daddy did."

I laughed. "Mommy will take care of setting up camp. You kids just have a good time."

And they did. While I put together the cookstove and blew up air mattresses and followed Polly's instructions for setting up our tent, the kids climbed the rocky red-soiled hills, explored the arroyos and hunted for lizards.

"Well!" I said, in happy satisfaction, as Polly and I finally relaxed beneath the scrubby shade of a few mesquite trees. "This is great. We're camping again! John would be so pleased."

Before Polly could reply, Andrew came hurtling down one of the hills. "Mommy! Mommy!" He had found something. But as he reached our campsite, he tripped. His hand fell open. A lizard scuttled off and disappeared into the rocks.

I was at Andrew's side before he had a chance to pull himself up. "Andrew, honey! Are you all right?"

"M-my lizard," he sobbed. "I lost my lizard."

"You'll find another," I soothed. "Here. Let Mommy tie that bad old shoelace."

When I returned to my lawn chair, Polly surprised me by shaking her head. "God, you baby that kid, Barb. He's almost six. Let him tie his own shoelaces."

41

"He hurt himself, Polly. When you're hurt, you like a little babying." I didn't say it, but to my way of thinking, Polly made her three children take on too much responsibility. Nobody stayed with them while she went to school. She seldom took her children out on weekends, as I did. Granted, her kids were a year older than mine. But I thought she asked too much when she told her son, Mike, to fix dinner every night!

But we valued our friendship too much to spoil it with fights over differences in child raising. So Polly shrugged and smiled, I smiled back and we changed the subject. The Colorado River was the first of many camping trips we would take together.

Like visits to the museums, our camping trips convinced me I was succeeding. I wanted to be more than a good single mother; I wanted to be, essentially, a double parent, an able stand-in for both mother and father. So far it seemed that I was reaching my goal.

But along with camping, that spring also brought a problem that would come back to haunt me years later. It was rooted in the skinny, scabby-kneed boy, Donny Hayward. Maria, my Mexican housekeeper, met me at the door one day, wringing her hands in consternation.

"Fight—boys fight, que sabe?" She made the motions of fist fighting and handed me a T-shirt, stained with blood.

Barty sat on his bed, holding a damp washcloth to his nose. His lip was puffy.

"I hate Donny!" he mumbled. "He won't leave me alone."

Barty still had the blue eyes and blonde curls his father had loved, but at eight, he was a round, slightly pudgy boy. He looked at me now, misery in his eyes.

"Make him leave me alone, Mom!"

"Donny's a bully!" Allison said from the doorway. Her eyes flashed with big sister indignation. "When I tried to make him go home, he chased me with a rock. Last week, he hit Maureen with a rock. He scares me, Mommy."

"I'd better talk to some of the neighbors," I decided.

The Haywards were recent additions to our neighborhood.

"And I sure wish they'd move away," said Bill Johnson, the high school math teacher who lived across the street. "Their kids are impossible, Barbara."

"I told his mother I'd call the police next time," Maureen's mother said. "He's the neighborhood bully, Barbara. Not that his mother seems to care. She slammed the door in my face."

Once again, I yearned for John. I was no good in confrontations. Hesitantly, I walked to the Haywards' house.

Mr. Hayward answered the door. Like his son, he was tall and wiry, with graying hair and glasses;. "We need to talk about Donny—" I began.

"I let my kids fight their own battles!" Hayward said. The door closed.

I stood, speechless, on his front stoop. A feeling of helplessness washed over me. Now what?

Finally, I simply walked home. "Can you stay out of his way, Barty?"

"I try, Mommy. But he comes after me."

"Well . . . let's try one more time. Okay?"

He nodded, but I could see disappointment in the slump of his shoulders and the shadow that hovered in his eyes.

Angry at myself, yet still feeling helpless, I retreated to my bedroom. Maybe, I thought hopefully, the fights will blow away.

But trouble continued, and not only for Barty; for the other kids, too.

"He's the bully of Kobe Drive," said Mary Johnson as we chatted in her driveway one morning. "Honestly, Barbara, it's beyond me how parents can let a child run wild the way the Haywards let Donny."

"There's something wrong with his parents, that's all. They must not care about their kids."

Even as we talked, Donny rode by on a makeshift bicycle someone had put together out of a hodgepodge of parts. Deliberately, he rode up a driveway where two preschoolers played, sending them scuttling for safety.

"Look at that!" Mary cried, outraged.

"I can't stand bullies! John detested them, too."

Mary looked at me slyly. "By the way, I've noticed a blue Pontiac in your driveway, lately. Anyone special?"

"Just a friend, Mary. A professor from school."

I could tell she didn't believe me, but it was true. A year after John's death, the small voice still echoed—"somebody love me, please, love me..." I wanted someone in my life again, someone to care about, who would care about me. Despite my attempt to play both roles, I yearned to give my children a real father so we could return to the happy *wholeness* of our Monterey days.

Frank Carter, PhD, was a balding bachelor in his early thirties with a shy, scholarly charm. Allison and Andrew seemed to like his company, but Barty scowled every time Frank walked through the door.

"How's the baseball, Barty?" Frank had tried at dinner a few nights earlier.

Barty scooped up a forkful of potatoes. "Okay."

"Barty wants to be a catcher," I said to break the silence. "His father was the catcher on the Navy team at Annapolis."

"Are you coming to my game tomorrow night, Mom?"

"Tomorrow...uh, what time?"

"Five o'clock. Like always. Can't you remember?"

"I'm sorry, Barty. Of course, I'll be there." Mentally, I rearranged my schedule. I tried to get to Barty's games—it was something I felt I had to do in my role as a double parent—but I marveled at the mothers and fathers who screamed and yelled in emotional frenzy over Little League ball games. How could they get so excited? Baseball bored me. If John were here, he'd love the games...but he wasn't here.

"I'd like to see you play," Frank said. "How about if I come with your mom?"

Barty scooped up another forkful of potatoes. "No thanks."

I felt a flash of irritation. Here was a perfectly nice man, willing to take some interest in Barty, and my son acted positively *rude*.

"Barty," I said crossly, "stop shoveling those potatoes into your mouth. Your manners are atrocious."

He looked surprised. "I'm not eating any different."

"That merely means your manners are always atrocious."

Andrew looked at me. "What's Ah-tro-shus?"

"Like a pig, Andrew."

"Barty eats like a pig?" Andrew was delighted. "Piggy—piggy—piggy..."

"I'm not a pig and you'd better shut up!"

"That's enough, Barty."

"Why're you mad at *me*? Andrew's the one—"

"I said, that's *enough*!"

"Well," he said sulkily, "tell Andrew not to call me a pig."

A devilish light appeared in Andrew's eyes. "*Oink, oink, oink!*"

Allison burst out laughing. I hid a smile myself.

Barty exploded. His chair clattered backwards; he jumped up, grabbed Andrew and started pounding him on his back. Andrew began to holler, and in the commotion Barty's milk spilled to the floor.

Frank stared, transfixed. Allison began mopping up milk.

"Barty!" I shouted, "Go to your room." I pulled him away from Andrew. "You're too big to beat up on your brother. Now go to your room until you calm down!" As an afterthought, I added, "Both of you!"

Grudgingly, they stalked off to the bedroom they shared.

"Barty gets mad so easy," Allison said.

I smiled weakly at Frank. He smiled back. But soon afterward, bachelor Frank disappeared from the scene.

A year and a half had passed since John's death. I had completed the remaining requirements for my undergraduate degree and was ready to enroll in graduate school.

Barty was nine now, still possessing the blond curls his father had loved, and the wide-set blue eyes. Andrew, too, retained his blond hair, but while Barty had the apple-cheeked cuteness of a Campbell's Soup kid, Andrew looked more like a slender elf. The boys were just as opposite in temperment.

Barty hated to be alone. He scooted out the door early every morning, looking for kids to play with. He always wanted to be part of the crowd.

Andrew, on the other hand, was forever involved in some solitary project of his own making. One day I found him in the garage, laboriously wrapping twine around two strips of Styrofoam.

"What are you doing?" I asked.

"Making water skis," he replied happily. "See?"

I did see and I marveled at his inventiveness. But I continued to fret about his progress in school.

He no longer needed speech therapy. Daily doses of Ritalin controlled his hyperactivity. We had all learned to recognize the high pitched "silly" giggles that signaled the need for more medication.

But although he was nominally in second grade at his private, special ed school, I learned that he also suffered from dyslexia, which meant he still wasn't able to read. His lack of small motor-coordination sent his handwriting wandering in an illegible scrawl across the page. He was very good with math concepts—but what good were numbers if he couldn't read?

It seemed as if I had worried about Andrew from the day he was born.

"You baby him too much," my mother said as we prepared to leave their house after a weekend visit.

"Now you sound like Polly," I retorted. "He's got a lot of special problems, that's all."

My father chuckled. "And oh boy, has he learned to use that to rattle Mommy's chain."

"Now, Daddy—"

"Don't neglect Barty," my mother cautioned me. But her voice was drowned out by the noisy shouts of the kids, who were tired of sitting in the station wagon and anxious to leave for home.

At home, Barty scrambled out of the car and ran to join a group of bigger boys who were playing ball in the cul-de-sac. I began carrying in suitcases and a sack of fresh fruit my mother had given me. Suddenly I heard shouts, followed by laughter and an unmistakable high pitched shriek from Bart.

I dropped the sack of fruit and ran outside.

"What's going on?" I called to Allison and her best friend, Boo, who watched from the sidewalk as a ninth grade boy laughingly sidestepped Barty's unsuccessful punches.

"The bigger boys tease Barty," Allison, explained, "'cause he always loses his temper. The latest thing is—"

"Is what?" I prompted.

She and Boo looked at each other. Boo giggled, then looked away, embarrassed.

"They call him Barty-Farty." Allison's voice took on a sing-song chant: "'Barty-Farty, Bart-the-Fart. Pulling on a pony cart.' It makes him *furious*, and he blows up and that makes the rest of them laugh and they tease him even more."

"Good heavens!" I was shocked. We were still contending with Donny Hayward. Now this? *Barty-Farty?*

"I've told him to ignore it and they'll stop," Allison continued. "But he gets real mad, Mommy. He gets mad about a lot of things. Lots more than he used to before Daddy died."

"Yes. Well..." I hesitated, not sure what to do. Would I make things worse if I ran to his rescue? Finally, I decided I would. Unlike Donny Hayward, these boys didn't appear to want to hurt Barty. Everyone had to learn to take a little teasing.

Allison and Boo wandered off towards Boo's house. As a sixth grader, Allison had given up dolls in favor of art work and week-long Monopoly games with Boo. She was still my easiest child to raise. With her wide spaced teeth and protruding overbite, she lacked the blond good looks of her brothers, but teachers and parents inevitably remarked, "What a cooperative child..." Or, "Such a sweet girl." Her report cards always showed A's.

The shouts and laughter had died down in the cul-de-sac. Apparently, the bigger boys had dropped their teasing of Barty. I walked back inside our house, thinking, again, how easy Allison was to raise and how much more I worried about her brothers. Although, I reflected as I picked up the sack of fruit, I didn't really worry about Barty. Oh, he could do better in school and he *did* have that explosive temper—but nothing like Andrew and his learning problems.

At that time I simply didn't understand the dynamics of childhood grief. It had never occurred to me that temper tantrums and a drop in school performance could be signs of hidden emotional stress.

By now, I was deeply embroiled in graduate school and had a job as an English teaching assistant. I was starting to look toward the future. I even thought I was ready to remarry. And I thought I had met the right man.

Malcolm Pritchard taught Romantic literature and looked the part. He reminded me of John. Not that they resembled each other or even had the same interests—but there was about Mal, as there had been about my husband, the ability to charm, to gather people around, to be a *center*.

The children liked him; even Barty seemed tolerant. He treated them with casual good humor, and although he seldom suggested activities that included them, he was an amiable participant if I made plans for "family outings."

In January, I told Mal that I loved him. It was the first time I'd spoken those words since John had died. Incredulously, Mal said that he loved me, too.

Happily, I made plans for marriage. Mal listened patiently as I ran through lists of wedding guests. Together we went to look at houses we might buy. He even went camping with us, although at the end of one weekend I couldn't resist teasing him, "Mal, are you definitely a hot-house flower."

But a few weeks before the wedding my dream of a family with a father was again shattered when he told me that he "just wasn't cut out for marriage or family."

I felt as if I were losing John all over again. I wept. I begged. But in the end he left, and I retreated to my bedroom and locked the door. "We never saw you," Allison said, remembering that time. "It was worse than after Daddy died."

I realized later that the devastation I felt at the loss of Mal hit as hard as it did because it brought home all the anguish I had still not worked through after John's death. My own buried grief might have given me insight into Barty's . . . but it didn't.

It did, however, make me think about moving from San Diego. In the early 1970s, as companies began to feel pressure to hire women, a thirty-one-year-old widow with a graduate degree was an attractive job candidate. Already a Midwest corporation had offered me a job in its public relations department.

"It would be a fresh start," I told my parents. "Andrew's teacher says he can handle public school if I hire a reading tutor. Allison will be in seventh grade and that means a new school *anyway*. And moving will get Barty away from that awful Donny Hayward."

We were sitting on the patio beside my parents' swimming pool. The children splashed and called to each other, or else to us: "Watch me dive! Watch me!" The most insistent voice was Barty's.

"What a ham!" my mother said fondly. "He so loves attention." Like John, she had a soft spot for this middle grandchild.

"It's a big decision," my father said. "We'll miss your tribe of Indians if you move."

"We'll still spend our Christmas holidays with you."

My father sighed as he watched the kids play. "Sounds

like you've made up your mind."

I looked at the hydrangea bushes and the tall purple bottle brush and the squat pineapple palms that stood sentry by the gate. I loved California! I thought about all that had happened in the nearly three years since John's death, how different life had turned out from the happy-ever-after I expected.

I had never held a full-time job. Could I handle the stress of fast track corporate public relations? Plus move my family to a new city? Plus help us all find new friends? I didn't know for sure, but...

"I guess I have decided, Daddy."

Somehow, I felt I had to try. I didn't realize then just how hard all the changes would be. Or what the move would mean to Barty, in particular.

CHAPTER FIVE

THE CHILDREN stared, wide-eyed, as we drove past rolling fields of soybeans and corn. Clumps of oak and elm trees shaded the suburban streets. It looked very different from the tropical expanse of southern California.

"I don't know if I like this place," said Andrew doubtfully. "Where's the ocean?"

"There isn't any ocean. But there are lakes. And horses. And a swimming pool. It's an adventure, Andrew."

"What about school?" Allison asked. "Is the junior high very big?"

"No bigger than San Diego, honey. You'll make friends. Wait and see."

Late August heat shimmered on the metal of the car. I had flown to the Midwest in July to manage the move and settle into my new job. The children had stayed with my parents until school started.

The physical act of moving in—hanging pictures, unwrapping dishes, arranging furniture—had brought me an unexpected feeling of strength. There was one moment, as I stepped back to admire a shelf I had hung, when I, who had always let John hang the shelves and pictures, felt an infinite sureness that I could do it! I could do it all! Succeed in a career! And succeed with my family!

"You'll love it here!" I said to the kids, enthusiastically.

But Barty, I noticed, was silent as we drove home from the airport. We reached our three-bedroom town house, one of a line of four in the apartment complex. I pointed to the clubhouse as we drove past, with its swimming pool and tennis courts, and I showed them the baseball field only one block from our townhouse.

"You'll like it here," I said again, hoping to convince them.

The children rushed inside, eager to see the familiar furniture and feel settled again.

But I caught Barty staring wistfully out the upstairs bedroom window.

"What's wrong, Barty?"

He looked at me solemnly, his ten-year-old face still kewpie doll cute, but reflecting an air of sadness.

"Back home, people knew my Daddy. What will I tell people here about Daddy?"

"Why—" for a moment, I didn't know what to say. The truth was, I found it difficult myself, to introduce the subject of my widowhood.

"Just say your daddy died," I finally replied. "Lots of daddies and mommies get divorced these days, so you won't be the only boy without a father."

"You still have a father when your parents get divorced," Barty objected scornfully. "People don't know what to say when you tell 'em your Daddy died. It makes them feel funny. They walk away." He looked out the window again. "I hate it here." His voice was so matter of fact, I felt a chill. Andrew, at least, was merely doubtful. Barty seemed to have his mind made up.

We spent the weekend getting settled. I introduced the kids to our neighbors—the Hammonds, and their children, Lisa and Mike. The Shapiros, and their children Rachel and Bobby. Jeannie Morris, who was divorced and whose son, Branson, lived with his father. Behind us, I pointed out, lived other kids. And look! We were only four blocks from the elementary school and a mile from the junior high.

The neighborhood children soon began calling Andrew "Andy." He decided he liked that. Barty told the kids his name was "Bart."

On Saturday, I introduced the children to Judy Kevinsky. A full-time housekeeper was beyond my budget in the Midwest, but I didn't want latchkey children and I didn't want to make Allison responsible for her brothers. An older teenager seemed like the answer.

"Judy will stay here every afternoon until five-thirty," I announced.

Sixteen-year-old Judy popped a piece of gum. "Hiya."

"A *baby-sitter*?" Allison said indignantly.

"To keep you from having to play referee," I pointed out. Already, Bart and Andy had argued furiously over who would take the upper bunk first. Allison's indignation quickly subsided.

Monday arrived. Despite his new pants and shirt and the Peanuts lunch pail he had picked out himself, Andy's face looked pinched and frightened as we entered George Washington Elementary School. In his Special Ed class back in California, there had been one instructor to every two students. Students worked at their own pace. Everyone understood that an eight-year-old might be on third grade arithmetic but second grade reading.

I opened the door to the third grade classroom. Rows of desks seemed to stare at us. Could Andy function in a classroom this size? I wondered, suddenly frightened myself. Protectively, I reached for his hand. He shook it off. "I'm not a baby," he whispered fiercely.

Andy, I recalled abruptly, hated to be the center of attention. I shoved my hand into my pocket. Mrs. Mancini, who wore her glasses on a chain and her hair in an outdated beehive, greeted Andy perfunctorily and waved him to a seat. He looked so vulnerable, sitting with shoulders hunched at a desk in the empty middle row, while around him boys who knew each other traded friendly jabs and noisy conversation.

But I couldn't protect him forever. And Bart was tugging at me. Unlike Andy, he was happy to hold my hand. We walked to the fifth grade classroom.

"You'll be one of the big kids," I said, brightly "That will be nice."

"I guess.'

But he entered his classroom willingly enough. I liked the looks of his teacher. Miss McGrail was young and had a cheerleader's smile.

"You going to be okay?"

"Sure."

"I'll see you tonight, then."

"Mom—wait!" He reached up and gave me a strong, tight hug. Surprised, I hugged him back. "You'll do fine," I whispered. This time, he nodded, and seemed content to have me leave.

Actually, next to Andy, the one I worried about most was Allison. The junior high was a big school—1,300 kids. And, although she would one day be a beautiful young woman, Allison, at twelve, walked with an awkward gait. Her hair had none of the blond bounce of her brothers' and her overbite and wide-spaced teeth were very pronounced. Kids her own age, I realized with some trepidation, might call her homely.

The red brick junior high echoed with the slam of lockers, the thump of sneakers and noisy shouts as kids pushed past us, bumping shoulders and screeching to friends, "Wait'll I tell you about *my* vacation!" Allison looked in dismay at the dress she wore. All the other girls seemed to be wearing jeans.

But when I offered to walk her to her first class, she demurred. *Like Andy and hand-holding*, I thought. I left her at the door to the office and headed down the freeway to work. Worrying all the way.

Since it was their first day of school, I planned to leave work a little early. But at four o'clock, my boss frantically beckoned me into his office. "Barbara, we've got a real brouhaha on our hands. *The Wall Street Journal* has heard a rumor..." he thrust some papers into my hand. "Track down this information for me so we can put out the fire."

Putting out the fire kept me at my desk until nearly seven. Already, on their first day of school, I was discovering the difficulties that face single working parents. It's not easy to balance all the commitments.

I quickly noticed other differences between life in California and in the Midwest. With no housekeeper and a full-time job, I needed a lot more help from the children around the house. But they weren't used to that. I was changing the rules of the game on them—and it created conflict.

"I don't need a husband," I sighed to Tina, the woman who had become my closest friend at work. "What I really need is a full-time, old-fashioned *wife*." Tina, who was single, laughed. She thought I was kidding. But it was no laughing matter, night after night, to meet the kids' demands for attention the minute I walked through the front door.

Usually, by the time I reached home, Judy had left. "How's she working out?" I asked Allison after the first week of school.

Allison shrugged. "All right, I guess. Mostly, she talks to her boyfriend on the phone."

"How about you? Making friends?"

"I get together with Rachel, next door. She's fun." Rachel was younger, still in sixth grade—never mind, I decided. Allison was not a sophisticated twelve-year-old. She would eventually find friends at school, too.

Andy didn't talk much about school, but he seemed to have found friends in Mike and Lisa Hammond and in

Bobby Shapiro, Rachel's brother. Mike was his age—eight; Lisa and Bobby were seven.

Bart was the one who was left out.

"This is a dumb neighborhood," he grumped as he sprinkled cheese on his spaghetti. "Nothing but little kids and girls."

"How about the boys in your class? Some of them must live fairly close."

"Judy won't let us go anywhere."

"Oh." I reached for the cheese. "Well, I'll talk to her. As long as you tell her where you'll be—"

Bart looked at me with ten-year-old disgust. "Mom, I can't just go up and ask a guy, 'Can I go home with you?'"

"Why not?"

A dab of red sauce smeared his chin. "You just don't do that." A fifth grade social rule that I, apparently, didn't understand.

"Then invite someone to our house."

"There's nothing to do here."

"Nothing to do? You've got your toys and a record player and games and a baseball field up the block..."

He stubbornly shook his head.

That Friday had been another long day. I was worried about approval on a brochure—the first brochure copy I had ever written. There were clothes yet to be washed. Bart had announced that morning that he was wearing "used underwear." It was already past eight and we hadn't finished dinner.

"Bart," I said with weary finality. "Quit the bellyaching."

"You don't care about us anymore. All you care about is your dumb job."

"That's not so!"

"You never come home when you say you will," he persisted.

"One night this week I've been late. One night is all."

"And you're always mad."

"Only when you kids give me a hard time. Like now."

"That Judy is dumb. You're wasting your money. She never pays attention to us."

"At least you're not alone after school."

"We're always alone in this dumb place," Bart sulked. "I hate it here! Why did you move us from San Diego?"

He hooked me on that one. I desperately wanted my children to be happy. I felt guilty, having moved them away from their grandparents and the neighborhood they knew. Why couldn't Bart act happy?

"Maybe it's *your* fault you can't make friends," I snapped.

Bart threw down his fork. "There's nothing wrong with me!" he shouted, shoving back his chair. I listened to the thud of his sneakers on the stairs. *Now why had I said that?* Allison and Andy stared at their plates.

I tried talking to Judy.

"Can you encourage Bart to invite friends home from school?"

For a minute, she looked blank. Then she popped her gum. "Actually, I been meaning to tell you. I start at McDonalds next week."

I had the feeling that losing Judy was no big loss.

Perhaps the kids would fare better on their own. Allison *was* twelve, after all. Maybe they would be better off alone until I got home.

Bart was the first to protest the new arrangement. "Allison's not going to be in charge of *me!*"

"Me, either," Andy chimed in.

An increasingly familiar irritation welled up. "No one has to be 'in charge' if you each do your share."

"I don't want Allison bossing me around," Bart persisted.

By this time I was out of patience. "Bart," I yelled, "shut up!"

Like prizefighters between rounds, we retreated to our corners.

We did enjoy one special weekend that fall. Thinking of the "family outings" that had been such a part of our lives in San Diego, I suggested a weekend in a rustic lodge at a large wooded lake a few hours away. My friend Tina went with us.

The kids were jubilant. It was not quite camping, but it came close. We hiked in the woods, admiring the oranges and yellows of fall foliage—so different from the tropical green and desert brown of southern California. Tina made jokes about her own "citified" growing up in Chicago. With no other demands on my time, I felt free to really listen as the children spilled out stories and anecdotes from school and—especially, I noticed—from past camping trips. All of us laughed a lot.

"Hasn't this been fun?" Tina said as we loaded suitcases for the trip home.

"Yes!" chorused the kids. "Yes," I echoed, and thought, wistfully, *if only every weekend could be so free.*

The hectic problems of daily life soon took over again. In October, I attended my first parent-teacher conferences.

"Andy doesn't participate," Mrs. Mancini told me. She fiddled, absently, at the chain that held her glasses. Her fingernails made small clicking noises against the metal. "He won't respond—even when I call on him directly."

I shifted on the hard wooden chair beside her desk. "He's afraid of being laughed at. Of giving the wrong answer."

"We all give wrong answers occasionally."

"But he doesn't realize that. I mean, kids with learning disabilities think they're 'stupid,' even though they're not. If you could encourage him more..."

"I have thirty students, Mrs. Bartocci. I can only do so much for one child. Some of that encouragement will have to come from home. Perhaps if you'd work with him after school..."

"But—"

Someone coughed outside her door. She smiled—a frosty twist of the lips that never quite reached her eyes. "I'm sorry to be so brief. Will you send in the next parents as you leave?"

In contrast, Darlene McGrail, Bart's teacher, practically bounced with enthusiasm.

"A handsome boy!" she said warmly. "And I can see his potential. But he seems unhappy and a bit angry. Any idea why?"

I explained that we were new to the midwest and that Bart had lost his father in Vietnam. Her expression softened.

"How sad! I'll spend extra time with him; encourage him to take that chip off his shoulder."

I thanked her warmly. Maybe she would succeed. Meanwhile, in days that already seemed too full, how could I find some extra time for Andy?

But while I focused on Andy, Bart got into more trouble. One evening, after I'd spent a particularly hectic day at work, Mary Hammond stopped me as I stepped from the car. She was angry.

"Your great big son hit Lisa today. Hit her hard! She has a bruised shoulder."

"Bart? Hit Lisa? He knows better than to hit a girl—"

"Barbara, as a friendly warning, let me tell you, your son does a lot of things he's not supposed to. If you were here more, maybe you'd notice."

I flushed. "That's not fair, Mary. With my husband gone, I *have* to work."

Mary Hammond did not work. Her shrug was eloquent.

It bothered me to be on the outs with a neighbor. I stalked inside our house—and encountered a living room littered, as usual, with children's belongings. Lunch pails, jackets, schoolbooks, a half-eaten apple, Andy's toy soldiers, Allison's paper and scissors, all were strewn across the living room. The TV blared so loudly no one heard me come in.

"What's going on here?" I hollered.

Andy jumped up. "Boy, am I glad to see you, Mom. What's for dinner?"

"Hi, Mom. Guess what Rachel and I did after school?" Bart didn't look up.

58

I threw Andy's jacket in the air, tossed a book from a chair to the carpet.

"I can't believe this mess. Didn't you hear me this morning? I said to have this house picked up!"

"In a minute—"

"NOW!"

"Aw, Mom—"

For the first time, Bart looked up. "I'm not cleaning their mess. Let Allison and Andy clean up their own junk."

"While you go beat up someone else?"

"I didn't beat Lisa up. I hit her. And she started it."

"I don't care who started it, Bart. Boys don't hit girls. Especially a little girl three years younger than you."

"She called me names."

"It doesn't matter. Boys don't hit girls."

"Bart should get his own friends," said Andy. "Lisa's my friend."

"Maybe I could, *toad*. If we lived in California."

"I'm not a toad. Mom, he called me a toad!"

"That's enough, boys. Bart, go to your room. I will not have you beating up little girls."

"She called me a girl's name. Goldilocks! Just 'cause I got these dumb curls. I ain't no sissy Goldilocks!"

"I don't care what she called you. Boys who hit girls are bullies."

"Why am I always the one you get sore at?"

"Bart, for once, don't argue! Go to your room! Or—" I glanced at the junk strewn around the living room—"Wait a minute. Go to your room *after* you pick up your share of this mess."

"Pick up your own damn mess!" He shoved past me to the front door, slamming it hard behind him.

All the frustrations of my work day, plus the after-school fight, welled up inside. I hurled my briefcase across the room—it narrowly missed a table lamp—and screamed at Andy and Allison.

"Pick up this living room right now! And turn off that

goddam TV." In a frenzy, I ran to the kitchen for my kitchen shears. "Here! This will keep the TV off!" With a strong snip, I cut the cord.

"Mom!" Andy wailed.

"Tell your brother, when he comes in, he's in real trouble with me!"

With that, I ran upstairs to my bedroom. Everything seemed to be falling on me at once. A wild desire took hold of me to just run away—find some island where job and neighbors and kids weren't piled on me, day after day. But I couldn't run away. And I couldn't yell at my boss or my neighbors. The one person I could yell at was the child who had caused the neighbors' wrath. I could yell at Bart.

The front door opened twenty minutes later. By now, the living room was straight. Allison was setting the table.

"Bart," I said coldly, ignoring the penitent look on his face, "you've been a troublemaker all day. Go eat in your room."

He hated to be alone and I knew it. For one long moment, we glared at each other. Then Bart stomped upstairs. I heard him mumble something.

"What did you say? Answer me!"

He turned. "I said you were a crappy mother and I wished you were dead, like my father!"

In hindsight, it was as if at this moment we had stepped on a giant slide and there was no way to go but down.

CHAPTER SIX

A COUPLE OF weeks later, I took Allison to the doctor for a physical—partly because she needed one for school and partly because she'd been complaining about backaches. After taking X rays, Dr. Vogel called us into his office.

"I'm afraid I have some bad news," he said kindly. "Your daughter has scoliosis. Curvature of the spine."

It was an affliction that was not uncommon in pre-puberty girls, the doctor explained. But if not caught and corrected in time, it resulted in permanent, crippling spinal curvature. We were lucky; a few more months and Allison's scoliosis would have required bed rest in a full body cast for a year.

I listened, horrified. When he told me what would be required in place of a body cast, I started to cry. For twenty-two hours a day for a minimum of two years, Allison would have to wear a neck-to-hip brace that would yank her head up, making it impossible for her to sit with any comfort.

I helped her into the brace the first day she wore it to school. Heavy white plastic, like a Playtex girdle only many times thicker, fit over her hips. Twin aluminum spines went up her back and front. I locked the thick metal neckpiece.

"Mom?" She had to turn her whole body to look at me.

"Yes, honey?"

"Will kids make fun of me?"

The idea of someone taunting my daughter made me sad enough to cry. I struggled to find some word of encouragement.

"Hey," Allison said, "don't look so worried, Mom. I'll be okay."

I laughed shakily. "I'm supposed to prop *you* up, not vice versa."

"More propping I don't need."

We both laughed at her small joke. It was the kind of laugh that's not far removed from tears.

Through the windows came the heavy clang of the trash truck and an accompanying chorus of dog yelps, while downstairs in the kitchen Andy and Bart wrangled over a cereal box. Allison walked carefully down the steps to join them.

"Wow," said Andy, when he first saw his sister. "You look funny."

"Thanks a *lot*."

Bart made room for her at the table. "You look okay to me. And if anyone gives you trouble, just let me know."

"Thanks, Bart." She made another awkward, full body turn—like the Tin Woodman of Oz, I thought—and gave her brother a kiss on the cheek. He kissed her back.

Twenty minutes later, I watched her start up the hill toward the school, taking small, jerky steps. A group of older boys ran past, turned, stared, snickered among themselves and ran on. Allison kept walking. I couldn't help thinking how small and lonely my daughter looked. I felt a helpless ache because I couldn't help her more.

Now I had Andy's learning disabilities and hyperactivity and Allison's spinal curvature to worry about. Bart had no obvious problem other than misbehavior. Why couldn't he just behave? I asked myself over and over again. Didn't I have enough worries with my other two children?

Soon it would be Halloween.

One Friday, I reached home as Jeannie Morris walked to her car. Jeannie was older than I—close to forty—and had been divorced for ten years. I waved. She waved back, hesitated, then motioned me over.

"Barbara, I'm meeting a girlfriend at Houlihans for Friday night happy hour. Want to come?"

"Oh. Why—yes. Yes, if you can wait a minute."

Since moving to the Midwest, I had tried to convince myself that career and family were enough. But Jeannie's invitation reminded me that something very important *was* missing.

I ran to the upstairs bathroom where I kept my makeup. "Allison, be a lamb and take charge tonight? Soup and peanut butter sandwiches. Tomorrow night, I'll fix a real dinner."

Bart followed me to the bathroom. "I need to talk about Halloween."

"Later, Bart. Okay?"

He watched me put on rouge and eyeshadow. "Where you going?"

"Just out. Grownup stuff."

"Picking up men, I'll bet."

"Bart, nothing of the kind." I ran downstairs. "Be good kids and I'll be back soon."

The door slammed behind me.

I was still asleep when Mrs. Isaacks, the condominium manager, telephoned the next morning.

"Mrs. Bartocci, please come to my office."

"Now?"

"Your son is sitting here. He's broken a window."

"Oh," I groaned. "All right. I'll be right over."

Dirty glasses and wadded-up napkins littered the clubhouse. Someone had apparently had a party the night before. I knocked on Mrs. Isaacks's door.

Bart sat on a chair against one wall. He looked worried, but his mouth had a stubborn pout.

"Mom, it was an accident," he said, jumping up as I walked in. "Honest!"

Plump Mrs. Isaacks, in her double-knit pants suit, quivered with indignation.

"It didn't look like an accident to our security guard. He said it looked as if your son took aim."

"I was just messing around. I didn't mean to hit the window. Honest."

"I'll pay for the window," I offered.

Mrs. Isaacks sniffed. "Very well. But keep in mind, this is a quiet neighborhood, Mrs. Bartocci—"

"I'm sure Bart is not the first child to break a window."

"No. However—" she paused and lowered her bulk behind her desk. I waited for her to go on. But after a long hesitation, she merely said, "Remember. This is a quiet neighborhood."

Bart and I started home in silence, scuffling our feet through piles of leaves. A calico cat scampered past.

"I'm sorry, Mom."

"You said it was an accident."

"And it was!"

But, as we turned up the street to our townhouse, I wondered...

Halloween, it turned out, was a big event at George Washington Elementary School. The PTA sponsored a huge carnival, with rides and duck-for-apples booths and a prize for best costume and plenty of hot dogs, popcorn, and cotton candy to eat. It was their major fundraising event of the year. After the carnival, the kids traditionally went trick or treating.

"Mom," Bart pleaded, "can I go as a pirate and wear Daddy's sword?"

"His navy sword?" I almost choked, thinking of that sharp pointed sword among a bunch of kids. "I don't think so. That's a real sword and it could be dangerous. But maybe I can pick up something nearly as good."

The next day, on my lunch hour, I ran to a costume supply house and found a fancifully plumed pirate's hat and a suitably wicked looking rubber sword. Bart was thrilled. I loaned him a satin blouse with long full sleeves and a wide colorful scarf for a belt.

By the time I reached home on October 31, it was already dark. Andy had on his red devil suit and was giggling as he made scary faces into the mirror. Bart pranced about the living room, brandishing his sword. Even Allison seemed excited. She and sixth grade Rachel were going to the carnival as ghosts.

"I'm meeting some of the guys at the carnival," Bart announced. "We're going trick or treating later, Okay?"

"Sure." I tried not to let on how thrilled I was to hear him talk about *the guys*. "Just be home by nine-thirty."

The door bell rang. Miniature ghosts, with mommies behind them, piped, "Twick or tweat." Allison handed out lollipops. A ballerina, skeleton, and cowboy appeared; they turned into Lisa, Mike, and Bobby. Andy ran for his own trick or treat sack. "Remember," I told him, "You're younger than your brother. I want you home by eight-thirty. And only trick or treat on the streets leading home from school."

"Okay, okay."

"I'll walk to school with you," Bart said grandly. "I'm meeting the guys."

"Have a wonderful time! All of you!"

I smiled happily as the door closed behind them. *I've been too impatient*, I thought. *Things are starting to work out. Bart just needed a little more time.*

But when Andy pushed open the front door at 8:30, Bart appeared behind him. His face had a pinched, forlorn expression.

"Home so soon?" I tried to keep the dismay from my voice. "What happened, Bart?"

"The guys left me. I guess they forgot I was supposed to go with them."

"We let him come home with us," Andy said. "Mommy, it was a *neat* carnival. Stevie Sherman came as The Cat in the Hat. He won a prize. And I did, too. See?" He pulled out a model airplane. "I tried to win a cake for you in the cakewalk but I didn't. But I hit the balloon with a dart. And I ducked for apples 'cept I only got wet and I shot a BB gun and—"

"That's wonderful, Andy," I interrupted. I glanced at Bart, who sat slumped on the couch. Again, a helpless feeling stole over me. I wanted all of my children to be happy. Andy and Allison had adjusted in spite of their physical disabilities. Bart had none of their problems, but he was the least happy of the three. Why couldn't he just fit in?

After the Halloween party, Bart seemed to give up on making friends with boys his own age. When I asked him about it, he muttered that the kids in his class were stupid jerks and he didn't want to talk about it. He began to hang around our townhouse after school, around the little kids. Soon, I began to get calls almost weekly from our neighbors.

"Barbara, Bart is bullying my son. I want it stopped."

". . . It's about Bart, Mrs. Bartocci. He's picked on Mike."

"Yeah, I hit Mike," admitted Bart. "But it's not my fault.

65

They pick on me! Bobby and Lisa and that dumb ol' Mike Hammond. My stupid *toad* brother told them about 'Bart the Fart' and now they call me that all the time. Just to make me mad!"

"Oh, Bart, I'm sorry." I felt a genuine stab of sympathy. "But the best way to make them stop is to pay no attention. Or to laugh it off."

"It's not funny."

No, I thought wanly, I suppose it's not. But it was no laughing matter, either, to see my son being tagged a *bully*.

That span of time between Halloween and Christmas has always reminded me of an accordion, the days all squeezed together.

My mother and father ("Mom and Granddaddy" to the kids) planned to arrive December 20. Excitedly, we began preparing for their visit.

Allison and Bart helped me pull out the cardboard box of Christmas decorations. We put up the Advent wreath and lit the first candle. We started the Wise Men on their traditional journey around our living room.

"Mom—Mommy, look!" Bart cried one Saturday morning in mid-December. He and Andy ran out the front door, so excited they forgot to put on their shoes. I followed them out, shivering in my bathrobe, but laughing, too. Snow! White, fluffy flakes that stuck to the eyelashes, perfect for making snowmen. Bart whirled around, his arms outstretched, his face lifted to the miracle of it. Andy packed together a snowball, tossed it at Bart. Bart giggled, threw one back. From other houses, kids began running outside in jackets and gloves.

"Come inside," I coaxed, "and get dressed properly. "And I—I'll tell you what. I'll fix waffles for breakfast."

Waffles had been a Sunday morning staple in San Diego. Here, cold cereal or scrambled eggs had taken over. Waffles took *time*. And there never seemed to be enough time.

But the snow created a magic. Allison felt it too. She followed her brothers outside after breakfast, walking more carefully in her back brace, but lifting her face, too, to the wonder of the fat, white flakes.

The Shapiro kids appeared with their sled. Through the kitchen window, I saw Bart pulling the smaller kids. They headed for the baseball field and the hill that sloped behind it.

Humming to myself, I put a Christmas record on the stereo. I'll build a fire, I thought. our first fire of the season. I even rummaged in the kitchen until I found some dusty packets of hot cider mix I had purchased on a whim months before.

It was close to lunchtime when I heard the commotion outside. Voices raised in anger—then a thud. I ran to the front door.

Bart and Bobby Shapiro were yelling at each other, tugging at the rope that pulled the sled. Bobby's father, Ned, appeared in his doorway. He ran toward the circle of kids. I ran out, too.

Bart's face was red with anger. Tears of frustration filmed his eyes. "But it's my turn!" he shouted.

"It's my sled!" cried Bobby Shapiro. "You go get your own sled."

"What's going on here?" Ned Shapiro demanded.

"Daddy, Bart's beating up on me. He's trying to take my sled."

"Listen, here, you young bully. You're three years older and thirty pounds heavier than—"

"But, they *said*—" Bart began.

"Please," I interrupted, "Whats *happening*?"

"They said—Bobby and Mike—if I pulled them home from the baseball field, I could take the sled by myself—"

"No, I didn't. It's my sled and he's trying to grab it. Big bully!"

"Liar! You did, too, say—"

"Who are you calling a liar, young man?"

"Please! Bart, be quiet for a minute!"

"I've had it up to here with your bullying son."

"Mom, honest! They said if I pulled them—"

"Daddy, tell him to stay away from us!"

"I certainly will. I'd better not see your kids anywhere near my kids and their sled. Is that clear, Barbara?"

My head felt as if it were spinning. "All right, Bart, come inside the house."

"But Mom, it's not fair. They *said*—"

"Bart! *Inside!*"

I spun on my heel, Bart trailing me.

Inside, he turned and screamed at me. Tears poured down his cheeks. "What kind of mother are you? You never take my side! They promised! They said if I pulled them home—"

"Bart, please! I know it's not fair. But it's still Bobby's sled and you're still three years older. You can't go pounding some little kid every time you get mad! Remember Donny Hayward in San Diego?"

"But they lied!"

"Maybe they did, but I can't do anything about that."

"Why can't you ever take my side?"

"I do take your side, honey. When I can. I got after the kids for taking your football, remember?"

"But you didn't stick up for me this morning."

"Because it *is* Bobby's sled. And even if he didn't keep his promise, that's no excuse for you to start a fight."

"I hate you. I hate this place. I hate—I hate *everyone!*"

He ran, still crying, to his bedroom. The door slammed. The vibration sent the record skipping. "These are a few of my favorite things... my favorite things... my favorite things..." The fire blazed. The air was fragrant with cider. But, standing alone in the living room, I began to cry, too. I ached for Bart's unhappiness but I didn't know what to do about it. I wanted to rescue him, but how? Out of my helplessness came anger. Damn! Why couldn't he simply get along?

My parents arrived and it was wonderful to see them. I proudly drove them to my office.

"How about that for your 'little girl'?" I teased my father.

68

"Not bad," he replied with the familiar twinkle in his eye. "Next thing I know, you'll be running the joint."

For all of us, the presence of "Mom and Granddaddy" seemed to release the tensions of fall.

My mother and the kids baked Christmas cookies. Mom took over the kitchen, fixing her special meat loaf and the mashed potatoes Andy loved, and the zucchini in cheese sauce that was my favorite.

One night we borrowed a projector and Daddy showed slides, all the familiar slides of Christmases past. There was John, his smile vibrant and alive as he held his Barty Boy; his Princess; his Andrew-Babe. A sweet sadness filled me as I recalled the happiness of those early family days. The children, I noticed, grew very quiet as the pictures of their Daddy flashed on the screen.

While I was at work, Mom and Granddaddy stayed with the kids. My mother began to notice something.

"Barbara," she said, as we stuffed the turkey on Christmas Eve, "Bart seems very unhappy. And unruly. I've had to stop several fights and most of them were fights he started."

I sighed and chopped another piece of celery. Little did Mom know that Bart's behavior was nothing new.

"Why not enroll him in a good Catholic school? That's what he needs."

The nearest Catholic school was too far for him to walk to, and I couldn't drive Bart and still get to work on time.

"He's fine," I said. "He's still getting used to things, that's all."

My mother didn't look convinced and I didn't blame her. But the problem of changing Bart's school was more than I could handle.

The day after New Year's Day we bid them goodbye at the airport. "I wish I could go with you," Bart said, clinging to his grandmother.

She hugged him tightly. "You can spend the summer with us. But for now—control that temper of yours. Don't get so *mad* all the time. Promise?"

He nodded.

My father gave us all a loving look. "Okay, you young whippersnappers. How about one for the road?"

We laughed. Everyone kissed him heartily on the cheek. We waited until their plane took off. As we watched I pictured it landing beneath the warm sun of San Diego and wondered if we should have stayed in California ... would everything be different if we had?

In the cold, confining months that followed, the question returned again. Winter only seemed to exacerbate Bart's quarrels and fights. I began to get calls from school as well as from neighborhood mothers.

"I've tried everything I know to reach Bart," said Miss McGrail, after Bart's third visit to the principal's office. Her usual cheery smile had vanished into a small, worried frown. "He seems so *angry*. So determined to get into trouble. I'm wondering ..." She hesitated. "Have you considered professional counseling?"

"You mean—a psychiatrist?"

"Or clinical psychologist."

"Bart doesn't need that. He needs to control his temper, that's all."

"But Mrs. Bartocci—"

"Look, I've got all I can handle, worrying about Andy and his learning problems. And Allison and that damn spinal curvature. I've done the best I can with Bart. Ever since his father died, I've tried—"

"No one is saying you haven't—"

"Then don't talk about psychiatrists. He's a normal kid! He's adjusting to a new environment, that's all. What he needs is a little more understanding from his teacher!" I stomped out of her office.

All that day, anger ate at me. I was mad at Bart. And myself. And Miss McGrail. And John, for dying. And God, for permitting it. By evening, my anger had grown into rage.

I stormed through our front door, slamming it shut. As usual, the TV was blaring and the living room a mess.

"Bart!" I screamed. "Come here!"

"What's wrong, Mom?"

I grabbed his arm and pulled him toward the hall closet. "I got another call from your school. Now I'm going to do what I shoud have done months ago." Still holding one arm, I reached for an old leather belt I usually shoved into my blue jeans. "Maybe this will teach you to stay out of fights, you troublemaking bully!"

"Mom, no! Don't hit me!"

"Stand still, Bart. Damn it, bend over! You're getting ten swats with this belt. Bend over, do you hear me?"

"No, Mom, no!"

He began to jump and screech as he tried to get away, while Allison and Andy, suddenly protective, started yelling, "Don't hit him, Mom! Don't hit him!" Scrambling to get hold of my wriggling son, I ran after him myself. The whole house trembled. I got hold of him once, but he slipped away. I grabbed him again, and this time he wriggled out of his T-shirt, sending me sprawling on the carpet. My shoes had come off and my hair flew in my face. Andy was pulling at the belt, trying to take it away from me. I shoved him aside and lunged again for Bart. This time I got him and pushed him to the carpeted floor, where I put one knee on his chest and flipped him over. He struggled and screamed all the more but I managed to get in a half-dozen licks. My flailings with the belt could not have hurt much—I had no leverage—but the panting, wild-eyed fighting terrified us all.

I let Bart up and he scuttled to his room while I screamed after him, "You're a troublemaker! Nothing but a trouble-maker!"

And then, feeling like a monstrous mother, I went, weeping, to my own room.

A scene from the old TV show, "Father Knows Best," flickered through my mind. I wanted us to be that kind of family, but I couldn't escape the truth of what our home was like—a battleground. And I was a failure—an exhausted failure.

Still, there was more at stake than my ideal vision of a family. My son was a boy consumed with pain, and his misbehavior was a cry for help. It was a cry I wasn't yet ready to hear.

CHAPTER SEVEN

AFTER WHAT seemed like a tortuous winter and spring, I sent the children to California for six weeks with a great feeling of relief. As they boarded their plane, it seemed as if anxiety lifted from me. Even the guilt I felt (what kind of mother was I to feel so happy to say goodbye to my children?) could not over-ride my feeling of relief.

I was free! For six blessed weeks, no fights with Bart. No sympathy pains for Allison. No secret worries about Andy's reading progress. Free!

To celebrate, I went with my friend Tina to an astrology lecture for single adults. Over the past year, I had tagged along with her occasionally to singles events. But the pressure of work and parenting had left me with little energy to consider the state of my own social life.

But now it was June. Tennis players lobbed balls on public courts. Bicyclists and joggers were visible on side streets. Picnickers flocked to the parks for free jazz concerts. Fireflies flickered in purple dusks.

And I was free!

I wore a new summer dress—a bold pink print—and walked into the lecture hall with a swing in my step.

Bill told me later it was the freedom of my walk—the

joy it expressed—that caught his attention.

He approached me after the lecture as Tina and I stood by the refreshment table.

What I saw was a man of medium height, somewhere in his late thirties, with a hairline that receded slightly and a waistline that protruded slightly. But when he smiled, his whole face lit with a warmth and—I searched for the right word—*kindness*. That was it. An unusual quality in a man.

"Well, did the speaker convince you?" he asked.

"To chart my horoscope? Not really."

"Me neither." He chuckled. "I only wish life were that simple."

"Me, too." I must have said it with unusual fervor because he chuckled again. "Let me guess. You're a single parent."

"How did you know?"

"Takes one to know one." This time, we both laughed. He asked if I were free the following evening for supper and a movie. (That's what he called it: supper, not dinner. I was struck by the quaint, but homey difference.) I said yes.

The next evening we ate hamburgers on a card table in his small apartment. The typical gold-carpeted, beige-walled apartment of the newly divorced male. He'd been married fourteen years, he told me, and his three kids were half grown. He missed them—missed the every-dayness of being with them and watching them grow.

I told him about John and my decision to move to the Midwest and—something about those kind eyes—I found myself describing my various problems with the children.

"I enjoy kids," he said, as we drove home from the movie. "I'd like to meet yours when they return."

A small silence fell between us. "I'd like that," I said, finally. We both smiled.

When he suggested we see the play at our local repertory theater the following Friday, I didn't hesitate. As I scrubbed my face clean of makeup that night, I found myself humming. What a wonderful summer it promised to be!

As if to reinforce the promise of summer, my boss called me into his office on Thursday. Papers, notebooks, file folders, and a Rolodex littered Dave's desk. He waved a hand at the disarray.

"I'm going bonkers, Barbara. We've tripled the size of the PR department since I came here. Jim [the V.P. of corporate communications] agrees that it's time to spread the work a little." He grinned. "We've created a new title: Director of Media Relations, and you're it, if you want it."

"Oh!" I was thrilled. "Yes. I'd love it."

"Good. You'll still report to me, but you'll be the one responsible for handling the media. I've put in for a raise for you, too." Idly, his fingers played with the cards in his Rolodex. "May mean a few late nights. Especially at first."

"No problem," I said quickly. "The kids are visiting my parents for six weeks. I can work late."

"Good." He grinned again. "You start your new job tomorrow."

Tina took me to lunch to celebrate.

"I hope I can manage," I said, as waiters clinked silverware and plates around us.

"Of course you can!"

"I mean, when the kids come back."

She speared a lettuce leaf. "By then, it'll be a piece of cake."

She's probably right, I thought. It occurred to me suddenly that I could share my good news with Bill the next night. But when Tina asked, "Why the happy smile?" I merely shrugged, "The new job, of course. What else?"

Tina was partly right. By the time the children returned in August, I felt I had a handle on my expanded job, though the workload was heavy. I was also seeing Bill regularly.

"What are those?" asked Allison, pointing to half-painted bookshelves drying on our patio on her first night home.

"They belong to a friend of mine," I replied. "You'll meet him tomorrow. I've asked him to dinner."

The children looked tanned and fit and seemed taller. Allison needed a new back brace, she told me; she was growing out of the present one. I helped carry in suitcases and Bart's new tennis racket and Andy's swimming fins and Allison's watercolor paint set.

The California sun had bleached the boys' hair. Their tans made their eyes appear bluer than I remembered. *What handsome boys*, I thought. I could hardly believe I had felt so relieved when they left. How good it felt to have them back with me now!

The Shapiro kids appeared. Rachel was developing a bosom. She and Allison greeted each other with excited squeals and hugs. Andy grabbed Bobby's arm. "C'mon. I'll show you my new rocket set."

Bart and I were left alone. He smiled shyly. I reached out and pulled him into my arms for a big hug.

No more fights between us, I promised myself. *This next year is going to be different.*

At dinner the next night, Bill described the canoe he had built with his son, Marc. "We use it for float trips. You kids ever been on a float trip?"

They shook their heads.

"Ever been bass fishing?"

"We go trout fishing," said Bart. "Our Daddy liked trout fishing best. He used to take us when we went camping in California."

"I like to camp. How about you and your Mom camping with me next weekend? I'll show you how to canoe. Maybe even how to fish for bass. Of course, I realize that won't compare to trout fishing."

"Wahoo!" shouted Andy.

"Darn. I promised to spend the night with Rachel."

Bart hesitated. A mixture of emotions ran across his face. The pull of the canoe won.

"Okay."

"Don't worry." Bill said to Allison. "There will be more

camping trips." He and I smiled at each other.

Bart's expression turned suspicious.

We set up our tent in a small grove of trees not far from the lake shore. Bill and I, with the boys helping, lifted the canoe off the top of his station wagon. Once in the water, Bill showed the boys how to paddle, made sure their life jackets were on, then pushed them out by themselves.

"You can go anywhere you want to in this cove. But don't leave it. Understand?"

"Oh, Bill!" I cried. "I don't know—"

"Barbara, this cove is very calm. We'll stay right here where we can see them. They're wearing life jackets. Both can swim. Stop being an over-protective Mommy."

The boys laughed, suddenly members of a species called "male" relating to a worry-wart species called "female."

I gave in. Bill waved the boys off. "Anyway," he said, sliding down beside me on the grass. "This way, I can hold their Mommy's hand, tell her she's beautiful, and not get jealous looks from her sons."

"Do you think they're jealous?"

"Bart more than Andy."

I sighed. "He never has accepted men I've dated."

"You just haven't dated the right one. Till now."

We looked at each other. Had it been only eight weeks since we met? I felt as if I'd known this man forever. Bill's hand on mine tightened.

The boys spent all afternoon in the canoe. They played pirate and explorer and Indian scout. Their shouts and splashes and gleeful laughter rang across the water. It was all we could do to get them to land at twilight.

"You boys fetch wood for a fire," Bill instructed. While the boys ran off to their tasks, he and I wandered, hand in hand, by the lake shore. Crickets and cicadas made summer evening music. Fireflies flickered. From across the water we heard someone laugh. A single sailboat drifted by, its sail ghostly in the deepening twilight. There was no need to talk.

Bart appeared so suddenly, he startled me.

"Mom, why are you spending all your time with him?"

"Bart? What do you mean?"

"All afternoon, that's what. Hanging around him. Sending us out by ourselves in that boat." Deliberately, he edged in between Bill and me.

Bill laughed. "Bart, we practically had to drag you out of that canoe. Stop playing games with your mother."

"She's my Mom! I've been gone all summer, and now you push us out in some dumb canoe so you two can play kissy-face."

"Bart, I didn't—"

"Why can't we go camping, just us? You and Allison and Andy and me? Just our family?"

"Look, son, that's enough! Right now, you're camping with me—"

"I ain't your son!"

"—and I sent you to fetch wood. Now get going or I'll find a piece of wood for your fanny!"

He sounded as if he meant it. Apparently, Bart thought so, too. He stomped off angrily, but I saw him bend down for a piece of firewood.

Later, though, when Bill showed the boys how to start a fire without paper and helped them whittle sticks for marshmallows, Bart seemed to forget his bad temper. In the firelight's glow, his cheeks grew ruddy with good humor and his laugh rang out as Bill told tales from his Boy Scout days. Bill is a lot like John, I thought. The two men had different personalities, but I sensed in Bill the same values I'd loved in John. It was apparent he liked kids.

Still, I couldn't forget what Bart had said earlier.

"Barbara," said Bill, after the boys had settled into sleeping bags, "don't you see? It's a game Bart plays. He had a *wonderful* time in that canoe. And what made it even better, he made you feel guilty, to boot."

I shook my head. "You don't understand."

"Yes, I do."

"No! I'm the only parent they've got left. I—" I stared

at the lake, at the moon shadows playing on the water. A fish jumped. "I may be wrong to even think of a life for myself until after they're grown."

Bill turned me toward him. I tried to turn away, but he forced me to face him. Even in the darkness, his eyes held me. "I love you, Barbara. And you're a person just as much as your kids are. You won't help Bart by burying your own needs."

He had never said "I love you" before.

I heard another fish jump and felt a sudden breeze off the water. I whispered, "I love you, too."

The next few weeks were magical.

"You look like one of those smiley-face buttons," said Tina, at lunch. "This guy must be some fella."

I sprinkled bacon bits on my salad. "He is." Noontime noises clinked around us. "But it's more than Bill. It's—" I waved a French roll expansively. "It's everything!"

Everything, I thought, in satisfaction, *is finally coming together.*

It had seemed that way ever since our camping trip, as if those whispered words on the shore of a lake had touched every aspect of life. I felt on top of my new job. At home, as we shopped for school clothes, the kids were cheerful and cooperative. Even Bart, after his outburst on the trip, seemed easier to get along with.

Dr. Vogel had looked at Allison's X rays and smiled. "We've arrested the curve in your spine. Think you can stand another year in this brace?"

Allison, her teeth now in braces, too, returned his smile. "I guess." She pointed to the hole rubbed in her T-shirt by the metal spine of the brace. "It's making me holy, anyway."

Her good humor lifted my spirits.

Andy met his fourth grade teacher, Frannie James. In her buttoned down shirt and penny loafers, she looked like a middle-aged preppie. She even spoke with a faint Maine accent.

"So you're the bright young man I've been hearing about.

Following in the footsteps of Albert Einstein and Franklin Roosevelt. Do you know who they were?"

Andy shook his head.

"Well, Roosevelt was president of the United States. And Einstein was one of the most brilliant scientists who ever lived. And you know what?"

She waited.

"What?" said Andy, finally.

"They had the same kind of reading problem you do. Letters looked backwards to them, too. At least, when they were boys. So they had to work a little harder to learn to read. Just as you do. We'll work together. Is it a deal?"

She stuck out her hand. Andy took it. They shook. Suddenly, Andy smiled as he never had the year before. I wanted to hug Frannie James.

Bart, too, seemed more confident that first day of school. He perched on the corner of my bed, watching as I put on makeup.

"Wait'll you see how good I do in school."

"I hope so, Bart. Sixth grade can be fun."

"I'll probably go to someone's house after school. Jake Ferrari's, maybe."

"That's okay. Just call me at work and tell me where you are."

"I'm going to make all A's this year."

"Good for you!"

I turned from the mirror. Bart jumped up and hugged me tightly. "You'll see," he repeated and ran downstairs.

But the honeymoon ended two weeks later. I arrived home from work, hot and sticky. The calendar said mid-September but the muggy heat felt like July.

"Let's eat sandwiches," I suggested, and was pulling out bologna when I noticed Bart's lip. It was swollen and bruised.

"What happened to you?"

Something about the way he and Andy exchanged glances made me suspicious. "What happened?" I repeated.

"I cut myself."

"How?"

"How? The way anybody does. I hit something. Jeez, Mom, you don't have to give me the third degree."

"Bart, were you in a fight?"

Again, that evasive exchange of glances. Outside the open kitchen window, a door slammed. Someone's car started. I wiped sweat off my forehead. Damn, it was hot.

"Well?"

"I didn't start it," he muttered. "Mike Hammond did. Calling me Bart the Fart again. I'd like to cream his ass!"

"Bart!"

"Mrs. Hammond said she's gonna talk to you," announced Andy, "She said she won't have another year like last year."

"Mom—" Bart's blue eyes were wide and beseeching. "I was just minding my own business. Honest. And they started in. That whole crowd of little twerps. They made me mad on *purpose.*"

"I'll speak to Mrs. Hammond, Bart. See if I can get the teasing stopped. But remember, you're too big a boy to lose your temper with little kids. Even if they tease you. Okay?"

"Okay," he agreed, obviously relieved that I was going to do something.

But when I talked to Mary Hammond, she shook her head in instant rebuttal. "I'm sorry, Barbara. My children don't use that kind of language."

"My son doesn't lie!"

"Oh? I don't think you know what your son does. When your children were away this summer, we all remarked that it was very peaceful in the neighborhood."

I was stung by her hostility. I'd always gotten along well with my neighbors.

"Bart," I said, when I returned home, "You've picked up a dreadful reputation."

"I knew you wouldn't take my side."

"It's not a matter of taking sides—"

"You never stick up for me. You don't love me near as much as you love Andy and Allison."

"Of course, I love you. You're my son—"

80

"No, you don't."

I recalled John's words that long-ago day on our patio. "Bart is sensitive." I thought of my own inadequacy in dealing with this middle child.

"You're totally wrong," I said shortly. "I love all three of you. What I *don't* love is your bullying behavior."

"I'm not a bully!"

"The neighbors think you are!"

"Why do you believe them? I'll tell you why. You don't like me."

"Bart, you're twisting my words—"

"You just don't want to admit it."

"Damn it! You make me so angry!"

"You make me more angry!"

"I've had enough of this! Go to your room."

"There you go again. Shoving me away. Trying to get rid of me. I'll bet you'd like to get rid of me forever."

"Maybe I would!"

"I knew you hated me!"

"I don't hate you, I love you! Now go to your room!"

He ran out of the kitchen. I wiped my face again. Why? Why did we always wind up this way? What could I do to change things?

CHAPTER EIGHT

I ENROLLED IN a class in parenting techniques offered by our local community college. Self-consciously, I tried out some newly acquired listening skills. The kids thought I was funnier than Richard Pryor.

"It's just—well, we know what you're doing," said Allison, with a good-natured giggle. "You sound like you're reading lines from a play, Mom."

"I must not read them too well," I replied, with a rueful laugh. The boys giggled, too. Oddly, it was a nice moment, a warm, sharing moment.

But, except for providing a few laugh-filled moments, parenting techniques was not the answer to the problems I saw accelerating in our family. I tried talking things over with Bill.

"The kids and I fight too much. Wouldn't you think they'd rather spend fifteen minutes picking up the house instead of listening to me nag? But, no. Every night, it's the same thing. The house is a mess and I rant and rave. God, I get tired."

Bill put his arm around me and pulled me close. We were sitting in his apartment. Beethoven's Sixth Symphony played softly on the stereo. Glasses of white wine sat on the coffee table in front of us.

"Your kids don't take you seriously," he said. "They know, in the end, you'll give in. Frankly, it appears to me that they've grown up with Mommy doing everything for them."

"I have to make up to them for losing their father."

"That's crazy."

"Oh?" I pulled out of his arms. It wasn't the first time we'd had this exchange. "Because I think parents have a certain responsibility to their children?"

"Responsibility for what? Were you responsible for John's death?"

"No, but just because I work, and just because there's only one parent doesn't mean my children should be burdened with—"

"Burdened with a few household chores? But you get mad as hell because they won't do chores!"

"I want them to pick up their own stuff. But you talk as if kids should do *everything*. You sound like my friend Polly."

Bill laughed. "I think I'd like your friend Polly."

"Oh, yeah?" I reached over and tickled him in the ribs. "Well, she's too pretty. I'd better not introduce you."

We both laughed, and then kissed, and after that, talk about kids was forgotten.

* * *

But our dialogue was not finished. A week later, I described the brouhaha Bart and I had gotten into over the dishes.

"Every last dish was still sitting on the counter from breakfast," I complained, "and you know what Bart said when I asked why he hadn't loaded the dishwasher? He said, 'But you didn't *say* to wash the dishes.' Well, no, I didn't. Not specifically. But he knew that's what I expected. 'But you didn't *say*—' he insisted. What do you think of that, Bill?"

"I think Bart sounds like a lawyer," Bill chuckled.

"It's not funny. We wound up yelling at each other again. I screamed like a banshee and then loaded the damn dishwasher, just to get it done."

Bill's grin vanished. "I know it's not funny, Barb. In fact, I see some bigger problems coming. Bart and Andy will be teenagers before you know it. You've got to establish respect for your authority before then."

"Don't you think I'm trying?"

"You try too hard to make your kids happy. But, my darling"—he wrapped one arm around my shoulders—"happy doesn't mean irresponsible. I've never seen a happy kid who didn't have limits set on his behavior."

Bill understood limits. I found that out one October Saturday. It was an incredibly beautiful Indian summer day. The air held the special crispness of autumn but the sun felt warm and mellow. He had telephoned early. "Let's take the canoe to the park. The kids can paddle on the lake and we'll barbecue hamburgers."

"Sounds terrific," I said.

We left home at ten o'clock. The boys clambered into the rear seat of Bill's three-seater station wagon. They loved the novelty of riding backwards.

"Leave the window open," they begged. The air conditioner didn't reach to the back, and it was hot.

"All right," Bill said, "but no standing up or leaning out. That's dangerous."

Allison and Rachel climbed into the middle seat, our picnic cooler on the floor between them. The sky looked like an overturned blue bowl; not a cloud in sight. A slight breeze rustled on our arms.

We had just turned into the park when Bill glanced in his rearview mirror. "Hey!" he growled. "Sit down back there!"

I twisted in my seat. Andy and Bart leaned out the open tailgate window, waving at the car behind us. Bill's growl sent Andy scurrying back inside, but Bart continued to lean and wave.

"Bart, sit down!" Bill hollered.

Bart pulled back slightly, but his head and shoulders were still leaning outside.

"If I have to tell you one more time, I'll pull over and paddle your rear with a belt!" Bill warned.

Bart didn't move. With a quick spin of the wheel, Bill pulled to the shoulder of the road and braked. Before I could cry more than "Wait!", he was out of the car, pulling the belt off his pants. Down came the tailgate. Bart was laid across it.

"Hey, you're not my Dad! Mom, tell him he can't touch me!"

"Bill, please—"

But without glancing up, Bill administered six strong whacks.

"Owww, woww, no, no!"

He shoved Bart back into the car, rolled up the window, jumped back in the driver's seat and proceeded along the parkway. Except for Bart's outraged cries from the rear, the entire car was silent. My fingernails dug into my palms.

"I don't think that was necessary, Bill."

"It was damn necessary. I know a kid who fell out of a car, pulling the same dumb trick. When safety is at stake and I give an order, I expect to be obeyed. Instantly!"

"Oh? May I say, you sound just a wee bit tyrannical."

"No, you may say I sound a *big* bit parental."

84

"Only you're not my son's parent."

We'd arrived at the picnic area. Conversation halted while we unloaded the canoe.

"Barbara," said Bill, after Andy and the girls had paddled out into the lake, "You and the kids come as a packaged set, and I know it. So let's talk about how you and I define *family*. To me, it's not a unit ruled by kids."

Silence fell between us. Was Bill making an oblique reference to marriage? We hadn't talked about any permanent commitment.

I replied carefully. "To me, a family is a group of loving, happy people. Look how angry Bart is." I pointed to the lakeshore, where he stood furiously pitching pebbles into the water.

Bill's expression grew more thoughtful. "Bart seems angry *all* the time. At everybody."

I felt small worry lines ridge my forehead. What Bill said was true.

Already, I'd been called by his principal, Mrs. McGregor.

"Bart can't seem to make friends with children his own age, Mrs. Bartocci. So he bullies the younger students." Her use of the word "bully" triggered memories of San Diego.

"A bully is despicable!" I said, admonishing Bart that evening. "You're getting to be as bad as that awful Donny Hayward. What am I going to do with you?"

"Send me back to California. Please! Let me live with Mom and Granddaddy."

"You think they'd want you now? They hate bullies, too."

Bart's face paled. I saw his change in expression. The sudden vulnerability brought a swift stab of remorse. But I felt resentful, too. All I wanted was a well-behaved child. Was that so much to ask? Bart was his Daddy's special boy, and damn it, he wasn't behaving the way John's son should.

As the weather grew colder, our fights heated up.

"Bart doesn't mean to be a bully," Allison said one wintry

night, after the boys had gone to bed. The evening had been filled with another shouting match between Bart and myself. Mary Hammond had complained again because Bart had pushed Mike Hammond off his bike and sent the bike careering, riderless, down the street. The result was a crumpled front fender.

"Deep down, he wants kids to like him," Allison went on. "But it's like—like everyone *expects* him to be a bully, now. So, he is. Do you see what I mean?" Her expression was earnest and troubled.

I sighed. I did see...sometimes. I remembered the infectious laugh and sunny good nature of our tow-headed Barty Boy. What a likeable little boy he had been. Where had he disappeared to, that child?

There were moments—becoming rarer and rarer—when Bart would hug me, his blue eyes wide and sincere, and say, "I'm going to get along with the kids today, Mom. You watch. If someone calls me 'Bart the Fart,' I'll laugh in his face." And I'd squeeze back and say, "Wonderful, Bart!"

I sighed, again. Did it only seem as if those were the very days when he got into the most trouble?

I turned toward Allison. "Enough of Bart. What's going on in your life, hon?"

She shifted, uncomfortably. The brace forced her to sit bolt upright. "Same old stuff."

"Seen much of Rachel lately?"

A pained look flashed in Allison's eyes. I saw it, and felt my own heart tighten. I knew what was happening. Rachel, in seventh grade, had blossomed. The bosom I noticed in August was more developed now. Her hair was thick and lustrous. Her eyes winked at boys through makeup. And the boys were winking back. They had noticed Rachel, all right. She no longer had time for a friend who was, in Allison's own words, a dork. "That's what I am, Mom. Let's face it. An eighth grade dork!"

I wanted to make things right for Allison. I despised all those awful kids who didn't invite my daughter to parties or ask her to sit at the "popular" lunch table. But what could I do?

"Listen," I said suddenly, "Remember how you used to say you'd like to own a dog? Why don't you talk to Bill? He and his daughter used to train German Shepherds. Maybe—"

Allison's smile was a happy silver glitter. "Oh, Mom, that's a wonderful idea!"

So we acquired Shasta, a friendly and engaging Yorkshire terrier. Everyone adored him; the boys as much as Allison. Andy had always been crazy about animals. But stormy confrontations, like the crackling midwest thunderstorms that billowed, gray and threatening, in early spring skies, continued to build in our family.

Bart accused Allison of "bossing." She accused me of expecting her to boss. The boys fought with each other over morning bowls of cereal, over what to watch on TV, over underwear, over who could take a bath first and who left the bathtub dirty for the next one.

"You always take Andy's side," Bart complained when I stepped into the middle of another fight between the boys. "He's your little baby."

"That's enough, Bart."

"Well, ain't it true? Allison's perfect, and Andy's your baby. Baby-baby-baby."

"Farty-Farty-Farty," retorted Andy. He slipped his hand into mine. "Bart beats up on me just because he's bigger."

"Bart—" I began, and then stoped. Did I favor Andy? If I did, it was surely because Andy didn't push me all the time. Neither did Allison. Bart wouldn't let things drop. It was as if he were determined to goad me into fighting with him. And, I thought unhappily, he usually succeeded.

Meanwhile, my job continued to expand. I loved my work, but found myself more and more pressured during the day, more exhausted when I did reach home, and more impatient with the kids.

It was good to have Bill in my life, but we had our own

stormy confrontations. Disturbing, lightning-flicked storms marred our attempt to define a relationship that included, besides each other, the baggage of past history and six kids between us. Even though Bill's children didn't live with him they visited often, and mixing two families was a big commitment. Was it a bigger commitment than each of us wanted to make? Time would tell.

I wrestled with my increasing frustration about Bart. His grades were going down. We had countless fights over his TV viewing. I had cut the cord so often that one night, when Bill was over, he discovered a television cord too short to repair. When I told him why I'd cut it—and how often— he stared at me in amused stupefaction. "Wouldn't it be easier to simply tell the kids 'No'?"

Of course! But I was feeling more and more helpless as a parent, which increased my resentment and anger—anger directed at Bart most often, because he seemed to cause the most trouble.

One day in early May, Bill watched Bart play softball in the field up the block. It was a pick-up game. Most players were in junior high. Bart was allowed in because he was big for his age.

His turn at bat. Crack! He hit the ball hard into the outfield, running past first in a bold try for second. But the second baseman tagged him out.

Bart had slid into base. He stood up with grass stains on his Levi's and dirt across one cheek. "Out? I'm not out."

"Sure ya are. I tagged you fair and square."

Bill reported the incident later. "He seemed to go berserk, Barb. He began punching that second base kid as if he wanted to mash his whole face in. I've never seen a kid so angry. He was angry at a whole lot more than being tagged out."

"He just lost his temper."

"No, it was more than that. He's really hurting inside. Have you thought of—"

"Don't you start in on me."

"All right. We'll drop it." But I could see, behind his glasses, a frown I hadn't seen before.

Bart's birthday arrived a few weeks later. He was turning twelve. "How about a party?" I suggested. Bart had always loved parties.

A sudden smile replaced his usual scowl. His blue eyes lit up and for an instant, I could see, again, the curly-haired, happy-natured baby I had enjoyed so much.

"Yeah. Could we go bowling?"

"Whatever you want. Bowling sounds fine. We'll go to Happy Joe's for pizza and ice cream afterwards."

"Terrific!"

"Okay. Invite six friends. I'll ask Bill to drive his station wagon. We'll leave at five o'clock on Friday. I'll come home early from work."

Bill and I reached my town house shortly after five. We walked inside and knew something was wrong right away. Allison and Andy were there, but Bart stood by himself in the center of the living room, a husky twelve-year-old who looked vulnerable and sad. He looked as if he wanted to cry but was ashamed to; as if he wanted someone to put loving arms around him.

No one had come to his party. Not one of the half-dozen kids Bart had asked. We stood around awkwardly, for thirty minutes more, saying to each other loudly, "Well, maybe they're just late." Then, finally, we just stood around.

Bart broke the silence. "Stupid dumb kids! Not even smart enough to remember the right day of the week! Why'd you move us here, Mom?"

"Please, Bart, don't get mad at me."

"Well, it's all your fault, moving us here! I want to go back to California!"

He pushed past me.

"Bart, wait!"

"Aw, go to hell."

"Let him go," said Bill.

"He shouldn't swear like that."

Andy snorted "Huh. You should hear him when you're not around."

Allison sighed. "Well, let's face it. We're the neighborhood untouchables."

"Allison, you don't mean that!"

"Oh, mother, sometimes you're so blind."

The doorbell rang. Mary Hammond stood outside.

"Barbara, the next time your son touches one of my children, I'm calling the police, do you hear?"

Mike Hammond stood behind his mother, blood still spilling out of his nose. Bart was nowhere to be seen.

I thought again of Donny Hayward, and how I had detested his parents for not keeping him in line. Now my son was the neighborhood bully. And I was the parent who couldn't keep my child in line. The old helplessness coursed through me.

Things in the neighborhood grew worse. One afternoon Mrs. Iverson, the apartment complex manager called. "Mrs. Bartocci," she said firmly, "we're getting too many complaints about your children. If you don't do something by the time your lease comes up, I'll have to ask you to move."

"I can't believe it!" I cried to Bill. "Nice, middle-class families don't get evicted!"

"Barb," Bill said quietly, "I think Bart needs professional help."

But what I saw was not a troubled child but a willful troublemaker. I began to realize I didn't really like my son. I tried to hide that truth from myself, but as children will, especially sensitive children, Bart sensed my dislike—and acted up even more. I still wasn't able to see that behind the troublemaker hid a frightfully lonely, hurting child.

The Fourth of July arrived. Fireworks were still allowed, and the neighborhood kids were all excited. I was talked into buying a large box at an outdoor stand.

It was a pleasant evening to sit outside. Distant pops

resounded from neighboring yards. Splashes of color lit the night sky and little kids waved sparklers.

I sat on the stoop while kids from six to sixteen grew more and more rambunctious as the fireworks made their colorful splashes. I wasn't close enough to hear Mike Hammond say, "Hey, I know what! Let's put firecrackers in the drainpipe. Wow, will that make a noise!"

"Great idea! Bart, you do it!"

"Me? I promised my Mom—"

"What's the matter, Bart the Fart? Scared? Scaredy cat, scaredy cat—"

"I ain't no scaredy cat!"

"You're backing off now."

"Oh, give 'em to me before anyone sees."

Wh-BOOM!

The sound rocked our neighborhood. Trapped in the clay cylinder, the fireworks sounded like a bomb exploding. Everyone jumped. Someone screamed.

"What's going on?" Mr. Hammond yelled.

"What are you kids up to?"

"It wasn't us. It was Bart Bartocci!"

"Bartocci! Is he causing trouble again?"

I found myself surrounded by parents.

"Do you realize the danger of fireworks?"

"Can't you keep an eye on your son? Just once?"

I felt as if the Scarlet Letter was branded on my forehead. I hurried over to Bart and pulled him, ignominiously, into the house. Behind us, in the dark, laughter echoed from the other kids.

"Mom, it wasn't just me. The other kids—"

"I don't care about the other kids! You were the one who did it!"

"But the other kids—"

"Don't talk back, Bart! You're finished for the night. Go to your room."

For once, he obeyed with no more arguments, but I saw anger reflected in his eyes.

The Fourth of July episode had permanent consequences.

Mrs. Iverson appeared the next day. "Mrs. Bartocci, last night was the final straw. The drainpipe is cracked, and your son did it! Your lease is up at the end of the month, and I want you out."

"You don't mean it!"

"I certainly do."

After she left, I slumped into a living room chair. My worst nightmare—eviction. I—who had grown up in a nice, middle class family, who went to church on Sunday and obeyed traffic laws, who was a product of the fifties Establishment—I and my family had been labeled "unfit."

I was humiliated. When Bart came downstairs and asked what was wrong, I said, in a flat, dead voice, "You're such a troublemaker, they won't let us live here anymore. Are you satisfied now?"

CHAPTER NINE

THE PROBLEM of finding a new place to live—and then moving—weighed on me heavily. So I gratefully accepted my parents' invitation to send the children to California for the summer, once again. I didn't mention our eviction. I was far too ashamed.

Bart boarded the airplane last. He wore wash khakis and a blue plaid shirt. With his wide blue eyes, his dimpled chin, and his longish blond hair curled about his neck, he resembled an apple-cheeked, well-scrubbed choir boy.

But anxiety showed in his eyes. "I'm sorry, Mom," he said again. How many times had he told me that since Mrs. Iverson had called? I swallowed. *He's only a boy. We all make mistakes.* But my hug was stiff, and although I said, "I know you are, Bart," there was no real forgiveness in my voice.

Bart's shoulders were hunched as he walked away from me into the California bound plane.

That evening, I met Bill at his apartment. He poured me a glass of white wine. From his balcony, we watched the sun set. Purplish-pink clouds puffed across the horizon. Chamber music played on the stereo.

"Kids get off all right?"

"Mmmmm."

"Feeling better?"

"No."

Silence, except for the soothing music. A mosquito buzzed. Cicadas began their summer strumming.

Bill cleared his throat. "It may be providential. Your moving out of the town house gives us a chance to find a house that suits us all.

"*All?*"

"All."

In the shadowy dusk, his chair scraped. He had pulled it closer to mine. I felt his hand, the fingers slightly rough.

"We've talked about it for months, Barb, but I had to be sure I could make the commitment—not just to you but to three fine kids. Now I feel ready. We can build a good family together."

"After all that's happened this spring?"

"Hey." His hands moved to my shoulders. He pulled me close. I smelled the faint aroma of his after-shave, the briar scent of his pipe tobacco. "I've got my eyes open. I can see we've got some problems. But together, we'll solve them."

Our kiss held a richness, a promise. But again, I hesitated, suddenly afraid. I, who had been pushing for commitment. "What if—what if it doesn't work?"

Bill kissed me again, slowly, sweetly. In the darkness that now surrounded us, his laugh was gentle. "We're not twenty-year-olds. You and I both know the hard work that goes into building a relationship. We'll make it work. I'll be a real father to your kids, Barb. I'll build on what their first father started. It will make a difference. You'll see."

But for all of our maturity and Bill's loving commitment, we both underestimated how difficult it would be to splice together a family. Especially when one child was hurting, emotionally.

Bill was production manager for a small company that made industrial water treating equipment. He took a day off from work, and the two of us began to househunt in earnest. Almost at once, we came across a vacant four-bedroom house for rent, a rarity in our part of suburbia. Best of all, it was in the same school district.

We decided to take it and moved immediately. As Bill helped hang curtains and pictures, I recalled how strong I had felt two years ago as I hung my own shelves in the townhouse. How sure I had been then that I could make everything work for my family.

Now, here we were, two of us. Would it make a difference, becoming a two-parent family again? Surely, it would.

There was one small surprise as we finalized plans for marriage. When I sat down to make changes in my will, my lawyer said, with a laugh, "You know, Barbara, it would simplify matters if you kept your own name."

"You mean remain Barbara Bartocci?"

"Sure. There's no legal requirement that a woman change her name when she marries."

I suddenly recalled those first years after John's death, when I struggled to see myself, not as daughter of ... or wife of ... but me. And that me, I realized, was represented by the name I had brought to the Midwest: Barbara Bartocci. Did I now want to change it to Mrs. William Shirley?

"I'm in love with Barbara Bartocci," Bill said. "It won't bother me if you keep your name." So I did.

The children were due back from California in August. Since Bill and I felt it would be better to present them with a *fait accompli*, I wrote them the news of our marriage the week before their return.

94

Allison appeared first in the group of passengers. We waved, and her face lit up. Behind her came Bart, more slowly. Andy ran toward me with ten-year-old eagerness. He gave me a hug, then looked curiously at Bill. "Are you guys *really* married?"

"We really are," Bill said, smiling.

Allison hugged Bill. "I'm glad."

Andy's eyes held a wait-and-see expression.

I reached toward Bart. My anger of a few weeks ago had dissipated. I felt hope for the future. We would be a family now, with a mother *and* a father. Bart hugged me tightly, but he said nothing to Bill, not even hello.

There were a lot of things to talk about on the way home. The kids babbled excitedly about their adventures in California.

"I found a lizard and named him Horace, but Mom wouldn't let me keep him."

"I learned to do a back dive off Mom and Granddaddy's diving board! Wait 'til I show you!"

"Sarah and I—remember Sarah, Mom?—we went to Disneyland on her birthday. It was *so* neat!"

"You'll like our new house," I said as we pulled into the driveway. "Each of you has your own bedroom."

"Yeah!" shouted Andy.

As they had two years ago, the children ran inside, anxious to see our furniture and to make the strange seem familiar.

Bill followed Bart into the bedroom. "Bart," he said, putting his arm around Bart's shoulder. "You had a wonderful father who loved you very much. I can't replace him. Nobody can. I can only succeed him as your second father."

Bart scuffled one sneakered foot against his canvas suitcase. "You may be the guy who married my Mom," he said finally, "but you ain't my father."

The stiffness in his shoulders seemed to say, *And you never will be.*

* * *

For the first time since John's death, a man's underwear filled the middle drawer of his tall dresser. On the stove, Bill's pot of tea simmered. His jug of cranapple juice squatted next to the orange juice in our refrigerator. His books were rammed next to mine on our bookshelves. The fragrance of his pipe tobacco mixed with lemon oil furniture polish. Everywhere, there was the subtle evidence of an adult male at home in our house.

Allison glowed. Her voice held a sweetly proprietary tone when she said, to a friend on the phone, "Well, *my* Dad says..."

And though Bart had groused, "You're just the guy who married my Mom," I noticed he found an excuse, in the mornings, to talk to Bill while Bill shaved. The house suddenly rang with excited discussions about football, good, sweaty "male talk," something the boys had never had with me.

The house we rented was twenty years old, and trees along the street made a canopy of lacy shadows against the August heat. I had seen a boy about Bart's age mowing grass a few houses from us. When I returned from work on Tuesday, he was sitting on our patio with Bart.

"Mom, this is Curt," Bart said.

The other boy waved a hand laconically without bothering to look up. I noticed two cigarette butts at their feet. Had he and Bart been smoking?

Don't be so judgmental, I thought. *He's the first friend Bart's brought home. Be glad.*

The two boys disappeared soon after I arrived. I saw them, through the living room window, heading down the street toward Curt's house. I smiled as I watched Bart swagger beside the taller boy.

Maybe our move was for the good, after all, I thought. *Seventh grade means a new school for Bart. Here's a new friend. We're in a new environment. Bart can become a happy boy.*

Humming, I went in to fix dinner.

96

* * *

Bill met Curt for the first time a few days later, after work. The two boys had just come upstairs from our basement. Curt's brown hair, like Bart's, hung to his shoulders but it had a stringy, unkempt look.

"Happy to meet you, Curt," said Bill. "What grade are you in?"

Curt glanced briefly at Bill, then down at the floor. "Uh, seventh."

"You're tall for twelve."

"Yeah. Well, actually I'm fourteen. I didn't go to school right away. And some ol' lady teacher wouldn't pass me one year. Hey Bart, ya comin'?"

Thoughtfully, Bill watched them hurry out the front door. "Barbara," he said, as we retreated to our bedroom, the only room in the house where we felt we had any privacy. "What do you know about that new friend of Bart's?"

"Curt? Nothing. Except that he lives down the street."

"Well, as the kids would say, I get 'bad vibes.'"

I told him about the two cigarette butts. Bill nodded, as if that confirmed something. "We'd better stay alert."

I was pulling off my panty hose, looking forward to the comfort of after-work jeans. "Okay, but don't rule out the boys' friendship. Curt is the first friend Bart has had since we moved."

"I'm not sure it's a friendship we should encourage."

"Oh, Bill! So he's not the All American Boy. That doesn't make him a rotten apple. Don't be such a worry wart."

"And don't you be so permissive that you blind yourself to facts."

"What facts? All you have are 'bad vibes.'"

"Yes. Well..." He grinned, suddenly. "You're right. The jury is still out on Curt. But when it comes to kids, my vibes are pretty good. So stay alert."

I said I would, but actually, my attention focused on something totally outside the family, something exciting in my professional life. I got a job offer to join a large downtown advertising agency as a copywriter. I was thrilled at the creative challenge, and the salary was higher, too. It reinforced the sense of promise and new start I felt with my marriage.

"Go for it!" urged Bill.

I took the job.

Andy came into my bedroom as I dressed for my frist day at the Agency.

"Mommy—"

"What?" I responded absently. My mind was on the uncertainties of my new position. I wondered if ad agencies were really the pressure cookers I had heard about.

"What's this?" He held up what looked like a handful of crushed, brownish-green leaves. I glanced at it briefly.

"I don't know. Andy, don't sit there! You'll wrinkle my suit jacket! Please, honey, I'm late for work. I don't have time for questions right now. Run along, okay?"

Andy shrugged and skipped out of our bedroom. "I found it in Bart's room," he called, as he left.

I didn't hear him. My mind was on the day ahead.

Ad agencies, I quickly discovered, *are* pressure cookers. Pressure was also building at home. Bill had some very specific ideas about what it meant to be a father, ideas that didn't square at all with what Bart and Andy expected. Conflicts arose particularly when all of us gathered at the table at dinner time.

"Bart, put your napkin in your lap," Bill would begin. And a few minutes later, "Andy, you're not a pig in a barnyard. Bart, that goes for you, too. Don't put your face in your plate. Sit up and eat properly. Please, show some manners."

For the first time in years, I looked, really looked at how the kids ate. Andy and Bart both hunched over their plates, scooping food rapid-fire into their mouths. I watched Andy cut a piece of meat. The bite was so big, he had trouble chewing.

I had grown up conscious of good manners. How had I

98

let my children's manners slip? Memory flashed. A puddle of light from the television set. The children, alone, TV dinners in front of them on the floor, me, retreating to my bedroom to cry. Of course. When had I been with them for dinner?

The boys reacted differently to Bill's criticisms.

Andy appealed to me. "Mom, I'm trying to eat the right way. Why does he always yell?"

Quickly, I capitulated. "Bill, they're trying to eat correctly. Give them a chance, okay?"

Bart tackled Bill head on. "I don't have to listen to you! You're just the guy who married my Mom. I wish you two had never gotten married."

Again I stepped in. "Bart, that's no way to speak to Bill."

"I'll talk to him any way I want to."

"We're trying to be a family. Don't always ruin things!"

"Just tell him to lay off, okay?"

"I can't stand it," Allison broke in. "All we do in this family is fight."

"I expect good table manners," said Bill firmly, and turned again to Bart. "Sit up straight, son, and eat properly."

An uneasy silence often fell at this point. It shattered when it came time to clear the table.

"Bart, it's your turn for dishes tonight."

"It's not my turn, Mom. It's Andy's."

"Oh, no, it's not. You traded with me last week, remember?"

"I'm not gonna do the dishes tonight. It's not my turn."

"It is so."

"No, it's not, toad."

"Bart, that's enough!" Bill said. "You could have had the dishes done by now."

"Oh, I'll do the darn dishes," Allison said. "Anything to stop the fighting."

Bill shook his head. "Sit down, Allison. Bart, if Andy has been unfair tonight, it will come out later. Meanwhile, do what your mother said. Get into the kitchen and start the dishes."

"Want to make me?"

"I will if I have to."

"Bart!" I was yelling now. "Go into the kitchen and start the dishes!"

"No. I'm going to my room."

"That's enough, son. Either do the dishes or bend over. And after that, you'll still do the dishes. Which will it be?"

"I said, I'm going to my—ow! Stop it, Bill! Stop it!"

That's how so many fights ended. Bill would pull off his belt. Bart would finally do his chore, but the echo of fighting and angry voices hung in the air like heavy fog.

Bill and I fought, too.

"If you could just be a little more tolerant. I want them to like you, Bill. How can they like you if you're always telling them what to do?" I lay against the pillows in our king-size bed while an errant moth fluttered around the bedlamp.

Bill sat on the corner chair, taking off his shoes. He scratched one ankle absently. When he looked up, his face wore an exasperated expression. "Barb, I want us to build a family where everyone contributes. The kids will like me—and themselves—a lot better once they accept some responsibilities. Kids feel they belong to a family when they invest something in it."

"You just want them to follow orders."

"Maybe it sounds that way right now."

He slid between the sheets and pulled me towards him. I turned off the lamp.

"I know what the boys fantasize," said Bill softly. "Bart, especially. They picture a father who's like Santa Claus. A Dad who hands out goodies and makes no demands." He ran his fingers lightly along my bare shoulders. "I believe parents should give kids freedom, but also make them accountable. These kids aren't used to that. Just give us time, Barb."

"But we're fighting more now than before you and I got married. If you would just let up a little—"

His chuckle fell into the darkness. "And magically, we'll have happy, well behaved kids who do well in school and have lots of friends, huh?"

"Well, I don't see how ordering them around all the time is going to do it."

"They need a little order and structure in their lives."

"I want a father who will love them, not structure them!"

"But that's one of the ways you show love."

"Maybe I don't think so."

Our voices rose. I moved away from Bill. Flipped on my bedlamp.

He blinked in the sudden light. "Barbara, your attitude doesn't help the kids."

"Oh? Well, they're my kids!"

"And mine, now, too."

I said nothing, but part of me responded, *No, they're not.*

"I think I'll read awhile," I said. Bill sighed and rolled over.

CHAPTER TEN

BEFORE SCHOOL started that fall, Bill suggested we go camping. It would be a family honeymoon, a chance to spend three days together at a special spot Bill knew about. "I used to take my kids there," he said, and I heard excitement in his voice. "It's a beautiful lake. The fishing is terrific and I know a special spot to set up camp, away from the main camp grounds. We'll have a great time."

We left on Friday afternoon after picking up Bill's four-teen-year-old son, Marc. This time, the back window of the car stayed up, and nobody, I noticed, even asked that it be lowered.

August heat shimmered on the highway. Fields of soy-

101

beans, approaching harvest, were turning from green to brown. Andy spied a hawk overhead. We played "Count the White Cars" and "Twenty Questions." It was a fun, laughter-filled trip. Soon we became part of a steady stream of campers and cars pulling boat trailers.

Bill drove across bumpy pasture land and up a small rise to a private grove of trees. The lake, miles of sparkling blue water, lay below us.

"Okay, kids," Bill shouted, as we piled out of the station wagon. "Let's set up camp. Allison, you pump up air mattresses. Andy, you unload food. Marc, you and I will put up the tent. Bart, you hike over to that well we passed and fill our water jug."

With an easy grin, Marc grabbed the tent and metal poles. "Sure, Dad."

No one noticed Bart's scowl until Bill said, "Bart, get moving. We'll need that water."

"I don't want to get the water."

"Bart," I said sharply, "everyone else is pitching in."

"I don't care. I don't wanna get the water."

I edged near him and pinched his arm hard. "Don't make a scene," I whispered. "Look how nicely Marc helps."

"Owww, you're hurting me!" he jerked his arm away, staring at the spot where Bill and Marc laughingly thrashed about beneath green canvas. "Get your own water!" he muttered, and took off at a trot for the woods behind our campsite.

"Bart, come back here!" Bill yelled.

"Let him go," Marc said softly. I looked from Marc to Bill to Bart's retreating back. At that moment, I was not only angry with my son; I disliked him thoroughly. Why did he always spoil things?

Bart returned to the campsite thirty minutes later. By that time Marc and Allison had filled the water jug and run down to the lake, while Andy trailed behind them, looking for lizards. Bill and I relaxed in lawn chairs beneath leafy oak trees.

Bart's walk was an unhappy slouch. He stopped at the picnic table, several yards away from us, toyed with the plastic salt shaker I had left on the table, picking it up, putting it down, picking it up, putting it down.

I pointedly ignored him, but, to my surprise, Bill got up and walked toward the table. I saw him bend down, put one arm around Bart's shoulders and say something. Bart nodded and followed Bill to the station wagon. A few minutes later, the two started toward the lake carrying tackle boxes and fishing rods. A fly, as my father liked to say, could have set up housekeeping in my open mouth.

Bart caught a mess of sand bass that evening. When I wandered down to the fishing dock, Bill was showing him how to clean them. "Mom, look!" called Bart proudly, and held up a bloody, headless fish.

"Good job!" I called back.

Nobody mentioned the water jug.

Yet underlying our weekend was a subtle current of something I couldn't quite put my finger on. I only knew that I felt as I did when I watched the slow buildup of storm clouds in the wide Midwest sky. A small black shadow appeared on the horizon at first, gradually growing bigger and bigger until dark gray billows threatened to blot out the sun. The smell of rain hung in the air but rain didn't always come.

Bill's expectations for camping behavior were very different from mine. Bart's good humor on Friday changed to scowls on Saturday when Bill told the kids to fix breakfast. Andy balked, too. "This is your mother's vacation, too," Bill insisted, even as I tried to say I didn't mind cooking breakfast.

Smiles came back when we rented a boat, retreated when Bill allowed Marc but not Bart to take the boat out alone.

On Monday, as we prepared to leave, Bill called, "Okay kids! Let's pitch in! We always leave a campsite cleaner than we found it."

"Boy, does that sound familiar," Marc said and began picking up trash that littered the area. Allison, after a puzzled glance at Marc, followed suit. Andy, dawdling, picked up just enough scraps to avoid Bill's wrath, but Bart wasn't having any of it. "That's stupid," he said and walked off to sit on a rock that overlooked the lake.

At first I was too busy packing the food to notice. Then I saw him. "Bart," I called, "come help. You heard Bill."

"No way," he called back. "I think it's dumb. Why should we pick up someone else's garbage?"

Marc laughed. "I used to wonder that, too, but you won't get anywhere arguing with Dad."

"Yeah? Maybe *you* won't."

"Bart," Bill said, sticking his head out of the tent he had just collapsed. "Get moving and help."

"I think it's dumb."

"So you think it's dumb. Do it anyway."

"I don't feel like it."

All my irritation from years of arguments welled up. I marched to where Bart sat on the rock. "Why," I said, through gritted teeth, "do you always make such an issue of things?"

"Camping with Bill is no fun," Bart complained. "All he does is make us work."

"That's not so. Please, for now, just help the other kids."

"I won't! I think it's dumb, I told you."

"Dammit, Bart, you're doing this on purpose!"

"Just 'cause I don't want to leave his dumb camp ground 'cleaner than we found it.'" His voice was a sing-song mimic.

Tears of frustration filled my eyes. What could I do with this boy? Hardly conscious of the motion, I hauled back and slapped him as hard as I could. "Sit in the car then and wait for us!"

As Bart, eyes wide, the red mark of my hand very clear on his cheek, stumbled toward the car, I marched back to the camp and screamed at the others, "So? Stop staring and pick up the damn camp ground!"

The camping trip marked the end of my dream of an instant happy family. Allison was now in ninth grade and

104

Bart in seventh. At Bill's suggestion, we put Allison on a clothing allowance and let her plan her own wardrobe for fall. Excitedly, she showed me her purchases. Her back brace stood in the corner of her room. She still had to wear it twelve hours a day, but for the first time in two years, she didn't have to wear it to school.

"Look!" she said, her voice filled with excitement as she spread out blouses and corduroy pants. "Clothes without holes!" We laughed together. Why was Allison so easy to deal with, I wondered, and Bart so difficult?

I noticed that the two of them did not walk together to the junior high. I supposed that was typical, but I also recalled the expression that had fleetingly crossed Allison's face when Curt's name came up at dinner, as if she smelled something distasteful.

Andy, now ten, was a slender, wiry boy whose reading problems were improving. Long blond hair fell almost to his shoulders and swept in shaggy bangs across his eyes. Years earlier, someone had teased him about having pointy "Mr. Spock" ears, and ever since, he'd insisted on long hair. Although Andy was still shy in public, his elfin sense of humor—his puns and corny knock-knock jokes—provided some of the few smiles our family enjoyed that fall. His inventiveness had focused on a new hobby: building rocket models. As with every hobby Andy had ever taken up, it totally absorbed him. When I'd come home from work to find him with plastic parts and model paint spread out on newspaper on the kitchen table, he'd look up startled. "Hi, Mommy. Are you home early?"

What Bill noticed about Andy that fall was his ability to solve problems. He was teaching Andy how to play chess. Privately he confided, "That boy's mind works like the proverbial steel trap, Barb."

"In school, he thinks he's dumb."

"Give him time. He'll grow into his own brains."

But there was another problem with Andy.

"Barbara," Bill said in exasperation, as I was running a comb through Andy's hair one morning. "Let him comb his own hair. You baby that boy terribly."

"I don't baby him. You forget he's had special problems."

"What does combing a kid's hair have to do with reading problems? Let him be more self-sufficient!"

Over his bowl of cereal, Andy watched closely. It was one of many quarrels we would have over Bill's insistence that I babied my youngest son.

Bart announced that he wanted to go out for YMCA football. My first reaction was to say no. I'd read of all kinds of dangers in contact sports at his age. Bill pulled me aside. "I've read the same reports," he said. "But I also coached Marc's YMCA team. The 'Y' is very safety conscious. Besides, Barb, don't you see what this means? A chance for Bart to be one of the 'good guys.' A jock! Not a bully! And maybe he'll find some new friends." Neither one of us mentioned Curt by name.

Bill finally convinced me when he offered to attend practices and check out the coaches. Bart was jubilant. "Wait'll you see me, Mom! I'm going to go out for fullback. Wahoo!"

"Remember one thing," Bill warned. "Once you sign up, there's no quitting midseason."

"Sure, sure. I know."

"Good. Okay if I come watch your practices?"

Just like the camping trip, twin emotions ran across Bart's face, like the shade-sun flicker of clouds in a dappled sky. "Okay," he said.

Once I got over my initial fears, I felt elated over Bart's decision. I remembered how much he'd liked baseball in San Diego. I should have encouraged organized sports a year ago, I thought. Maybe we never would have had all these problems. Once again it seemed as if we were on our way to better times.

Bart came home from his first practice beaming. "The coach says I'm the right size for fullback."

"You don't have the position nailed down yet," Bill cautioned, but if Bart heard, he didn't respond. His enthusiasm for football was all-encompassing. Again, I saw the smiling, happy boy I remembered from our Monterey days. Gone were the dinner table fights, the stubborn refusal to do chores, even his usual quarrels with Andy.

But two weeks into practice Bill and Bart came home from the field, shouting at each other. "Fullback isn't the only position, Bart. Offensive tackle is important. I played tackle myself in high school."

"Who gives a damn what you played!" Bart hollered throwing his shoulder pads at the couch. "Offensive tackle sucks. So does the coach. Playing favorites, that's all. I could be a good fullback."

"You've got the size, but not the speed."

"What does he know? I'm not going to play on their stupid team!"

"No quitting. Remember?"

"I'll quit if I damn well please. Football and I are through!"

Their shouts had brought me running from the kitchen, Allison and Andy from the family room. "What's going *on?*"

"The coach wants Bart to play a line position."

"Because he doesn't like me," Bart said.

I looked from Bart to Bill and back again, not sure how to respond. Before I had a chance to say anything, Bart grabbed his shoulder pads and stomped off to his bedroom. The door slammed.

Bill shook his head. "Bart can't seem to deal with authority," he said. "Me . . . the coaches . . . his teachers."

"That's not fair." I bristled. "We haven't heard any complaints from his teachers."

". . . yet. But I predict we will. He shot his mouth off at the coach this afternoon."

"What's wrong with tackle?" I knew very little about football.

"It's not the kind of spot where you can star, and Bart wants to star. But he can play offensive line and still be part of the team, if he'll stop badmouthing the coach. Otherwise, I'm afraid the coach will bench him. Then he won't play at all." He sighed. "He wants so much to be part of something, Barb. But this anger of his keeps getting in the way. There's something about it that I can't quite put my finger on." He sighed again, and shook his head, this time in obvious frustration.

When I went to fetch Bart for dinner, his room was empty. He came in at nine o'clock, surly and bad tempered. He'd been at Curt's, he said. When I started to say I'd wished he'd told me where he was going, he walked off while I was still speaking.

Bart didn't quit the team, whether because of Bill's insistence or because of a forlorn remnant of his earlier hopes, I couldn't tell. But his good-natured enthusiasm was gone.

We went to the first game, played on one of ten YMCA football fields that spread across what had once been acres of farmland. Parents and children streamed into the bleacher sections that surrounded each playing field. Cheerleaders waved pom-poms and practiced their cheers. Vendors hawked Cokes and popcorn.

Bart, in a blue jersey, wore Number 72. I watched for him as the game progressed, but he warmed the bench until the end of third quarter. Bill, who had roamed the sidelines, came and stood at my side. "He should have gone in sooner. He's a better tackle than the other kid. But he started mouthing off again at practice yesterday. The coach warned him he wouldn't play much today if he didn't shut up."

Bart's team won. The boys hollered a victory cheer and rushed off to a snack stand for Cokes. Bart ran and hollered with the rest of them, but when he joined us in the parking lot, his face had slipped into a sulky, disappointed expression. His uniform had the telltale whiteness of a player who hadn't seen much play.

He spent a lot of that season on the bench, even though Bill said he was a better tackle than the other boy who played the position. Bart couldn't keep his mouth shut at practice. At home, too, arguments and fights had become, once again, a daily staple. It didn't seem to matter what the subject was.

108

"Bart, will you take out the trash?"

"It's Andy's turn."

"He's not here. Come on. The bag's dripping."

"I'm busy. You always dump those chores on me."

"Bart! Take out the trash!"

"Why do I have to do it? You baby Andy. He gets away with murder."

"You could have dumped the trash by now. Don't argue!"

"But it's not fair. You always make me do stuff. You don't tell Allison and Andy to—"

"Bart! You make me so mad! Now take out the trash!"

"I'll take it out later."

"Oh! Sometimes I wish you weren't—"

"—born? That's what you wish, isn't it?"

"No! Yes! Oh, for God's sake. Maybe so!" He'd pushed me too far again. "Now take out the trash!"

"Go screw your damn trash!"

And out he ran, while I stood with the dripping bag, hearing the echo of another hurtful argument and feeling the familiar mixture of guilt and helplessness. *What could we do with this boy?*

CHAPTER ELEVEN

E VEN BIGGER fights arose over Bart's smoking.

"You're only twelve!" I protested. "I won't allow it."

"Who says I smoke?" he fenced.

"You smell of it. And I find cigarette butts on the patio. And you hang around with a boy who smokes."

Bill stepped in. "We can't *make* you stop smoking if that's what you're going to do, but we won't allow it in our house. Understand?"

"I'll smoke anywhere I want to. You can't stop me."

"Don't try me!"

"Oh, sure, just 'cause you're bigger'n me. Just wait, Bill. One of these days I'll be bigger than you and then—"

"Don't make threats, son."

"I'm not your son. I'll never be your son!"

"Bart, please, Bill only—"

"And I'll smoke anywhere I damn well please!"

"Not in this house, you won't!"

But Bill was shouting at Bart's retreating back as he ran into his bedroom.

My new husband I looked at each other. The debilitating effects of daily family quarrels were beginning to take their toll.

It was a relief to leave home in the morning for work. The ad agency was located on the twelfth floor of what was, for our city, a skyscraper, thirty stories high. One of the client companies assigned to me was a hospital. David, the art director, and I were putting together a series of ads that included local TV production. It was exciting, creative work. The two of us brainstormed endlessly with files of medical pictures strewn in front of us.

I knew David was married. "Do you have any kids?" I once asked him.

"Me? No way!" He shook his head so vehemently that the gold chains around his neck made a clinking noise. "Kids are a hassle. I got me a dog. Big ol' Huskie. He don't give me no shit!"

I laughed—David loved to play the good ole boy—but I felt a twinge of envy. David was right. Kids are a terrible hassle. *If I had it to do over again*, I thought, *would I...*? Even asking the question made me realize how backed into a corner I felt with the children.

"Maybe Bill should cool it a little," Tina advised over lunch, as I rehashed our ongoing problems. "Remember Marty Williams? She got married again, and before the wedding she and her hubby-to-be agreed that he would stay out of her way where her kids were concerned. Of course, her ex-husband is a real involved father. Maybe that makes a difference."

"Of course it does."

I wondered, though, if it would be easier if Bill didn't get involved. Then I laughed ironically. How could I forget all the problems leading up to our eviction? A big reason for my marriage was to give my children a father, not just a man who married Mommy.

But I had also heard of second marriages breaking up over problems with the children. "Tina," I said, with a sigh, "be glad you're single."

"I am," she said, and with no comfort to me, added, "especially after I talk to you."

"Mom," Allison said.

"What, honey?" We were sitting at the breakfast table, munching Raisin Bran. Bill had already left for work, and the boys were still in their bedrooms.

"Kathy and I think we'll go to the Harvest Hop."

"Good for you!" Kathy was Rachel's replacement, a best friend who, like Allison, was a late bloomer. Kathy wore silver wire on her teeth, wire frames on her glasses, and had a body that was lean and wiry, too. With her bone structure, she would look gorgeous at thirty, but at fourteen, neither she nor Allison had started to date.

"I thought you decided not to go."

"Well, a lot of girls say they're going. Will you or Bill drive one way?"

"Of course." The Harvest Hop was the fall school party, and I was happy Allison was going to chance it. I hated knowing that she got left out of things the popular girls did. Bill had no such worries. "Give her ten years," he said. "In her twenties, she'll have it all over those little junior high cuties." Maybe, but I was more concerned about now. "We'll drive both ways if you need us to," I promised.

Bart liked girls, and he wasn't bashful around them, but when I asked if he'd like a ride to the Harvest Hop, he shook his head. "I'm not going to that dumb party."

111

Bill picked the girls up afterwards. "Oh, Mr. Shirley," Kathy said, sliding into the back seat. "You should have seen the excitement! A bunch of boys were caught smoking pot out behind the cafeteria."

"That so? What happened?"

"A couple of them ran. I guess they called the parents of the others. Do you think they'll go to jail?"

Allison's voice was very low. "I think one of the boys was Curt."

"Oh?" Bill said nothing more, but his expression grew thoughtful.

Although Bart had stayed on the football team, the only friend he ever brought home was Curt. I had already noticed that if the two boys were sitting in our living room when Bill or I reached home, their voices always halted abruptly.

"It's not as if we know Curt has done something wrong," I pointed out. "Allison isn't really sure she saw him that night."

"I know," Bill replied. "And it's judgmental as hell to say this, but, Barb, Curt's a loser, and I'm afraid that's how Bart sees himself. Otherwise, why would he hang out with him?"

Because he can't find anyone else to be friends with, I thought, painfully.

"And have you noticed how Bart looks, lately?" Bill went on.

I hadn't. A crisis had occurred at the ad agency—a client insisted we redo an entire fall campaign. "God dammit," George Castleman had shouted. Castleman, the agency president, was a mercurial man, "a creative genius," said older hands in advertising, and also, they added, "a real SOB to work for." He scared me, especially as he stomped and shouted and ordered us to produce "stuff that works, do you hear me? Or you'll be out on your asses, every last one of you!" Fearing Castleman's threats, I was working nearly twelve hours a day and coming home exhausted.

Now I took a good look at Bart. He was husky and still

112

a little pudgy around his middle. His wavy blond hair hung almost to his shoulders, but long hair has to be kept clean and well trimmed. Bart's was neither. And where were all the nice clothes we had purchased before school? The back pocket of his jeans hung loose and there was a large hole in one knee. His shirt, which he said a friend had loaned him, was shabby and too big for him.

"You look like a slob," I said.

"Ma, this is how they dress in junior high. Don't bug me."

"Maybe it is," I said to Bill. "I remember my parents were horrified because I wore my father's old shirts with my blue jeans."

Bill shook his head stubbornly. "I don't think so."

A few weeks after the Harvest Hop, on a blustery mid-November day, I arrived home late, tired and cranky from a long day and a godawful traffic snarl on the freeway. But tired as I was, I didn't expect Bill to meet me at the front door.

"Barbara," he said, "before you go inside—"

Adrenalin shot through me, hundreds of tiny white-hot needles. "Who's hurt?"

"Nothing serious. Not in the hurt department. It's Bart. He's been suspended from school."

"Suspended!" In my mind, I heard echoes of "Evicted!"

Bill gripped my free arm, the one without the briefcase. "I knew it would upset you—there was a fight, and both boys are suspended until their parents meet with the school principal."

Before I could explode, Bill held up a hand. "It's not the fight that concerns me. Take a look at Bart when you go inside. Look at his eyes, especially."

"What do you—"

"Just look."

Fearfully, I walked inside. Bart was sitting in a chair in the kitchen. Two glasses of milk, half drunk, sat on the table. Apparently, Bill and Bart had been talking.

Bart looked shamefaced. "I'm sorry, Mom. I didn't mean to start it. Honest."

I glanced at Bill, then back at Bart. I saw what Bill meant. The pupils in Bart's eyes looked enormous, and his whole posture had a loose, rag-doll appearance.

"Why don't you go lie down?" Bill suggested to Bart. "You've had quite a day."

Bart smiled. "Sure thing." His gait, as he headed toward his room, had the same uncontrolled ease.

"I'm not worried about the fight," Bill said quietly, "or the suspension. But if Bart's taken some kind of drug, that scares me a lot. I think we need outside help, Barbara."

Suspended! Possible drugs! I finally agreed with Bill.

The next morning I made an appointment to see Dr. Steven Brusheski, a child psychologist. Then we met with Edwin Morris, assistant principal of the junior high. In his office, we learned what had happened.

It had begun in the gym. Through the accident of heredity, Bart had large hips and a sway back. He was built like his father. And one day, the boys in his gym class noticed.

"Hey, Bart, you got a big butt!" one of the eighth graders shouted after a sweaty game of basketball had brought them all to the showers. A boy snickered, and another picked it up.

"Yeah, Bart, you got a butt that won't quit!"

"The biggest ass in school!"

Sticking out his rear end in an exaggerated fashion, the first boy pranced across the showers' tiled floor. Laughter seemed to roll up against the tiles. It echoed and re-echoed and brought memories of the earlier jibe, "Bart the Fart." With giggles and shouts, other boys pranced across the floor, their rear ends stuck out.

"Bart the Butt, Bart the Butt," the boys chanted. Bart, the son John had called sensitive, was caught in a circle of boys taunting "Bart the Butt! Bart the Butt! Biggest ass in

114

school! Bart the Butt! Bart the Butt! Biggest ass in school!"

The five-minute bell rang. Classes! Boys began scrambling into their clothes. Locker doors clanged, then were silent, until, at last, Bart was alone. Carefully, he reached down and picked up his white towel, which had been tossed to the floor. It was too wet to use. Slowly, he began to dress, pulling his clothes gently over his damp body.

A few days later, jibes started again. It was the period just before lunch. The cavernous gym echoed with the noise of sneakered feet on the basketball court and boys shouting to one another. Sunlight slanted through the high windows.

"Hey, Bart," someone hollered, "How's your butt?"

"Yeah, how's the biggest ass in school?" joined in an eighth grader named Jim.

Bart was standing near the edge of the basketball court, holding a basketball. Suddenly, he exploded, throwing the basketball as hard as he could at Jim's face.

"Hey, oww! Ohhh!" Blood gushed out, bright red against Jim's white T-shirt.

Noisy shouts brought the gym instructor running. "What's going on?"

By then, Jim had wiped his nose. "Nothing," he mumbled.

The teacher looked at the huddle of boys, the red stain on Jim's T-shirt, the scared look on Bart's face. He started to say something, thought better of it, rumbled instead, "I'd better not have any trouble. You hear?" and stalked off.

Jim and his friends surrounded Bart. "Okay, Big Ass. You want a fight? You got one. After school. Behind the library."

Bart swallowed and shook his head, but the other boys only laughed. They were still laughing after showers when the bell rang.

It was the kind of news that spreads fast in a school. Curt met Bart at the end of fifth period. "Hey, boy, don't worry. You'll whomp that turd."

Bart's face had a gray cast. "No, I won't," he whispered.

115

"I'm not much good in a fight, Curt. I'm—" he swallowed, turned his head. "I'm not much good," he repeated.

"Don't worry. I got something to help. Here."

The final school bell rang. A crowd of boys gathered behind the library. Curt ran toward Bart. "You can take him!"

The afternoon was chill and overcast, yet Bart felt sweat trickle moistly down his armpit. His heart thumped in an odd rhythm. It didn't feel like his heart. He was breathing heavily, as if he had been running. He bounced on his toes, tried not to look at the jeering faces. Jim was nearly a head taller. The two boys circled each other. Bart lifted his fists. He was sweating all over.

"Come on..." "Come on..." the watching boys shouted. Traffic noises hummed in the background. Suddenly, Jim lunged. Startled, Bart lifted one hand to protect his face, jabbing, futilely, with the other. A fist slammed his side and knocked the wind out of him. One more blow and he fell awkwardly. Fists were in his face.

"Stop—stop—" he yelled. He heard other shouts, but they seemed far away. Then, abruptly, he was yanked too his feet. Mr. Morris, the assistant principal, held Bart by one arm, Jim by the other.

"There's no fighting allowed on school grounds," he said sternly. "You two come with me."

That was the fight that led to our first visit with Dr. Brusheski.

CHAPTER TWELVE

DR. STEVEN Brusheski was a tall, balding man. He looked more like a genial truck driver than a child psychologist, but he knew how to talk to kids.

"What's this crap you're dishing out?" I heard him asking Bart as they disappeared together into his inner office.

Nervously, I glanced around the waiting room. Another child, a girl about fourteen, had just come out. She sat, slumped, in the chair opposite me. A strand of dark hair fell across one eye. After a few minutes, the waiting room door opened and a tall, heavy-set woman stuck her head in. "Let's go, Gloria." Obediently, the girl stood up, smoothed her hair, and followed her mother. I wondered what their problems were. They looked perfectly normal to me.

I supposed we did, too.

"Bart is very, very angry," Dr. Brusheski said a few weeks later. We were in his inner office. Around me were pieces of South American sculpture, an oriental rug hung on one wall, and a game table sat in one corner. It didn't look at all the way I expected the office of a child psychologist to look.

"First of all," Brusheski continued, "God punished Bart by taking away his father, a fact he still hasn't fully accepted."

"Not accepted?"

"Well, after all, they never found the body. So who's to know if his father really died? Maybe he got to shore somehow and is hiding out or has amnesia—"

"Surely, Bart doesn't think that!"

"Part of him does. It gets in the way of his relating to Bill. Plus, he's hated you, you know." His voice was quiet and matter-of-fact. I shivered. "You dragged him off to this Godforsaken Midwest where nobody knows about his father and he has no friends and his mother is always at work. Why shouldn't he hate you?

"But at the same time," Brusheski went on, "you're his mother, and he loves you. Loves you passionately, intensely, and with great fear, because he senses you don't like him. He's lost one parent. What if he loses another? What will become of him? So he's all torn up inside, hating you but

117

loving you. Afraid that his hate will make his worst nightmare come true, and you, too, will disappear. And all wrapped up in those emotions is this terrible anger. Bart wonders, why can't he grow up with two loving parents as other boys do? Why must he cope with all this other awful stuff?"

His words brought a spasm of pity for my son, and amazement as well. How could I have lived with a child all these years and never had an inkling of such deep-rooted feelings? I tried to remember those days and weeks and months after John died, tried to recall Barty, but all that came to mind was Andy and his red toy telephone. And, yes, a memory of my anger because Bart never cried.

So both of us were angry. With each other.

"Do all families live with such secrets from one another?" I wondered aloud.

Brusheski nodded. "Quite often."

Weekly visits with Dr. Brusheski helped me understand more of what caused Bart's actions. I began to understand the debilitating effect that buried grief can have on healthy emotional recovery after a death, especially in a child. I began to see, too, that pain can masquerade as anger and that Bart's angry acting out was, in fact, a cry for help.

At first, Bart had strenuously objected to seeing Brusheski. "What do I need a shrink for? I'm not crazy!" But now he waited amiably for me to drive him to his appointment.

Football season ended, and we went to the football banquet. For once, Bart willingly put on the nice pair of pants and new shirt I'd bought him. In the cafeteria that night, he introduced Bill to other kids as "my Dad."

I beamed. "How about that?" I whispered. Bill squeezed my hand and smiled.

At the football players' table, Bart seemed as merrily rowdy as the other boys. *It looks as if Dr. Brusheski was the answer*, I thought.

The psychologist suggested we give up our arguments against smoking. Bill agreed, reluctantly. "You know we don't approve," he told Bart, "but if you insist, we'd rather you smoked in front of us than behind our backs. No more hiding, okay?"

Bart looked startled but pleased. "Okay."

Dr. Brusheski and I also talked about my difficulties in relating to Bart. "Why do you get so angry?"

"Because I feel responsible. I want my children to be happy, and Bart's been terribly unhappy for a long time. Nothing I do seems to make any difference. I resent that, so I guess I wind up resenting him. Besides—"

"Yes?"

"I want him to be a boy John could be proud of. He's his father's namesake, and he was always special to his father. I'm angry that he's so *unlike* his father."

"I see," he murmured. "But are you aware that the two of you are very much alike? You're both enthusiastic, creative, impulsive. Wide mood swings."

"Bill says I turn into another child when Bart and I fight."

He nodded, as if that explained something. "Bart feels you treat him differently from the way you do Allison and Andy."

I pondered that on the way home.

We seemed to have reached a truce in family fighting, but problems still hovered on the horizon. For one thing, Bart never seemed able to show us his schoolwork. He always had excuses: "I forgot it," or "It got lost."

"I smell trouble," said Bill. "Bart's hiding something."

"For heaven's sake," I sputtered. "He's like most kids. Loses stuff a lot. Why borrow trouble?"

"I told you, I smell it."

"Oh? Well, I'll buy you a new nose for Christmas."

He laughed, as I had intended, but his chuckle was brief. Midterm report cards proved he was right. Bart's grades were C's and D's, more D's than C's.

Christmas brought my parents from California, and with them an uncomfortable undercurrent. I couldn't put my finger on it until Bill introduced a tradition he said his family had always followed. After Christmas breakfast and before opening the gifts beneath the tree, everyone helped clean the kitchen and pick up the house. "Our gift to Mother," he explained.

"*Before* the tree?" asked my mother, her mouth pursed. "To me, that's unnecessary." My mother, I realized, considered Bill a guest, not a family member. It was obvious she did not see him as a father to her grandchildren.

"Can't we clean the house after the presents?" Andy said.

"Yeah," echoed Bart. "That's how we do it in *our* family, Bill."

"Oh, well," my father joshed more easily, "I suppose I can wipe a dish or two right now."

I gave him a squeeze. "Thanks, Daddy."

My parents had brought a special gift for the kids. "Close your eyes," my father ordered after all the other presents were opened. "Come on, you whippersnappers, get those eyes shut."

Andy giggled. Allison and Bart, their faces alight in anticipation, obediently crinkled their eyes.

My mother and father went to the garage and returned, pulling something. "Okay," my father said, and as the children opened their eyes, he and my mother stepped aside.

"Ohhh!" cried Allison.

"A sled!" shouted Bart and Andy.

"Not just any sled," my father amended. "This was your grandmother's Flexible Flyer when she was growing up."

Bill, who always appreciated good workmanship, gave a small whistle. "Looks like you nearly rebuilt it."

"It's had a little work," my father agreed, pleased that Bill had noticed.

"Wahoo!" shouted Bart. "Now all we need is snow!"

As if in response, heavy white snow fell the very next weekend, a few days after my parents left. Bart and Andy ran outside early, pulling the sled behind them. It was a wonderful sled, longer and—despite its age—sturdier than any I had seen in stores.

The trouble occurred when Bart ran back inside for a few minutes. "Gotta pee," he cried, racing past me, pell mell. A few minutes later, he headed outdoors again. I was in the living room, wrapping up ornaments we had taken off the tree. Suddenly, the front door banged open.

"That—that *toad* ran off with the sled," cried Bart. "He was supposed to wait for me, but he just ran off."

"Oh well"—I remembered the sledding incident back in the town houses—"don't get too bent out of shape, Bart. He'll bring it back pretty soon."

"But, Mom, it was *my* turn, not Andy's! He said he'd wait while I went to the bathroom."

"He'll come back, Bart. Why don't you go wait for him?"

"No, dammit." Bill's shout startled us both. He came striding into the living room, one sock on, and a shoe dangling from his hand. "Dammit, Barbara, don't always expect Bart to give in to Andy."

"Bill, you're mistake—"

"No, I'm not. Now, this is one time Bart is in the right and I'm going to see that he doesn't give in to his brother. Bart, go find Andy and send him in to me."

"Bill," I protested, "you're going to cause trouble where there doesn't need to be any. Andy will come home soon."

"You're letting him off the hook, Barb!"

"All brothers fight. I'm sure he wasn't even thinking when he took that sled."

But Bill was insistent. "Andy," he said, when Andy showed up, "you're grounded in your bedroom for the rest of the day."

"Grounded! Mom, that's not fair. I thought Bart went inside for good. I didn't know he was coming back."

"Liar! You did, too, know!" Bart screamed.

"Bill," I interrupted, "don't you think all day is a little—harsh?"

"I do not."

"Well, I do."

"And I think you mollycoddle your youngest son and pick on your oldest."

His words stopped me cold. Even the boys looked surprised. Bill did, too. Obviously, the words had just popped out, but they triggered all kinds of guilt in me. Dr. Brusheski had said Bart thought I dealt with him unfairly. Was it true? Was I the cause of our problems? Or was Bill picking on Andy?

We were barely into the new year when a major crisis occurred. Bill called me at work and asked if I could meet him at our favorite restaurant. As soon as were settled in a corner booth, he said, trying for nonchalance, "I seem to be out of work, as of today."

"Oh, Bill, no!"

"The company is folding, Fred tells me. How's that for the world's best-kept secret?"

"I'm so sorry, honey."

His attempted nonchalance failed. Harsh worry lines appeared between his eyes. "There's not much chance of my finding a job in my field locally, Barb. Would you be willing to move?"

"Oh, Bill, it's taken so long for the kids to adjust as it is. And my own job—it's a good one—I mean, I don't know. Move?"

He poured us each a glass of wine. "Well, there is an alternative, but it's pretty risky. I've always dreamed of going into business for myself. How would you feel if I hung out my shingle as a management consultant?"

"If it's that or move out of the city, I say, go for it!"

"It could be a while before I earn any income."

I thought about Bill's alimony and child-support payments, and our own expenses, including Dr. Brusheski. I thought about uprooting our family at this point. Besides, if this was something Bill had dreamed about, we ought to take a chance. "I think you should try," I repeated. Bill smiled and we clinked our glasses to the future. But what

122

was really in our future—and the terrible expense of it—
neither of us foresaw.

Semester report cards arrived. Allison's grades were A's
and B's, Andy's B's & C's, and Bart's three D's and two F's.
"Bart, this is terrible!" I said. "You're too smart for these
grades."
"It's not my fault," he sulked. "Davison hates my guts.
And Sherril only pays attention to her pets."
But Bill and I both knew something more was going on.
We made appointments with Bart's teachers. They all gave
us similar reports. "He seemed cheerful and cooperative at
first. Then, he just stopped working."
"He's quite disruptive in class," added Gerry Sherril, his
English teacher. "Frankly, it's almost as if he wants to get
into trouble."
I went home worried, and seething inside. Why were we
still having such problems? Weren't we seeing a psychologist? What more could we do?
We became convinced Bart would fail seventh grade unless we did something drastic. Bill devised a study plan.
"I'm going to get in touch with each of your teachers," he
told Bart, "and tell them you are to bring home a signed
note each week saying you have completed both homework
and classwork satisfactorily. Incomplete work will be made
up on the weekend."
"You've got to be joking," said Bart.
"Meanwhile," Bill continued, as if Bart hadn't spoken,
"no more television on school nights."
"You can't boss me around."
"Bart," I pleaded. "You know how important school is.
You saw me go to college. And your Daddy..."
"Yeah, I saw you go to scho-o-o-el!"
"What does that mean?" Worried about being able to
support the family, I hadn't considered how much Bart and
the others might have resented the time I had spent in
classes, away from them. Bart didn't answer me; his atten-

tion had returned to Bill. "I'll study when I damn well want to! Not when you order me to!"

It was as if he had locked horns with Bill. The two of them glared at each other, fair-haired Bart, with his blue eyes narrowed and his chubby face etched into lines of anger, and Bill, hands on hips, his mouth in a firm, straight line, his own eyes filled with worry. But Bill contacted the teachers.

For three weeks, they sent notes home, all saying the same thing. Bart was not completing his work satisfactorily. He also refused to bring any books or work home on the weekends.

"Look," Brusheski advised, "drop the teachers' notes. Bart has dug in his heels. It's become a point of pride with him now not to give in to you." I could see the frustration in Bill's eyes. I felt it too.

We tried something else. After dinner, Bart was sent to his room. "You're to spend at least two hours on your schoolwork before you come out," ordered Bill.

Bart scowled. "I'll go to my room," he said, "but there ain't no way you can make me study."

And, of course, we couldn't. In his room, Bart read comics or slept.

"Do you like being a failure at everything?" I said, standing in his doorway. "Is that what you want to be in life? A failure? A dropout?" Stony-faced, Bart rolled over on his bed.

CHAPTER THIRTEEN

THEN BART made a complete turnaround, in a way we would never have predicted. I arrived home from work one night during that transition season in March, when the weather hovers between the frozen deadness of winter and the first greening of spring, to find him in a paroxysm of excitement.

"I've got a job!" he announced. For the first time in weeks, a happy light showed in his eyes. His whole face had an open, boyish air.

"A job!" Andy said. He sounded impressed.

"It's delivering papers!"

But this was no ordinary paper route, we soon learned. Bart had to get up at three a.m., be at work by four to roll papers, then ride with the delivery truck until six, tossing out papers. The hours were terrible for a boy his age.

"Let him do it," Brusheski advised. "He got the job himself. It's tough, but if he succeeds, it will do wonders for his self-image."

So we bought Bart an alarm clock, and he began getting up in the dark. Half asleep, I would hear the front door open and close. I began listening for it. Sometimes, when I didn't hear it, I would stumble out of bed and wake Bart, who had overslept, but most mornings, he made it on his own.

Again we began to feel hopeful that our family problems would work out. Maybe what Bart had needed, all along, was a situation where he could succeed on his own terms.

He also discovered, that spring, a special friend in our next-door neighbor, Mrs. Winifred Sheehan. Mrs. Sheehan was a plump, sixty-year-old widow, who might have reminded Bart of his grandmother. He began going to her house after school, and they talked while she baked cookies. I was pleased. I hoped she could give him something I apparently couldn't. Besides, when he was at her house, he wasn't with Curt.

Curt had started the paper route, too. He was the one who first heard of the job, but he quickly dropped out. Bart conveyed that news with a touch of pride. A tone that said, Curt couldn't hack it, but I can.

Yet, after a short breather, I wondered if the paper route, after all, was merely an island in a turbulent sea. Even with

125

Dr. Brusheski's help, not a week went by without some strident family argument. Nor did Bart's schoolwork improve.

"He's exhausted," I complained to the psychologist as the end of the seventh grade approached. "Are you sure we should allow the paper route?"

"If you make him quit now," said Brusheski, "he'll be so resentful he'll make damn sure he fails. Let it go till summer." We decided to follow his advice.

At the ad agency, spring campaigns got underway. I was in the middle of a client presentation when a secretary stuck her head through the door of our conference room. "Your daughter's on the phone," she told me quietly. "She said it was important."

Allison sounded scared. "Something is wrong with Bart. He's real sick, Mom. You better come home."

Allison was not the panicky sort. I felt the sickish presence of fear in my gut as I made my apologies to the client and hurried to the parking lot.

On my drive home I thought of the season and how good I had been feeling about it until Allison called. The brown hills of winter were turning green with April foliage. At noon that day, several of us from the agency had walked a few blocks to a small outdoor cafe. Pulling up chairs to an umbrella-topped table, we had ordered wine and submarine sandwiches and let the sun warm our pale wintry skin. Conversation had flown freely, filled with laughter and gossipy speculation about people in the ad world.

People who work in advertising always seemed to me to have it together. I knew that was how people regarded me. How surprised my associates would be, I thought, if they knew how uncertain I felt about the one role women are supposed to have down pat, the role of mother.

Shasta barked his usual greeting as I pulled into the driveway. Allison met me, her eyes wide with worry.

Bart lay on his bed, with sweating face and hands, apparently in delirium. His forehead felt hot, his eyes were glassy. I tried to rouse him, but he only mumbled. Spittle trickled from the corner of his mouth. My first thought was that the paper route had taken its toll. All those early mornings with no sleep had lowered his body resistance and he'd contracted some disease. Mononucleosis, spinal meningitis—my mind raced over the terrible possibilities.

"Call Bill," I told Allison. He had rented a small office not far from where we lived. Allison ran to telephone while Andy hovered anxiously at the doorway to Bart's room.

Bill, too, thought it might be some virulent infection. "Let's get him into the bathtub," he said. "Get his fever down while I call the doctor." Bart was a dead weight, but we managed to drag him into the bathroom. I started the water while Bill pulled off his clothes. Suddenly, Bart retched. Vomit splashed across the tiles, hitting the bathtub, Bill, me, even the toilet.

"Yuuuk,"cried Andy, from the doorway.

Bill sniffed. Abruptly, he turned on his heel and marched back to Bart's room. I was still cleaning vomit when he returned.

"You can relax. He's not dying." He held up an empty bottle of Bourbon. A half bottle that had been sitting in our liquor cabinet.

Bart wasn't sick; he was drunk. Stinking drunk!

In our relief, we burst into a crazy mixture of tears and hysterical laughter. "Oh my god," I gasped, "I thought he had spinal meningitis." Bill leaned his forehead against the doorjamb. His shoulders shook. "I didn't know what the hell it was." Shakily, Allison and Andy began to giggle, too. Bart wasn't dying. He was just drunk! Dead-to-the-world, passed-out stinking drunk!

But later, after Bart was put to bed, his head still lolling backwards, and after I had thoroughly scrubbed the bathroom, Bill and I met in our bedroom. He looked at me with real concern. "You know, it's one thing to sample booze. Most kids do that. But hiding in your bedroom, all by yourself on a sunny afternoon, deliberately drinking yourself into a stupor, that doesn't strike me as a simple teenage experimenting, Barb."

Dr. Brusheski didn't think so, either. "Bart feels bad about himself and his world, but he doesn't think he's responsible. It's the world that's screwed him—which means he doesn't see any way he can make changes." He tapped his fingers together thoughtfully. "Better stay alert for signs of harder drugs."

But again, like a dance, one step up, two steps back, we appeared to be standing in place. Bart wasn't getting any better, but neither was he getting worse. The drunk episode seemed to have scared him.

Summer approached, our third in the Midwest. Air conditioners hummed. Ice tinkled in iced-tea pitchers. Shorts and halters were pulled out of drawers, and the summer smell of chlorine drifted above the neighborhood swimming pool.

For the first time, the children would not fly to California. Bart, because of his failing grades, had to pass eight weeks of summer school if he hoped to enter eighth grade. Allison had accepted a baby-sitting job for a working mother and Andy was enrolled in day camp.

With his paper route wages, Bart purchased a 10-speed bicycle, a beautiful deluxe European model, painted red. Bill helped him pick it out.

"Mrs. Sheehan," Bart called, as he and Bill lifted the bike off the roof of the station wagon. "Come look!"

Our widowed neighbor bustled out her front door and over to our driveway. "It's beautiful, Bart."

He beamed. "I earned the money myself."

"Imagine." She nodded to us. "You can be very proud of your boy."

At that moment, I was. I gave Bart a hug.

He willingly agreed to ride six miles each day to school, no small feat in a city where summer temperatures can reach 100 degrees. We complimented him. Once more, Bart was showing new resolve. I, too, resolved to be more under-standing.

"You watch," he called, as he peddled off the first day of school, "I'm gonna make straight A's."

"Good for you!" I called after him.

Although he didn't make A's, his two-week report showed solid B's. "See?" I said, pleased. "You can do it."

Bart looked pleased himself.

The following week he was caught smoking in the boys' restroom. In summer school, smoking meant automatic expulsion. Bart had forgotten his resolve. I forgot mine.

"Why?" I screamed. "Why do you always get into trouble? Your father would hate the person you are today."

The misery on Bart's face deepened to an ugly scowl. "Yeah? Screw my father. He shouldn't have died."

"You will not speak that way!"

"Oh yeah? Screw you, too. Sometimes I wish—"

"Yes?"

"Never mind."

"I know what you were about to say. Sometimes you wish I were dead. Well, who knows, maybe I'll die tomorrow in a car crash. Then you'll have your wish. Both your parents will be dead. And it will be all your fault!"

His face whitened. I felt a sickening wrench inside. What had I said?

"Bart, I'm sorry. I didn't mean—"

But it was too late. He ran from the room.

Two days later, Bill phoned me at work. "Barbara, I'm at the police station with Bart. You'd better come."

The police! On the way to the station, my imagination ran riot. Once more I remembered Donny Hayward in San Diego and the neighbors' desperate threats to call the police. I thought of John and his deep respect for law and order. I remembered the day John had called his oldest son, "special."

Bart sat huddled in a chair against one wall while Bart

129

and a blue-uniformed police officer talked. "Bart and Curt were caught shoplifting," said Bill. "Bart swiped a tape cassette."

I stared at my son. "You don't even own a tape player! Why?"

He shrugged, not meeting my eyes. "I don't know."

Because it was a first-time offense, charges weren't filed. Bill requested the store owner's name. "You're going to pay him a personal visit," he said, "and make restitution." I nodded in vehement agreement. But again, I wondered with a growing sense of despair, What more could we do? Why wasn't anything working?

What happened next was no more than unhappy coincidence. Mrs. Sheehan, Bart's special friend next door, received an out-of-town visitor, her grandson. Suddenly, the nice lady who baked Bart cookies and spent hours talking to him was busy with another boy. At a time when he especially needed a friend, Bart felt, again, as if he'd been abandoned. No one guessed the extent of his seething resentment. I didn't even know Mrs. Sheehan had a visitor.

Then, on a steamy July night, Bart asked if Curt could sleep over. We agreed reluctantly. I would have said no but Bill prevailed. "Look," he said, "We can't stop Bart from seeing Curt, so we're better off with them at our house. At least here we can keep an eye on things."

Curt came over after supper, and the boys immediately disappeared into the basement. Bill and I went to bed early that night. Humidity was high and the cicadas seemed noisier than usual, but I was tired and fell asleep quickly.

The next morning, as I walked down the driveway toward my car, my mind was on the day ahead. Then I noticed my neighbor's property. I gasped and closed my eyes against the vicious red paint that spilled like bloody gashes across Mrs. Sheehan's car, the ashes from the fire that had been started in her mailbox, the strands of toilet paper that hung like Spanish moss from her trees.

"No," I whispered, "Bart couldn't have done this." But

with a sick certainly, I knew he had. My eyes went back to the hideous red streaks that slashed Mrs. Sheehan's white Ford.

That was the day Dr. Brusheski recommended residential treatment.

CHAPTER FOURTEEN

I SAT ON the edge of a hardbacked wooden chair outside Dr. Kruepper's office at the Boys' Home. In the chair opposite, Bill read the parents' handbook.

Boys' Home. The very words left a sick, queasy feeling in my stomach. Boys' Home meant unloved, abandoned youth. Boys in trouble. Orphaned boys with no parents. *What are we doing here?* I wondered wildly, and it was all I could do to keep from running to our car and driving away as fast as I could.

"Barbara," Bill said quietly, "read this." Reluctantly, I accepted the manual he handed me. The Boys' Home, said a line in bold print on the first page, offered residential psychiatric care to fifty-eight boys between the ages of twelve and eighteen.

"The boys who come here are anxious and disturbed," I read. "They have difficulties controlling their thoughts and impulses. Treatment includes three kinds: milieu therapy, which means a carefully structured environment; reality therapy, which helps the boys develop responsibility within themselves for socially acceptable behavior; and psychotherapy, which puts a boy in touch with his fears, doubts, and troubling emotions through one-on-one meetings with an individual therapist."

It was not a hospital, stressed the handbook. Nor was it an institution for the insane—those who have let go completely the ties to reality; those who hear voices or who inhabit worlds populated by their own disturbed imaginations. But it was a place of deep emotional pain. Boys in treatment felt overwhelmed by feelings of anger, rejection, and low self-esteem. In nearly every case, the boy's family system had floundered, become dysfunctional, so the boy and his parents no longer communicated. Home was a place of constant uproar.

Before I could read further, the door opened, Bart stepped out, and Dr. Kruepper beckoned us inside. He gestured to two cracked leather chairs from a scarred oak desk. For a minute or two, as we nervously seated ourselves, he simply puffed on his pipe. Then, in the folksy twang I would come to know well, he said, "Your son is stuck at age seven emotionally. A very angry seven. He'll stay stuck all his life if you don't get help now.

"Oh, he'll appear superficially to grow up," he continued, "but all his life, that seven-year-old anger will bob to the surface in unexpected ways. It will get in the way of marriage and job. He'll be handicapped emotionally."

I listened, wide-eyed, as he painted an incredibly accurate picture of Bart. How had he seen him so clearly in only thirty minutes?

"But why residential treatment?" I asked. "Why can't we get the help we need outside?"

"Because it just isn't workin' at home," Kruepper said with another puff on his pipe. "An hour a week isn't enough. Bart needs more. Most of all, he needs a fresh environment, needs to get away from the fights and failures. Until then, he won't be free to work on his emotional problems."

An odd mix of feelings stirred within me. Failure. Guilt. Fear. As if from a distance, I heard the psychiatrist say, "It's going to be rough. Very rough on Bart. And on the two of you. But..."

It was the *But* that I clung to. *But* if we did this, things would get better. Was that what he was saying?

Despite my shame and deep sense of failure, when we left, I had the feeling that we would return.

As a wild animal caught in a trap will chew off its own leg, each boy at the Boys' Home acted out in a desperate thrashing effort to still the pain he felt, which succeeded only in creating more uproar at home, more anger, more rejection, more self-hatred. It was into this milieu that Bart was dragged, screaming and kicking, on that hot July day when we left him at the Home.

The two dorm staffers, Schotte and Connoli, took their struggling charge into a room in the Northwest Dorm. It held a bed, a dresser, a desk, a chair, and an open doorway.

While Bart unpacked, one of the boys stuck his head in the room. "Hi. You smoke?"

Hesitantly, Bart nodded.

The boy grinned. "Then you'd better hide your cigarettes. Schotte will search you for sure."

"Uh, thanks." Bart looked around for a hiding place.

"Here, I'll show you." The boy lifted the mattress and pointed to a spot between the bed springs.

"Thanks," Bart said again. He pulled four packs of cigarettes out of the bottom of his suitcase and extended one to the boy.

"A whole pack?"

"Sure. Maybe you can show me around."

The boy nodded. "I'm Tom," he said. He left as Schotte returned.

"All right," Schotte said. "Let's see where you've got your cigarettes stashed away." The heavyset counselor started searching the room, but the boy's hiding place was a good one. Schotte didn't find them.

"Smoking is against the rules," he said. "And I come down hard when you break the rules. Remember that."

When he left, Bart finished unpacking and sat down on the bed. Sounds of a television set and a sudden burst of loud laughter came from somewhere nearby. He heard a dog bark. Otherwise, it was quiet. No one walked by the open doorway. He sat on his bed for a while, his hands resting on his knees. Still, no one came by. At last, hesitantly, he got up and walked into the hall. The sound of the television got louder. He smelled the faint odor of Lysol.

Bart followed the noise to the dorm rec room. Two pool tables took up an alcove. A couch with a hole in the upholstery stood in one corner. A group of boys, watching a large TV set, eyed Bart carefully. He sat down in the back row of chairs, his shoulders tense. After a while, most of the boys lost interest in him, so he relaxed a little.

When the TV show ended, a boy in the front row got up and left. Bart asked if he could have his seat. He'd only been in it a minute when a tall, wiry black boy came into the room and swaggered toward Bart.

"Get outa that chair."

"It's my chair," Bart said. "The boy who had it said it was okay."

"I don't give a shit. I want that chair."

"I ain't getting out of it," Bart insisted. The black boy socked him. No warning. Just pow. Bart winced from the sudden pain, but he wouldn't give in. "It ain't your chair and I'm not getting out of it."

As the black boy raised his fist again, Tom suddenly appeared. "Hey, Ghetto, leave him alone. He didn't do nothing." The black boy paused, looked at Tom, shrugged, and dropped his fist.

"Thanks," Bart said to Tom.

"Don't worry about it. Ghetto's always picking fights."

Bart watched TV for a few more minutes. When another show ended, boys began to disperse. Tom leaned toward Bart.

"How about it? Want to smoke?"

"Sure. Where do we go?"

"The bathroom. Follow me."

He showed Bart the procedure. You sat on the toilet seat, so if anyone came in, you could stick the cigarette under the ledge of the seat quickly.

They were half way through a shared cigarette when Schotte walked in. Bart stashed the butt fast under the toilet ledge.

"Give it here!" said Schotte.

"Give what?" Smoke poured out of the bowl.

Schotte yanked him off the stool and dropped the cigarette into the water. "That cigarette burning your ass is what. Now fifty pushups, both of you. And when you finish, Bart, I want every last cigarette you managed to hide."

This time he got them.

After Schotte left his room, Bart threw himself back on the bed. He listened to the noises of the dorm—boys' voices, sneakers hitting the tiled floor, a sudden thump as something fell. His first day at the Boys' Home. He didn't try to wipe away the tears.

CHAPTER FIFTEEN

TO BART, Mrs. Tabor seemed proof positive that his life was screwed up by other people. He stalked into her office for their first meeting with unconcealed belligerence, but the tall, rawboned, gray-haired psychiatric counselor had worked with troubled children for nearly thirty years. She regarded Bart calmly.

"Why do you ask so many damn questions," he demanded after a few minutes.

"I'm interested in you. I want to find out why you're so angry."

"I'll tell you why! It's because of Bill, my stupid son-of-a-bitch stepdad who conned Mom into bringing me to a crazy home for kids."

"Do you really think it's Bill's fault?"

"Of course. There's nothing wrong with me. We were fine when we lived in California. We were fine until Bill came into the family. That's when everything fell apart."

"How about your problems in the neighborhood before your mother knew Bill?"

"Who told you about that?" A sulky expression crossed his face. "It was nothing serious, anyway. It's Bill who ought to be talking to you. I don't belong in this place. I don't belong here, I tell you!" Now, he was yelling.

"Well, you are here," said Mrs. Tabor, patiently. "And you're going to have to work hard to get well so you can go back home to your family."

"I am well!" he hollered. "Except I got some quack old lady telling me I'm crazy and that I got to work hard like it was homework or something. I'll tell you something—"

"No, I'll tell you something," she shouted back. Her hand smashed down hard on her desk. "I'll tell you something. And you'd better listen. You do not refer to me as some 'quack old lady.' You will call me Mrs. Tabor. Do you understand?"

Bart stared, a stunned expression on his face. Mrs. Tabor looked too old to yell like that. She looked too frail, like a skeleton. For another long minute, he simply stared. Then, with a hard swallow, he whispered, "Okay. I'm sorry."

"What?"

"I said I'm sorry for calling you a quack. But I want to go home. How will things get better *there* if I'm stuck *here*?"

"Those are good questions," she said calmly. "We'll work on the answers when I see you tomorrow."

Bill and I stood in the drab yellow hallway outside Mrs. Tabor's office. Two staff members of the treatment center walked past and nodded, but I turned away.

"What's wrong?" asked Bill as he felt me tense.

"I feel like such a failure. Everyone here thinks we're parents who can't raise our children right."

"That's silly. We've got a troubled boy, and we're getting help. That doesn't make us failures."

"If I'd done my job right, Bart wouldn't need help."

Before Bill could answer, the office door opened, and Mrs. Tabor beckoned us inside. Months later I would overhear Bart describe her as a "tough old lady," and she was

136

that, but it was the toughness of love. However, neither Bart nor I knew that at first.

"You and Bart need a rest from each other," Mrs. Tabor said at our initial meeting, "so you won't be seeing him for a while. But I did suggest he write you."

I took, with trembling hands, the letter she handed me.

"Despite what you read," she added, "we're quite satisfied with the way he's settled in."

I looked at the uneven penciled scrawl that spilled across the lined notebook sheet.

> Dear Mom, you said if I didn't like it here, you would take me out. That's the only reason I said I'd come. Well, I hate this place. I don't have any friends. I just plane [sic] don't like it here. You said you'd take me out if I didn't. Please don't go back on your word. You promised. Get me out of here. Please! Love, Bart. P.S. It won't be "Love, Bart" if you keep me here.

From outside the office window, we heard shouts of boys at play. A faint metallic clink told me dinner preparations were under way. I glanced across the small, cramped office. A large poster announced, "Today Is the First Day of the Rest of Your Life."

Bart needs to be here, I reminded myself. But he thinks we have abandoned him. "Maybe I should—" I began.

"No, you shouldn't," said Mrs. Tabor firmly. "Your son is where he needs to be. Remember that. Now," she added briskly, "let's talk about you."

"What about us?" I felt defensive and scared. An outpatient psychologist was one thing, Mrs. Tabor something else. This tough old lady was calling the shots, even telling us when we could see our son.

"You'll have to work as hard as Bart. Everyone will have to make changes before Bart can come home again. But tell me how things are at home, now that Bart is here."

At home, Allison and Andy were as scared as Bill and I. They had watched Bart pack his suitcase with wide, frightened eyes. Andy ran into his bedroom and wouldn't come out to say goodbye. When I went to him later, he backed away from me.

"Andy, what's wrong?"

He looked at the bedroom wall, at the stuffed tiger on his bed, at the library books about snakes that reflected his latest interest, at everything but me. "Are you going to send me away, too?" he said finally.

"Andy, we didn't send Bart *away*! I mean, yes, he's going away to a—well, a kind of school—but that's so he can get help. We're not sending him away from the family."

Now, Andy did look at me with a sober, intense gaze that made me want to cry, for I read in that gaze, very clearly, the message. *I don't believe you.*

"Bart will be gone for a long time, won't he?" Allison said simply.

I nodded. She said nothing more, but her chin trembled.

Our days fell quickly into a new pattern, a pattern whose center was the Boys' Home. We grew used to the sound of our tires on the freeway pavement, then the blacktop, then the graveled entrance road to the Home. We came to expect the boisterous greeting from Dog, a black and white mutt who romped with the boys whenever he wasn't racing cars pell mell up the drive.

On Tuesdays, we met with Mrs. Tabor. Wednesday evenings were reserved for our parents group, under the leadership of Dr. Kruepper and Mrs. Tabor.

Summer twilights linger so it was still light outside as we entered the dining room for our first group meeting. Three cafeteria tables formed a U.

Betty and Art Lehman sat on one side. In wash khakis and sports shirt, with horn-rimmed glasses on a narrow, intelligent face, Art Lehman looked every inch the college professor that he was, while Betty's long brown hair and high cheekbones gave her the appearance of a sensitive, artistic woman.

In stark contrast were Cora and Harry Stacker. A beefy road construction worker, Harry looked like a cartoon character who sits, drinking beer, in his undershirt. Cora, who worked as a motel cleaning lady, was overweight, with flabby skin hanging from her upper arms. Most startling of all was her mouth. She had no teeth.

Howard and Millie Boynton completed the group. Howard's thinning hair, slight middle-age paunch, and well-tailored pinstripe suit marked him as a corporate executive, specifically, corporate legal counsel. Millie appeared to be a traditional homemaker who deferred to Howard on everything.

Bill and I were the newcomers.

"Well," said Dr. Kruepper, as we settled into chairs with cups of coffee. "How did the weekend visit go, Cora?"

Cora smiled. Her toothless gums appalled me. Again came the thought, like an inner wail, *What's a nice girl like me doing here?*

"It went real good, didn't it, Harry? Harry and Benjie talked some. Harry even looked at one of Benjie's drawings. And ya know what?" Something warm crept into her eyes, something even I responded to. I told myself that love and compassion wear many faces. "Harry hugged Benjie good-bye."

Harry looked embarrassed. His ruddy face turned even redder. "You folks been pushing me to do it. But I'll tell ya, you got to watch that sissy stuff with boys. Makes 'em fags."

Benjie, I learned later, was twelve years old. I saw him in the hall one evening; a small, slight boy who looked closer to ten than twelve. A year ago, he'd tried to hang himself.

He was a boy caught in the middle. His two older sisters were favored by their father, who in return for "woman's work" at home offered them affection. Benjie's two younger brothers, carbon copies of their rough-hewn, macho father, won his casual, offhand approval. Benjie, however, was a mystery to Harry—a small, pale boy who ran from fights, who preferred art and music to sports, and wept easily. Most of the time Harry ignored his middle child, but every so often, never predictably, he'd blow up at "the sissy."

Finally, Benjie did something macho. He tried to hang himself.

Millie cleared her throat with a dry, nervous cough. "I think it's very nice that Harry hugged Benjie." She glanced sideways at her husband. Howard appeared not to hear.

Betty Lehman leaned forward. Her voice was as soft as her eyes. "Art and I went to a party last Saturday."

"And Betty was right out there, talking and laughing with everyone else," Art said. I couldn't understand why he sounded so proud, or why the others at the table clapped and shouted, "Bravo!" "Good for you!"

As if sensing my puzzlement, Betty smiled at me. "I'm trying to get over my—shyness," she said. "It will help when Jacob comes home."

Jacob was sixteen. Tall and thin, he looked strikingly like his mother, and seemed outwardly as shy. But eighteen months ago, he had started firing a BB gun randomly through the quiet neighborhood where he lived with his mother, his sister, and his new stepfather. Luckily, no one was hurt. Like the red paint on Mrs. Sheehan's car, I thought, it was really a cry for help.

The only one who didn't speak that night was Howard Boynton. He sat stiffly in his chair, arms folded tightly across his chest. His face had a closed, disapproving expression. I noticed Millie Boynton glancing at him every so often, like a frightened wren glancing at a cat, I thought.

Actually, Howard wasn't the only silent one. Bill and I didn't talk, either, and no one pushed us to. Only toward the end of the two-hour session did Cora look my way. Despite her toothlessness, her smile was warm.

"How old's your boy, Barbara?"

I felt the group pause, saw their eyes on me, and felt a strange suffocation engulfing me. I gasped quickly, trying to get air. And it seemed, then, as if I stood outside myself, as if the real me stood alongside this poor creature in the chair. The real me raised two arms in anger and shouted, "Leave her alone! She doesn't belong here!" The me they saw only shook her head and swallowed.

Bill answered. "He's thirteen."

"This here's a good place," said Cora. "Me 'n Harry, we're gettin' a lot of help. You will, too."

I couldn't stand it. How could I be compared to her? I had been raised to do things right. I came from a loving, churchgoing family. I had wanted all my babies. I had a master's degree. And I had worked so damn hard. Why was I here?

I shoved back my chair and ran from the room. Bill found me, sobbing uncontrollably, as I leaned against the cold yellow wall of the hallway.

My terrible depression started then.

"Barbara." A hand nudged my shoulder. Nudged it harder. "Barbara, wake up."

As if swimming up through depths of water, heavy dark ocean depths, I struggled to respond. At last, my head burst the surface. My eyes opened. Bill's face swam into view. He looked worried.

"Barbara, I've been trying to wake you for five minutes."

My mouth felt furry, my head groggy. I blinked, worked my mouth, managed to say, "Sorry." Slowly, I pulled myself up, pushed back the sheets.

"You slept for ten hours."

I glanced at my alarm clock. Eight o'clock! I was usually at my desk by 8:15, but somehow, it didn't seem to matter. All I wanted to do was fall back into bed.

Bill stood by the dresser, waiting, so I struggled to my feet and staggered toward the shower, where I waited for the hot needles of water to revive me. I felt as if I were drugged.

Even after John died, I couldn't remember such depression. Then, there had been deep, aching sorrow, a grief that was physical in its pain, but nothing like this gray fog into which I had fallen, this nothingness that seemed to clog my eyes and ears and brain.

At the ad agency, I sat in my office with the door shut, staring mindlessly at job tickets. Occasionally I doodled a few words on paper, but they were meaningless words. A TV script was due for our hospital client, and a print ad for an industrial account, but I couldn't make the deadlines seem important. Footsteps went past my door, paused, then went on.

At home, I fixed super like a robot and headed for bed immediately afterwards. Allison followed me into the bedroom, her face anxious.

"Mom, are you sick?" She pointed to the summer sky. At 8:30, it was still light.

"Just tired, honey."

Her anxious expression didn't lift, but I couldn't find the energy to care.

At our next parents' group meeting, I sat without speaking, my hands clenched tightly in my lap. Cora poured coffee into styrofoam cups. A plate of home-baked oatmeal cookies made the rounds. The Boys' Home had a good cook.

"Well?" Dr. Kruepper said. "What's happenin'?"

Betty Lehman twisted a strand of her dark, shoulder-length hair. "I'm very angry," she said in a soft voice at odds with her words.

"At whom?"

"At my mother. *Very* angry." Her voice rose slightly. "Last Friday, she called. Told me I should get out more, wear brighter colors, stop being a stay-at-home bookworm, what kind of example was I setting for Melanie? And I nodded my head and said 'Yes Mama, yes Mama,' just like always, and after I hung up, I wanted to throw up, I was so angry."

"It doesn't sound as if you're mad at your mother," said Mrs. Tabor.

"Nope, your mama's not acting no different," said Cora. "Sounds like you're mad at *you*."

"When are you gonna tell your old lady to butt out?" Harry demanded.

"That's what I asked her," Art murmured.

Betty played with another long strand of hair. "I gave in to her again, didn't I?"

"Aw, it's easy to do. I'm always falling into that with Harry. Start thinking I ain't worth nothing, 'cept to cook and clean."

Betty was silent. Suddenly, her voice soared. "Damn it, mother, I don't like bright colors! I hate joining groups! I love to read! So take your advice and—and shove it! It's me I'm going to listen to!"

"Good for you!" cried Cora. Her mouth parted in a smile.

Art Lehman gave his wife a hug.

Bill and I didn't understand it all that night, but over the next weeks and months, we learned the Lehmans' story. Betty had been adopted as a baby by a middle-aged couple who wanted a Shirley Temple. To them, shy, introverted Betty was a great disappointment, and they told her so constantly. Yet, in their own way, they wanted the best for her. They dressed her well and sent her to a good college. There, she met Dan, a charming textbook salesman in his twenties. In the spring of her freshman year, they eloped. It was Betty's one small moment of revolt. But five years later, Dan left her. Devastated, Betty returned home with her son and infant daughter.

By some genetic quirk, the little girl was the blonde, dimpled Shirley Temple type her grandparents had yearned for. Jacob was quiet and shy like his mother. For years, the grandparents played favorites. Jacob, too, was called a disappointment, a misfit.

To support herself and her children, Betty went to work in the administrative office at the nearby University. On her own, she pursued a lifelong interest in art. At a traveling exhibit of Thomas Hart Benton paintings, she met Art Lehman.

After they married, Art had tried to help Jacob feel better about himself, but it was too late for simple solutions. One day, quiet, withdrawn Jacob struck back and shot up the neighborhood. Now, at the Boys' Home, he was coming to grips with his years of suppressed anger. Both he and his mother were trying to create new self-images.

"When Jacob first came here, I felt as you do," Betty said gently, and I realized she was addressing me. "I felt so awful about myself...."

"Wait a minute!" I bristled. "I don't feel awful about me. I feel awful about..."

"Yes?" prompted Kruepper.

"...about being here, that's all! I'm ashamed! Everyone in this room has failed as a parent. I don't want to know you people! I just want my son to get well and come home!"

"We all want that," Cora said comfortingly.

Howard Boynton loosened his hands briefly from their clasp on his pinstriped vest. "I understand what you mean. It's incredible to me that I sit in this *place*"—his voice held a querulous astonishment—"week after week. What would my colleagues think!"

"Do the rest of you feel like failures as parents?" asked Dr. Kruepper.

His question drew a pause. Betty spoke into the silence. "I used to, but now I realize that I did the best I could. I was a hurting person, too. How could I protect Jacob from his grandparents when I didn't know how to stand up for myself?"

Art reached over and squeezed her hand.

"Believe me," said Dr. Kruepper, his eyes moving from Betty to me, "I've seen many, many parents who did their absolute durn-tootin' best and still their child became troubled."

He puffed on his pipe for a moment, then continued. "Children and parents are individuals, with a predisposition to certain behavior and emotional response. And you have to remember, events shape a child's life as well, events over which a parent has no control. It's a mighty big mistake to think parents are the only ones at fault for a child's emotional

144

illness. When parents and society get rid of that notion, a lot more kids who need it will get help."

Believe me, he had said, but I didn't. I was lost in gray fog, convinced that I'd failed, certain that outsiders look at a family in emotional turmoil and blame the parents. If the parents had done their job right, their kid wouldn't be in trouble, wouldn't be sick, wouldn't need psychiatric treatment.

As my fingers clenched more tightly in my lap, Kruepper watched me thoughtfully. When our session ended and Bill and I prepared to leave, he stopped us.

"If you don't start coming out of this depression, Barbara, you call me," he said, and his folksy twang had entirely disappeared.

I said nothing, but Bill nodded in relief.

My sense of shame was such that I couldn't bring myself to tell anyone where my son was. Not even Tina, my closest friend, knew.

When she asked, "Where's Bart?" I mumbled, "boarding school," and changed the subject.

I couldn't bring myself to say anything at the agency, either. Advertising is built on surface perceptions. Advertising people see themselves as winners, people who do things "right." How could I admit how wrong everything had gone in our family?

George Castleman called me into his office and said, "You've been a little off feed, Barbara."

I stared miserably at my feet. "I know I missed a deadline last week—"

"Two."

"I—I've been under some strain lately."

Castleman played impatiently with a paperweight prism. It was an award from the Ad Club's annual creative competition.

"Unfortunately, our clients don't care about your problems. They just want good ads. Time to get up and at 'em,

145

hmmm?" His jovial tone was forced.

I swallowed and nodded, barely managing a smile. "You bet, George."

Back in my office cold, clammy panic swept over me. I knew what George's real message was, and now, especially, I couldn't afford to lose my job. Bart's treatment cost fifty-five dollars a day.

But still the fog of depression clung.

CHAPTER SIXTEEN

I THOUGHT NOTHING could make me feel worse than I did. I was wrong.

Although Bart could not come home, he was allowed to write letters, not only to us, but to his grandparents. He wrote to them in California: "Mom and Bill sent me to a boys home. It's real tough here. The bigger boys beat up on me. I miss my family terrible. Please write. I'm so lonely."

My mother's outraged phone call came immediately. "What does he mean a *boys' home*? What have you done with our grandson?"

"Mom, it's a residential treatment center. For boys with emotional problems."

"Bart is a loving child, Barbara. What he needs is the attention of his mother. And maybe a good Catholic school, not some home for orphan boys!"

"It's a psychiatric treatment center."

"Psychiatrists? Bart's not crazy. I know my own grandson. Something has happened to you since you got married."

"Mom, no. You don't understand."

"Barbara, if you're having problems you can't handle, send Bart to live with us. Don't leave him in a *boys' home!*"

146

When I hung up the telephone, I was shaking as if I had palsy. I rubbed my hands up and down my arms. My skin felt cold.

It was obvious that to my mother I was the victim of sinister forces, persuaded by some midwestern Rasputin to deny my son and send him away. How could she, halfway across the continent and from another generation, understand why we had her grandson in a residential psychiatric treatment center?

On the other hand, could she be right? Maybe I should send Bart to his grandparents, or bring him home and try a Catholic school...

"Barb," Bill said when he heard, "your mother doesn't know the situation. She doesn't realize that Bart is ill. He needs help he can't get at home. You have to hang in there. For his sake."

Mrs. Tabor, at our next meeting, spoke drily. "Bart's letter was designed to play on his grandmother's sympathies. And on yours. He's very good at manipulative behavior. Most of the boys here are." Her hand, the paper-thin flesh barely covering the bone, clasped mine for a moment. "You are doing what is best for your son. Trust yourself."

But my parents and I were close, and I had always respected their views. Besides, I had been raised to be a dutiful daughter. My mother's outraged concern increased my own torment and self-doubt. Whom should I listen to?

I leaned back wearily in the chair beside Mrs. Tabor's desk. I had come alone this week. From the kitchen across the hall I heard the now-familiar noises of dinner preparation, and through the window distant shouts of boys. It was late August, nearly the sixth anniversary of John's death. What would he think? He had counted on me to take good care of our children.

"Mrs. Bartocci," Mrs. Tabor firmly said, "you want to be a perfect parent. You feel you have failed. But how many perfect people do you know?"

"I was raised to be a good mother."

"Good does not mean perfect. It is damn hard to be a single parent, to cope with grief and still give your children all they need, to bring a step-parent into a family."

She doodled absently on a sheet of scratch paper. "Certainly, there are patterns to change in the way you deal with Bart, but first, Mrs. Bartocci, you have to unload this overwhelming—and unrealistic—guilt and shame. You're human. That's all."

Tears filled my eyes. Embarrassed, I rummaged for a tissue. Was she saying I was not the worst of all mothers, that I was merely human? The idea took my breath away. I could not believe it, not yet, but for the first time in weeks, a tiny bit of the depression lifted. When I left her office, I felt, at least for the moment, committed to remain on this path we had selected. Bart—and his parents—would stay in treatment at the Boys' Home.

A fundamental part of that treatment was *milieu therapy*, which meant that the boys in residence lived totally structured lives. Every minute was supposedly accounted for and supervised by a therapist, a dorm counselor, a recreation director, or a teacher.

Bart met with Mrs. Tabor, his therapist, five days a week. The rest of his days were divided into summer school, sports, recreation, and chores. The boys set tables, did lawn maintenance, took turns with KP, cleaned out the stables, and so forth. Some boys also met in group therapy.

Gradually, we learned a few stastistics. The average age of admittance was thirteen years and most boys stayed about eighteen months. Fifty percent of the residents had spent some time in a psychiatric hospital ward. More boys came from two-parent families than single-parent households (although the difference was only a percentage point or two), and three-fourths were diagnosed with a personality disorder or psychoneurosis, indefinite labels that meant nothing to me. Virtually all had been in outpatient treatment before a residential placement.

"For all kinds of reasons, seldom just one, a home environment may stop working for a child," Mrs. Tabor said. "When that happens, the boy feels like a Ping-Pong ball, ricocheting off walls. Therapy has little chance of success.

"What we must do first, before a boy can begin to examine his feelings, is bring his life back under control. We do that by structuring his environment. Totally. From the time he wakes in the morning until he goes to bed at night."

The boys fought the structured environment. They stayed constantly on the lookout for ways to circumvent it. And they had their own pecking order.

The highest positions in the social scheme were held by the boys between sixteen and eighteen. They recruited the younger boys of thirteen or fourteen to do their dirty work, like "running up" for cigarettes or making their beds. The boys who were Bart's age were made to serve the older boys and they, in turn, commanded the ten- to twelve-year-olds. The youngest boys, from eight to ten, were called Rug Rats. They lived in a dorm by themselves.

Most of the boys in Bart's Northwest Dorm wing were older, sixteen to eighteen. Some, referred by the courts, had been raised in the rougher areas of big cities, came from foster homes, or were wards of the state. Ghetto was known as Head Honcho. Nobody messed with Ghetto, not even the boys who were bigger and older.

A week after Bart arrived at the Home, Ghetto and his sidekicks, Mike (Diablo) and Jimmy (Diego), decided Bart needed an initiation. It was late afternoon, the quiet time between afternoon sports and dinner. Caught without warning outside his room, Bart was dragged to the basketball court and pushed into a pine box used for holding baseball bats.

"Hey, what are you doing?" he cried, but it was too late.

"Okay, Bart boy," Ghetto whooped, locking the lid. The three of them began to shake the box. Nails and splinters of wood scraped Bart's skin and snagged his clothes.

"Let me out!" he hollered, but they just shook the box more. It was dark and suffocating. He began to cry.

"Come on, you guys, let me out. Please!" The box shook again.

"Not till you quit crying, Bart boy."

That made him mad. "Aw, fuck you, Ghetto, you son of a bitch!"

"What did you call me? Now, you asked for it!"

They flipped the box upside down, so hard Bart crashed down on his head. He began to scream and cry in real terror. His screams scared the older boys. "Hey, pipe down before someone comes. We'll let you out. Stop your hollering."

They opened the top of the box. The first thing Bart did was go for Ghetto, fists flying. He was screaming and cursing and tears ran down his cheeks.

That's when Schotte appeared. "What's going on?"

"Nothing," Ghetto said quickly. "We were just teasing Bart a little."

"What were they doing?" Schotte said to Bart.

"Nothing," he lied. "We were just messing around."

Schotte looked at them suspiciously. Bart's nose was running. He sniffed. Still, no one said anything. "All right. Go to your rooms. All of you."

Bart walked shakily to his room.

With nearly sixty troubled teenagers in residence, it was inevitable that boys tried to sneak around the rules. The wonder was not that they did, but that the staff controlled them so successfully. The goal of milieu therapy was to encourage the boys' transition from the tight structure of external controls to their own internal controls. To accomplish this, the Home also used the Level System.

"Think of the levels as something like school grades," we were told. "A boy climbs from freshman to senior, although we have six levels, not four, and when he reaches the top, he graduates back into the real world."

"Earning new levels will give Bart a visible measure of his success in taking charge of his own life," Mrs. Tabor said.

All incoming boys started at Level 1. To move to the

next level, the boy had to make written application, stating why he deserved the higher level. Each new level brought new rewards.

On Level 1, a boy had access to a lock box for treasured personal belongings. He received some allowance and could use the recreation room, but if he wanted a radio in his room and a bigger allowance, he had to earn Level 2. On that level, he could go off grounds on occasional group activities, but for a weekly off-grounds trip—the boys took in frequent movies and sporting events—he had to reach Level 3. Then he could also have a stereo. On Level 4, he could go off grounds twice a week and spend some time unsupervised. On the highest levels, 5 and 6, a boy could go to a high school dance or football game. Some even held part-time jobs.

The requirements for earning a level were specific to each boy's behavior goals. If Eddy lost his temper frequently, he would have to control it; if Jimmy was too withdrawn, he would have to mix more. A boy could be "busted" a level, too.

"The Level System is also an observation tool," Mrs. Tabor said. "If a boy stays on one level too long, we know something is wrong and we reexamine our treatment plan. Through the Level System, Bart will soon see that certain behavior brings certain rewards."

"Like behavior modification?" Bill asked.

"Essentially. Nothing is taken for granted," she added, "not even a visit home, although we don't tie home visits specifically to levels. But they're not automatic, either. Don't expect a visit home from Bart for at least sixty days, maybe longer."

"That long?" I cried. "But surely—"

"Mrs. Bartocci, life has been hell for Bart. And his family. As I told you before, you all need a little breathing room."

Bill had insisted, as my depression continued, that I call Dr. Kruepper. The psychiatrist gave me a prescription. "These are kinda like cold pills," he said. "They won't cure

151

the cause of your depression, but they'll help the symptoms—pull you outta that black hole you're in. And you gotta pull out of it, Barbara, or you'll wind up in the hospital."

The prescription helped. My fog began to lift. And I discovered Mrs. Tabor was right. It did seem as if there was suddenly room to breathe at home. It was a giddy, almost physical sensation. One night at dinner, Andy started telling knock-knock jokes. They got sillier and sillier.

I passed around the platter of pot roast and vegetables. "More carrots?"

"I don't car-rot all for carrots," Bill quipped.

"Ohhhh," Allison groaned. "You're corny."

"Not corny," Andy shouted. "He's carroty!" Wild uproarious laughter from us all.

Andy speared another piece of meat. "I sure like dinner time better without Bart," he said.

My fork clanged against my plate. "That's an awful thing to say. Bart is your brother!"

"So? Dinner's still more fun without him."

"I won't let you say that."

"Calm down, Barbara."

"I won't calm down! Just because Bart isn't here—"

"Hey, wait—"

But I had thrown down my napkin and run to our bedroom. Bill followed. He stood inside the doorway, as I lay across the bed. Strips of twilight filtered through the blinds, making a pattern on my hand.

"You're taking your own feelings out on Andy," he said with irritation. I turned my head away. The mattress sank as he sat down beside me.

"Barbara," he said more gently, "Don't blame Andy because he voices what we all feel. Dinner *is* more fun without Bart right now. Bart probably thinks dinner without us is more fun, or, at least, more peaceful. This family was at war. Who wouldn't enjoy a truce?"

A tear trickled slowly down my cheek.

"Don't be ashamed of how you feel," Bill whispered. The

trickles came faster and faster, and I never was quite sure if I wept from relief because Bart wasn't home or from shame that I felt so relieved.

CHAPTER SEVENTEEN

AUGUST ENDED and school began. Was it only a year ago that Bill and I had married, that we had gone camping on our "family honeymoon," that I had felt such high hopes for our new family?

At the Boys' Home we were still not allowed to see Bart. But we continued to get letters from him, delivered each week by Mrs. Tabor. They were usually penciled on lined notebook sheets, often with drawings attached. The content was never predictable.

Dear Mom, [I read, shortly after his first angry letter.] I am sorry for my last letter. I talked it over with Schotte, my dorm counselor. I've decided I'll stay here. But you have to admit that what you told me about this place was a bundle of tricks and lies. Which I don't like!

(To Andy) "Write me more often. I feel you and Allison are the only ones who care how I feel. There are a lot of tough guys in this place."

(To Allison) "Hi. I am making you a leather change purse in shop class. It looks like this. [He drew a picture.] I hope you like it. I can hardly wait to leave this place. Love, Bart."

"P.S. to Mom. Can you bring some Pringle's next time you come? I get awful hungry here."

And later, another letter to me.

Dear Mom, I ain't right for this place. I am getting beat up for something I didn't do. Someone else put cigarettes in my room, and they thought I stole them. Mrs. Tabor said it would stop [the beating up]. She's a liar! Please take me home. Also, send me some Pringle's. I don't like starving. Send three cans. I don't hate you but I am mad and sad. I better get out of here soon. Love, Mad Bart

Shortly after his arrival, Bart was given a battery of psychological tests. In response to one Rorschach card, he said he saw a butterfly "with broken wings." Asked to look at a picture and tell a story, he replied, "It's a boy who had his dog killed and his parents are dead and he has to stay all alone. He feels sad, for too many things have been happening to him."

"Bart lost important nurturing," Mrs. Tabor said as we sat alone in her office. For some time, Bill and I had been visiting Mrs. Tabor separately. Through her window, I could see spatters of September rain. My gaze swerved to a crudely drawn picture tacked to her bulletin board. It showed a very large house and a family of stick figures, all big. Alone and very small and off to himself was another forlorn stick figure.

"Your grief was so intense when your husband died, it was as if Bart lost his mother as well as his father."

"But what about Andy?" I protested. "He's two years younger than Bart. Did he lose nurturing??"

"Andy had special problems," Mrs. Tabor gently said. "You were very concerned about Andy, remember? You paid close attention to him."

"And not Bart?"

Her fingers came together in a steeple. "You've told me, yourself, what difficulty you had relating to Bart. Yet his teachers in the early grades, his grandmother, his father, they all noticed that he needed more attention and appreciation than most children."

"What you're saying is I failed my son."

"I think you did the best you could. Your own grief and the necessity to restructure your life caused Bart's special needs to just . . . get lost."

* * *

"Tell me," she asked, another day, "how do you feel about being a parent?"

I thought of a bumper sticker I had seen. "It's easy to have a baby . . . hard to raise a child." How easy it had been to have babies, to nuzzle and love them, to change diapers and wipe noses. But later, especially after John died—

"I hate being a parent!" I burst out. "I love my children dearly, every one of them, but all the demands for so many years. Coping with John's death. Finishing school. Getting a job. Handling a tough boss. Doing well. And then raising the children on top of it, twenty-four hours a day, no relief. I know you're supposed to make rules and be consistent, but it's so hard when there's only you. I hate it, if you want to know the truth! I love my children, but if I had my way, I wouldn't be a parent at all."

"What would you be?"

"Oh—" I smiled. "A friend. I'd like to be a friend to my kids, to have fun with them."

"I see." But she said nothing more.

I was able to be a friend to Allison. True, she had needs, but they were simpler. Or maybe my response was different.

The night before school began—Allison's first year of high school—she called me into her bedroom. "Mom, what do you think? Have I outgrown my Dork Days?" She looked at me inquiringly. Her back brace was off for good now, and it seemed to me that I could already see changes in the shape of her jaw, thanks to the orthodontist. Her hair, spilling to her shoulders, was heavy and full, and over the summer she had started plucking her eyebrows, which made her deep-set blue eyes—her father's eyes—stand out more.

I looked at her carefully because I knew that's what she wanted. Then I smiled. "Definitely beyond Dork. Especially with your nice thick hair and your pretty eyes."

"Now that you can see them," she said. "Mom, didn't you ever notice that your daughter's eyebrows met in the middle? I was Dorky Allison One-Brow."

I burst into laughter. "Oh, dear, no. I didn't notice. You always looked pretty to me."

"Only a mother would love the world's bushiest eyebrows!"

We both giggled. "Allison," I said fondly, "you'll do just fine in high school." To myself, I added a quiet wish. Please, let it be so.

Allison was starting ninth grade, Andrew sixth. After years of tutoring, diagnostic tests showed he could now read at his grade level, and his body was outgrowing the earlier hyperactivity. I was thrilled and tried to encourage Andy's own perception that he was not only as smart as any other kid, but a little brighter than most. Andy, at eleven, was still quick to crawl up beside me on the family room couch and give me a hug. Our relationship was warm and affectionate, but Bill felt he saw definite problems.

"Damn it!" I heard him holler, one evening. "What happened to the ice cream?"

I was putting on my after-work blue jeans. Hurriedly, I fastened my belt buckle and headed for the kitchen.

"Andy ate it," Allison said as she pulled out silverware to set the dinner table.

"Ate it all? There was a half gallon last night."

She shrugged. "Ice cream never lasts around here."

Bill spied me and held out a nearly empty ice cream carton. "Look what I found in the freezer. Andy ate it!"

"So?"

"He ate it in one sitting, Barb. No one else had a chance!"

"Oh well..." I looked at Andy, who had heard the noise and followed me into the kitchen. We laughed. "Andy's an ice-cream-holic. So am I."

Bill's expression darkened. "Are you willing to let him get away with this?"

"I suppose he should eat less sugar but—"

"Less sugar! Barb, why should one member of the family hog a whole half gallon of ice cream? Doesn't Allison deserve some? Or you? Or me?"

156

"Bill, if you have a craving for ice cream, I'll go get you—"

"No! Dammit, that's not the point. Don't you see?"

My own voice hardened. "I agree, Andy didn't need to hog the ice cream, but I don't see it as a capital offense."

Bill held out the empty ice cream carton to Andy. "Did you eat all of that?"

"Yeah."

"Okay. Barbara, from now on, when we buy ice cream, I will divide it into quarters, and mark the quarters, one for each member of this family. You can eat your quarter any time you want, Andy, but if you eat Allison's or mine or your mother's, you're in deep trouble with me. Understand?"

I clapped my hands and laughed delightedly. "I think that's a wonderful idea!"

Allison smiled. "Me, too."

"It's okay with me," said Andy.

"It's a desperate measure," said Bill. He didn't smile at all. Dinner that night was silent.

When Bill reported the incident to our parents' group, his voice grew angry again. Usually, the parents didn't talk about their boys in group, at least not directly. The value of group, Dr. Kruepper had explained, came from insights we could give each other about our own personal development and our marriage relationships.

"I don't understand," I said. "What does Andy's hogging the ice cream have to do with Bart? Why are we talking about this?"

"Anyone here want to answer?" Kruepper asked.

Art Lehman's eyebrow lifted quizzically. "Kids like our Jacob and your Bart and—" he nodded towards the Boyntons—"Gene Boynton need the Boys' Home structure because for one reason or another their parents have lost control. Sounds like Bill thinks you don't have any more control over Andy than you had with Bart. And he's worried."

157

"Wait a minute," Howard bristled, "I don't need you telling me I lost control."

"You don't think you did?" Kruepper asked.

"No. I gave Gene everything. Howard Junior, too. But I set standards, high standards, because, dammit, that's how you succeed in life. By aiming high! No sir. No loss of control in our house. Gene just never measured up."

It was the longest statement I'd heard Howard make. As if realizing that, he shut up and settled back into his familiar, closed posture, but Bill pursued. "What do you mean, Gene never measured up?"

Howard shrugged. "I suppose he can't be blamed. That spinal meningitis at two, it damaged him."

Millie cleared her throat. "I—I do think Gene is a—a better person than you give him credit for, Howard."

"Isn't your defense a bit absurd after what happened, my dear?"

Millie turned pale. I wondered what had happened, but she seemed, suddenly, so shattered that I couldn't bring myself to ask.

Besides, Art's statement made me bristle, too. "What do you mean, I've lost control?"

"Don't rile up," Kruepper said. "Think for a minute. Do you feel in control as a parent?"

I stared at the psychiatrist. I wanted to say "Of course," but a familiar tug of helplessness stole over me. Reluctantly, I shook my head.

"No child becomes emotionally ill in a vacuum," Kruepper said. "The whole family is involved in some way. We can bring structure into a boy's life here at the home and, with therapy, help him solve his emotional problems, but if we send him back into the same environment, he'll fall right back into old behaviors. Parents have to change as well as their boys."

"But—"

"You need to feel as if you're in control before Bart comes home again. This little ol' ice cream caper"—a chuckle ran

158

around the table—"gave you a chance to practice. Do you see?"

I could see I was outnumbered, so I nodded, but I really didn't see at all.

CHAPTER EIGHTEEN

WE WERE permitted our first visit with Bart two weeks later. Bill and I arrived at the Boys' Home fifteen minutes early. My palms were sweaty, and my stomach felt as if I were about to go on stage...

Mrs. Tabor ushered us into her office. Bart knocked on the door a few minutes later.

"Hi, Mom. Bill."

He looked taller. Thinner. And his hair was cut short. Was his smile diffident? Uncertain? Or were those only my feelings?

I wanted to reach out and hug him, but something—an awkwardness—held me back. It was as if he belonged to the Boys' Home now, not to me.

"You look good," I said, instead.

"Thanks."

A small silence fell. Bill cleared his throat.

"Settling in all right, son?"

"It's okay." His voice was stiff.

"We miss you at home," I said. "Allison and Andy say hello. They miss you a lot, too."

"I'll bet they do. They're probably glad to have me gone. I'll bet it's real peaceful now."

"That's not true," I said quickly. Too quickly.

Suddenly, tears swam in Bart's eyes. "Oh Mom, why did you put me here? I hate this place. I want to come home so bad. I'll be good. I promise—" his voice had dropped, but I heard the sob—"please say you'll take me away from here."

Oh, my baby boy. I felt as if I were melting, as if my bones and skin and very self were turning into liquid gelatin... then I felt Bill clasp my hand. I took a deep breath.

"We want you to come home, Bart. But not right now. Right now, you need something we can't give you. The Boys' Home—"

"Screw the Boys' Home! It doesn't have what I need!" His tears, suddenly, were gone. "I need parents and a family. Not a bunch of juvenile delinquents with asshole staff members following us around." He turned to Bill. His voice rose. "This is your doing! You don't want me around, so you conned my Mom into sending me away. I want to go home NOW!" He was almost screaming. A desperate sort of scream. "You'll be sorry if you don't take me out of here, Mom. I'll run away. Or I'll kill myself. How will you feel then? Huh? Huh, Bill, you lousy son of a bitch homewrecker—?"

"That's enough," said Mrs. Tabor. She stood up and gestured toward us. "You'd better go. I'll see you next week. Bart will be all right."

"Go?" I said stupidly. Bill reached for my hand, propelled me out the door. It shut behind us. I looked at my husband, too stunned to cry.

All I could think was: *What in God's name have I done?*

Mrs. Tabor called me at work the next day.

"I just want to reassure you," she said. "Bart settled down after you left. He's doing fine." She paused. "I wish we had a little space between visits, but I just got a call about our court date. It's set for day after tomorrow. Can you drive with us to the courthouse?"

The court date. Of course. Bart's vandalism against Mrs. Sheehan.

Bart slid sulkily into the front seat of my station wagon. It was obvious he didn't want to go. How could I blame him? Neither did I. Mrs. Tabor slid in beside us. She seemed cheerful. The air held the crisp golden clarity of early fall. If it weren't for our destination and memories of our last visit, I could have been cheerful, too.

I headed down a back-country highway; a shortcut to the courthouse, said Mrs. Tabor. Two kids about Bart's age rode by on horseback.

Suddenly, Bart spoke up. "When are you going to take me out of that shit house?"

I swallowed. "I thought we covered that the other day, Bart."

"To hell with that. Answer me! *When?*"

"When you and I learn better ways to relate to each other." I glanced at Mrs. Tabor. She smiled her approval and said firmly, "Now, Bart, you already know your mother is not going to take you out of the Boys' Home. So stop playing games."

"I'm not playing games. I want to go home! Now!"

I groped, again, for the right words. "We love you very much, Bart. And we want you home. But not until we're both ready. Not until you've worked out your anger and become the loving person I know you are, deep inside."

My words had the opposite effect of what I hoped.

"*Me* become loving? You're the one who doesn't love me! You never have!" Like an awful echo of the other day, his voice rose. "How could you send someone you love to a goddam Boy's Home?"

"Bart, settle down," said Mrs. Tabor.

"Aw, fuck you, bitch. And you too, Mom. You bitch. You whore. I'll bet you and Bill have a great time with me out of the way. You goddam fucking slut. I hate you. I hate you, do you hear? Hate you hate you HATE YOU!" Suddenly, he grabbed the wheel. "Stop the car! I want out!" His foot reached across mine, stomped hard on the brake pedal.

"Bart, sit back!" I screamed. The car zigzagged crazily across the road. Frantically I pushed at his leg, trying to release my foot from the gas pedal. Mrs. Tabor pulled at

161

Bart's arm and got him off balance just enough so that his foot lifted slightly. I clutched the wheel and manuevered the car to a jerky stop. A truck roared past us, its horn honking.

My heart was pounding wildly and I could hear my breath come in short, shallow gasps. Bart was breathing hard, too. I didn't look at him. For a minute, I just clutched the steering wheel.

"Get in the back seat," said Mrs. Tabor. Her voice held a tone of crisp authority. "If you try to run away, the state will take custody. Do you understand, Bart?"

For a long, long minute, Bart didn't move. The car was silent, except for our breathing. Then, grudgingly, he climbed over the seat into the back.

Mrs. Tabor and I stood outside the hearing room. Bart had already been escorted inside, chastened by the show of official judiciary. "I'm sorry," Mrs. Tabor said. "I misjudged how—" she paused "—how irrational he might become. But I assure you, Mrs. Bartocci, he *will* be fine."

For the second time in a week, Mrs. Tabor sent me home after another wrenching display by Bart. I crept away like a small, wingless creature, no longer able to fly.

The court hearing was short. Since Bart was a resident of the Boys' Home, the judge said nothing more was needed. Mrs. Tabor telephoned a member of the dorm staff to pick them up. She chose Benjamin Percy, a 250-pound black man whose ambition was to be a pro lineman. Bart didn't give him any trouble.

Back in her office, Mrs. Tabor and Bart sat quietly. Neither one spoke for awhile. He stared at the poster on her wall: "Today is the First Day of the Rest of Your Life."

Finally, she said, "Bart, what did your outburst accomplish?"

"Felt good."

"Did you enjoy calling your mother a slut and a whore?"

162

He winced. "What if I did?"

"What would you do if a friend called your mother those names?"

"I'd kill him!"

"But it's all right for you? What would your first father say?"

"He wouldn't say nothing! He's not around."

"But if he was?"

"He'd probably kick my ass. But he's not around. If he was, I wouldn't be here talking to you. We'd be a nice, normal, happy family, like we were before."

Mrs. Tabor grew quiet. So did Bart. Usually, he'd break the silence first. But this time she spoke.

"How about drawing some pictures?"

"Huh? Okay. Sure. Beats talking." He took the paper and crayons she handed him. "What should I draw?"

"How about a boat?"

"Okay." He drew a sailboat with three sails flying. The boat traveled horizontally across the page. It was a sunny day and he drew some seagulls, the kind Allison had taught him. Then he drew a big wheel near the back of the boat and a captain to steer the wheel.

"Who's the captain?"

"I dunno. Me, I guess." He added some finishing touches. A pirate flag.

"Why the skull and crossbones?"

"No reason."

"Where is your ship traveling?"

"Nowhere." Suddenly, he crumpled up the paper and started to cry. Mrs. Tabor put her arms around him until he cried himself out.

CHAPTER NINETEEN

THE TWO confrontations with Bart brought back the depression I had hoped was lifting. Once again, I felt as if fog wrapped around me.

My face must have reflected my feelings at the next parents group. "What's wrong, Barbara?" Cora asked as she took a chocolate chip cookie from the plate being passed around.

"Is it Bart?" Betty asked softly.

I hadn't said much at the last few group meetings, sitting as stony-faced as Howard Boynton. I still chafed over what Dr. Kruepper called the Ice Cream Caper. But now I nodded gratefully to Betty's question. In a flat voice, I described the courthouse ride. "Bart was *enraged*," I said. "I've never seen him so angry at me."

"Maybe it wasn't just you," Millie Boynton said. She spoke, as always, with a dry nervous cough and quick sideways glances at Howard, as if looking for permission. "When Gene beat me up—"

I gasped.

"Didn't you know?" Howard said. "I thought the whole goddam world knew."

Millie looked down quickly, hiding her face as best she could. It was not the physical pain, I realized later, but the emotional pain of knowing that her child—child of her womb, once nurtured with her blood—had beaten her nearly senseless one night, spilling her blood across the gold shag carpet of their $160,000 home.

"He was so sorry later," she whispered. "He said, over and over, he didn't mean it, he was sorry, he was sorry, he just—"

164

". . . just couldn't take it no more," said Cora. "Like Benjie. Only Benjie didn't beat up on nobody else. He beat up on himself. The worst way, by trying to kill himself."

"Jacob thought about suicide," Betty Lehman admitted.

"Anger is a secondary emotion," Kruepper said. "It usually masks other feelings, a hurt of some kind. And depression is anger turned inwards."

"Gene tried," Millie whispered. "He tried to measure up to Howard's standards, but Howard has always done so well, you know"—she glanced admiringly at her husband—"Howard Junior, too. Gene said he—he wanted me to—to support him more." Her face crumpled. "But it's so hard to know what to do. I think Howard's right—people should succeed in life. . . ."

"Ah, 'What doth it profit a man. . .'" Art said softly.

Howard, who had once acknowledged being "a church-going man," glared at Art with undisguised hostility.

As the Boyntons' story unfolded, I identified with Howard in may ways. Hadn't I, too, been raised in a family where one strived for excellence? I understood the belief that average is mediocre. The goal was to be outstanding.

Howard, Jr. was. He was a handsome, straight-A honor student with precocious musical ability. It was assumed he would follow in his father's footsteps and enter a prestigious law school.

Eugene, on the other hand, was sickly as a child. He never earned above a B in school and was mediocre in high school track. He ran an acceptable race but never won a medal.

"Jacob felt like Gene," Betty said. "No matter what he did, he couldn't please his grandfather."

"Just a minute," Howard said. "It's not a matter of *pleasing*. It's a matter of competence. I gave both our sons every advantage. Gene never performed. But I blame the meningitis. He was damaged, that's all."

"You sound like a quality control inspector," Bill said.

At Harry's snort of laughter, a muscle tightened in Howard's cheek. He leaned back in his chair, folding his

165

arms across his chest again. This was Millie's signal to sub-side, but tonight, with a sudden flash of ire, she spoke up. "Howard makes everyone feel like damaged goods when they don't meet his standards."

"Tell Howard, not us," Dr. Kruepper said.

Millie turned toward her husband. "You make me feel—" She erupted into a paroxysm of coughing. "Oh! I need some water," she gasped. When she returned from the drinking fountain, Dr. Kruepper looked at her again, but she shook her head.

She doesn't see herself as an individual at all, I thought. No wonder Gene got angry. He must have yearned for a mother who would stand up for him against his father's harsh expectations. Why can't she see that?

I was grateful, suddenly, for my own strength, for the abilities I had found in myself after John died. But later that night, as I was falling asleep, it occurred to me that Millie and I were alike after all, for didn't I, too, have a son who yearned for something his mother had been unable to give?

I still hadn't found the courage to tell my friend, Tina, the truth. She looked at me, sometimes, with a puzzled frown, when we met for lunch. "Is there something I don't know about, Barb?"

I always got very busy with my salad or luncheon plate. I wanted to tell her about Bart, but whenever I tried to say, "Bart is in residential psychiatric treatment," the words stuck in my throat.

Yet, despite the continuing turmoil with Bart, two re-assuring incidents occurred. Allison announced she had ac-cepted her speech teacher's invitation to join the school forensics club. "We compete with schools all over the city. You should see our trophies!"

"What's for-en-sics?" Andy asked.

"You give speeches and readings and—oh, all sorts of things!"

"You'll do great, kiddo," Bill encouraged.

She beamed, and startled me even more by adding, "I'm trying out for the fall play, too."

Andy, too, found a special niche, in a most unusual way. He came running toward the house one Saturday afternoon, yelling and waving what I thought was a crooked stick. Bill and I were both in the kitchen and at Andy's shouts, we hurried outside. I thought he must have hurt himself.

"Don't be scared, Mom!" he hollered.

Me, scared? Then I saw the stick move.

"It's a garter snake," he called. "He won't hurt you. I've named him Hercules. Can I keep him? Please?"

He was close enough now that I could see the flicking tongue of the gray striped snake. I shuddered. "Keep a snake? Not on your—"

"Wait a minute, Barb," Bill broke in. "Andy, do you think you can care for a snake?"

"Sure. I know all about herpetology. What snakes eat and everything. Please."

I backed away from the wriggling, three-foot-long snake, while Bill's expression grew thoughtful. "Tell you what," he said. "If your mother agrees, we'll let you keep the snake on a one-week trial basis. I'll help you build a cage, you show us you know how to care for your snake and"—he smiled—"keep it away from your mother, and maybe Hercules can stay. Okay, Barb?"

"But what if it gets out?"

"It won't, Mom. Honest!"

I remained skeptical, but Hercules entered the household, followed, in the next few weeks, by a string of kids eager to see Andy's snake. Almost overnight, Andy exhibited the air of confidence I had hoped to see in him that fall.

"All because of a snake?" I asked, bewildered.

Bill chuckled, "Hercules makes Andy unique. Who else do you know who owns a snake?"

"Who else has parents crazy enough to allow it?" I retorted. But I was overjoyed to see Andy blossom.

* * *

We were halfway through October before Mrs. Tabor let us try another meeting with Bart. He had been concentrating on getting along at the Home. Unfortunately, to Bart getting along did not mean getting along with staff or moving up the Level System. Accepting the Level System meant accepting the Boys' Home and admitting he needed to be there. All Bart wanted, that fall, was to gain acceptance from Ghetto and his gang. One way was by "running up" for cigarettes.

The Boys' Home was out in the country, but about a half mile away was a tavern and, beyond that, a small convenience store. Despite stringent staff attempts to curtail it, boys periodically tried to escape the confines of the Home by running up to the store for cigarettes.

Running up was considered exhilarating because a boy left the grounds. It was like executing an attack mission or committing a crime. If a boy got away with it, he was a hero to the other boys. If he got caught, punishment was severe—loss of allowance and a night's room restriction or getting busted a level. That only added to the exhilaration for Bart.

Most of the boys in the Northwest Dorm smoked. Smoking meant dignity to them. As long as they smoked cigarettes and planned ways to get them, they were not caving in to the system. The key was not to give in, not to admit you might need help.

Bart liked to run up, but Fuller didn't. Fuller was a skinny kid of twelve with a terrible stutter. It wasn't just a stutter like a record skip. When he got stuck on a letter he would draw it out as if a doctor were holding down his tongue with a tongue depressor. His neck would stretch like a turtle's and his facial muscles would contort with the effort. Ghetto had it in for Fuller, but when they were alone, Bart tried to help him. "Come on, Fuller, spit it out. Just spit it out," he'd urge as Fuller, red-faced, tried to speak.

One day when Ghetto forced Fuller to run up, Fuller got caught. "Spill it," growled Schotte. "Did someone force you to run up?" Fuller hesitated, then nodded. "Was it

Ghetto?" Fuller hesitated again, but finally, nodded. "Okay," said Schotte. The next day he put Ghetto on room restriction.

It didn't take Ghetto long to figure out who had talked to Schotte. Two days later, he pulled Fuller aside in the dinner line. "You little narc," he whispered in a low, mean voice. "You're gonna be real sorry you blabbered." Fuller's face turned pale. Narcs were total outcasts. Even the wimpiest of boys could have a field day with a narc and no one would come to his defense. Bart saw Fuller looking at him. He bent down and pretended to tie his shoelace.

That night, after lights out, it started. Someone gave Fuller a hotfoot. He woke up screaming. Two of his toes were blistered.

The next day, Ghetto organized a blanket party. While Diablo stayed down the hall, playing lookout for staff, the rest of the boys in the Northwest Wing invaded Fuller's room. He was lying on his bed, and he screamed, but it got muffled by the blanket Ghetto tossed over his head. "Okay, narc. You're gonna get it." He started hitting on the blanket, waving to the rest of the boys to join in. Everybody started beating on the blanket. Fuller squirmed and jumped and started crying. His stutter sounded frantic. The boys laughed and imitated it.

Bart held back until Ghetto yelled, "Come on, Bartocci!" Then, he jumped and screeched and waved his arms in the air with the rest of them. But he only pretended to hit the blanket.

Sudenly, a whistle signaled Schotte was coming. Ghetto jerked off the blanket and everybody ran. Out of the corner of his eye, Bart saw Fuller huddled on the floor with his hands over his head.

A few days later, the word went out again. "Meet behind the trash cans." The boys gathered shortly before dinner, giggling as Diego dragged Fuller to the center of their circle. He was so scared that he fell on his knees in front of Ghetto and started crying and blubbering and trying to talk but his stutter just got worse and worse.

169

"Okay, narc," growled Ghetto, "You want forgiveness?"

Fuller nodded. His head bobbed on his skinny neck like a toy on a wire spring.

Ghetto grinned. "Okay. I'll forgive you if you kiss my asshole."

Fuller stopped crying. He swallowed. His face got white. "AAaaaall Rrrrrrright."

Ghetto winked. He turned and pulled down his pants and stuck his brown, hairy rump in Fuller's face. Fuller swallowed and leaned forward. And right then, Ghetto blew a fart.

"I wouldn't let your lips touch my ass in million years," he said.

The boys laughed hysterically. They rolled on the ground, they laughed so hard. Ghetto smirked and pulled up his pants.

Bart laughed too. As he felt Ghetto's eyes on him, he made himself laugh even harder.

Ghetto was head man in every situation but one—therapy. Bart and Ghetto had their therapy sessions at the same hour, and sometimes, because the walls were thin, Bart heard Ghetto crying or cursing.

One afternoon, after therapy, he ran into Ghetto in the hall outside their caseworkers' offices. Ghetto's dark skin had a gray pallor. "Hey, Bartocci," he said, "Let's grab a butt."

Ghetto inviting him to share a cigarette! Bart was elated. They sneaked away to a spot behind the dorm where the trash cans were kept. Ghetto slumped down with his back against the wall and fished a crumpled half-pack of cigarettes out of his shoe.

"Shit, man, what do those shrinks want?"

Bart didn't know what to say, so he remained silent.

"Asking me what I wanted from my old lady. Hell, all I remember about my mother is a booze-hound with a bottle. She didn't care nothin' about me. Just an alley cat. What am I s'posed to want from her?"

170

They both inhaled. In the quiet, Bart heard shouts from the dorm and the whirr of a tractor-mower out near the stables.

"You ever been in a foster home?" Ghetto asked.

Bart shook his head.

"I been in five of 'em. Makes you feel like you don't belong nowhere. The last one—she wasn't so bad. Ma Turney, we called her. Know what she said?"

Bart shook his head again.

"Told the judge"—Ghetto paused and gave a sort of laugh—"told the judge I was smart. 'A boy worth saving.' So they sent me here when I got picked up for stealing that car. Coulda sent me to the boys' reform, but she convinced him I was 'a boy worth saving.' Ya ever heard such crap?" He said it with a sneer, but Bart thought he seemed proud, too.

All of a sudden, Ghetto threw down his cigarette and ground it under with his heel. "Shit, man, I never knew they'd start messing with my brains in this place. Asking me how I feel about my booze-hound old lady!" He jumped up and ran off, leaving Bart alone, blinking in the sunlight that bounced off the metal trash cans.

CHAPTER TWENTY

WHEN BILL and I met with Bart next, it was very different from our first meeting. He entered Mrs. Tabor's office with a wide smile. "Hi, Mom, Hi, Bill. I'm real glad to see you."

Inwardly, I held my breath. "It's good to see you, Bart."

His smile broadened as he sat down. Our knees nearly touched in the cramped office. "Mrs. Tabor says I can come home for three hours next Sunday!"

"If—" she added.

"If I reach Level Two by the weekend."

"Tell your parents the other news. About your name."

"Oh, yeah. I have a new name. Well, actually, it's an old name. You're supposed to call me John, now."

John. His birth name.

"It's symbolic," Mrs. Tabor said, smiling at John. "A new person is being born. A person who feels good about himself, who knows how to control his anger and his anxieties. Right, John?"

"If you say so."

"I say so. The change won't come right away, but it will come."

Now I, too, smiled broadly. A visit home. His reborn name. Maybe Bart—quickly, I corrected myself—maybe John would be able to come home before the eighteen months were out. I smiled again. "That's wonderful, John," I said and meant it.

Mrs. Tabor's requirements for reaching Level 2 were not complicated. John was expected to follow the rules, avoid losing his temper, and actively participate in his therapy sessions.

He succeeded in all three and on Sunday, the whole family drove out to pick him up. I felt excited but scared. Oh please let it work please let it work please let it work. The words kept rhythm to the sound of our spinning tires. We turned up the familiar graveled road and were greeted exuberantly by Dog. Andy looked around in surprise. "Hey, this doesn't look like a prison!"

"It looks like a school," Allison said as I parked in front of the group of red buildings.

"Well, of course," I said. "What did you expect?"

Andy shrugged. "A prison."

"Wow," Allison said suddenly. "Look at Ba—uh, John."

John waited outside the main building. His hair, so long and unkempt all the previous year, was now neatly trimmed. The pudginess around his middle was gone. I had worried about their feeding him enough, yet I had to admit his new ranginess looked good. He waved to two older boys as he climbed into the car.

"Are those guys crazy?" Andy asked matter of factly.

"No," John said, equally casual. "But they're JDs."

"JDs?" I asked.

"Juvenile delinquents. You know. The court sent them here. Ghetto lives in my dorm. The other guy—Ed—killed his old man."

I stared, aghast.

John chattered happily as we drove home. He was exuberant, without a trace of his earlier anger. When we pulled into our driveway, he raced indoors, ran to his room, stood in the doorway for a minute, then walked around slowly, touching his bed, the familiar Mexican bedspread, his posters of "chicks" hanging on the walls, the picture of his father, his desk and bookcase, his swimming trophy, his clock radio.

There was something terribly poignant about the way John touched, ever so gently, each of his belongings. I turned quickly and went to the kitchen.

I knew that most residents at the Boys' Home felt, initially, torn away from their families and cast off. They couldn't understand the long range benefits. To them, their parents were simply getting rid of them. In John's careful touching, I saw what that sense of abandonment meant.

As I put my home-made lasagne in the oven, I heard John pick up the phone in the hallway. His voice, still high pitched, carried easily to the kitchen.

"Curt, hiya . . . it's me, Bart . . . yeah. I been gone. You mean, you didn't know? . . . Oh, you and Tom, huh? . . . Well . . . yeah, they sent me to a boys' home . . . The older guys beat up on you, but it's not so bad . . . yeah. Sure. Okay . . . see ya around."

I stepped into the hallway. John still had his hand on the telephone. His eyes had a suspicious brightness.

"What d'ya think of that? Curt didn't even know I was gone." He shrugged elaborately, and I saw him swallow, as if something hurt. Then he shrugged again, and with a defiant swagger headed outdoors. In a minute, I heard our basketball hitting the driveway with fury.

John cheered up over lasagne. We had to eat quickly because Mrs. Tabor had been quite specific. "Three hours, no more. John has to learn that rules are rules, and not to be bent, not even by fifteen minutes."

"Wait a minute," Bill said at the door to the house. With a thoroughness that surprised me, he frisked John. John exploded.

"Take your hands off me. I'm no jailbird! What the hell are you doing?"

"Just making sure you're not smuggling cigarettes."

"Didn't find any, did ya? Mom, that's what makes me crazy, stuff like that. Please, please bring me home. Mom, don't let 'em treat me like a prisoner. I'm not a bad boy, please." He caught my hands. His warm breath fell on my cheek. Quite suddenly, I remembered a sunlit early year, holding my baby boy, and the soft milky fragrance of his breath on my cheek.

A surrealistic sense of unreality caught me. This was my boy, my child. What were we doing frisking him like a common thief, afraid to keep him home for more than three hours? What craziness had we embarked on? At that moment, the Boys' Home seemed preposterous.

"Leave him alone!' I said angrily to Bill. "He's my son, not a thief."

John smiled, all cheerful schoolboy again. "Where are my goodies?" he demanded. Leaving us, he ran to the kitchen, returning with the grocery sack I'd packed with Pringle's, M & M candies, and tortilla chips. "Man oh man," he laughed, "we're gonna have a real party tonight!"

He could have been any schoolboy taking snacks back to his friends in the dorm. Was the rest just an act to manipulate Mother, as Mrs. Tabor called it? It was all too confusing. I shook my head helplessly and climbed into the car.

Later, when I noticed a five dollar bill missing from my

purse, I didn't connect it with John. I felt I must have simply miscounted.

At our next parents group, everyone asked about John's first visit home, everyone, that is, except Howard Boynton, who sat with his arms folded across his chest, his face a mask.

Autumn nights closed around us now. In the dark window across from me, I could see my own shimmering reflection. This evening, wind gusts sent a tree branch rat-a-tat-tatting against the window. Every few minutes, like a small punctuation mark, the branch drummed against the glass.

"Everything go okay on Sunday?" Cora asked with genuine warmth in her eyes.

"He called his friend, Curt, and Curt didn't even know John was gone."

Betty Lehman played with a strand of long brown hair. "Poor John," she said softly. "I know how he felt."

Art squeezed her shoulder. "You think people forget you even when they don't." Something passed between them, something warm and loving.

"You're helping me think otherwise," she said and smiled.

"Everything else go well?" Mrs. Tabor asked.

The tree's small drum roll filled the pause. Then Bill spoke. "Not exactly. I frisked John for cigarettes before we came back. Just like you told me to do. He got mad as hell. And, you know, I'm mad, too."

I looked at him, surprised.

"I'm sick and tired of always playing the heavy, Barb. After we got married, you dropped out of parenting."

"That's not so!" I cried.

"Oh yes, it is. I feel as if I'm the one stuck with setting up rules for the family and jumping on the kids when they ignore them. You don't help. You never support me. Half the time, I have to fight with you—as if it's you and the kids against me."

He glanced at the other parents around the table, then

back at me. "Dammit, Barb, stop acting like a big sister and start acting like a mother. I want a parenting *partner*."

"I know what you mean," Cora sighed. "Harry ain't never believed he has to do nothing as a father. 'Cept get mad if one of the kids makes him wait on supper. When I'm working and Harry's laid off on account of bad weather, he sits around the house watching TV and all hell could break loose but he won't do nothing. Unless it gets in *his* way. Then, watch out!" Almost to herself, she added, "It's like he don't want to be bothered."

"Speak to Harry directly, not to us," reminded Kruepper.

"It's like you don't want to be bothered," Cora repeated turning toward her husband. "I got to do it all—scrub and clean and cook and run herd on five kids." Her lips parted in a good-humored, toothless smile. "Sometimes I feel like I got six kids, and one of 'em is sitting right here!"

"That's not—"

"I don't think—"

Harry and I both spoke at once. A titter ran around the table.

"I didn't drop out of parenting," I protested. "It's a relief to have someone else do it for a while, that's all. A father. For years, I've wanted my children to have a father."

"Then let me be a father. Don't fight me every time I set down rules."

"But I don't always agree with you."

"Then let's agree beforehand and stick together. The kids are confused. Dammit, there's no consistency."

"I've done the best I can, Bill."

"Well, your best isn't very damn good."

I felt as if I'd been slapped.

"Whoa," Kruepper said. "Don't get your dander up, Barbara. Let's see what's eating on Bill. Let's look at this *parents as partners* thing."

A lot was eating on him, it turned out. He felt as if I said one thing, acted another. "You're as bad as the kids, Barb. You're looking for Santa Claus—some nice man who won't make waves."

"No, I want you. But you're so demanding."

"Because you're so lenient."

We stared angrily at each other. For the first time, I realized that we had problems, too, not just problems with John but with each other.

Bill wanted a partner. He also wanted me to deal differently with Andy.

"Don't you *see?*" he said a few nights later, as we got ready for bed. He slapped his hand against his bureau for emphasis. "Everyone in this family has been conditioned to give in to Andy."

"But he's had learning difficult—"

"Barbara, I know! You always remind me! But his learning problems are being corrected, he's about to go off Ritalin, he doesn't need babying any longer."

"What babying?" I'd been sitting on the side of the bed. Now I slid beneath the covers. I had still not adjusted to the chill of Midwest Novembers.

"Lunch. Lunch on Saturday, if you need an example."

I tried to recall Saturday. As usual, it had been a hectic day, filled with errands and forensic competition for Allison.

Bill threw his hands in the air. "You didn't even notice. That's why you don't remember. Look. You were standing in the kitchen, unloading groceries. Allison came in, and you asked if she wanted lunch. When she said yes, do you remember what you said?"

Perplexed, I nodded. "I pointed to a loaf of bread and told her to make a peanut butter sandwich."

"Right," Bill said. "And thirty minutes later, Andy walked in, and you asked if he was hungry. Remember?"

"You make me feel like someone on trial. Yes, your honor, I remember."

Bill ignored my sarcasm. "So what did you do?"

"Why—" I tried to visualize the scene. Andy coming in the back door, blonde bangs falling over his eyes, hungry from a game of tag football. Me, with grocery sacks still stacked along kitchen counters. "I guess I fixed him a sandwich."

"Aha!"

"Aha, yourself! So what?"

"So," said Bill, pacing the floor in front of our bed, "Allison is fifteen. Andy is eleven. They're both old enough to fix their own sandwiches. Why the devil did you fix Andy's for him?"

"Oh, for heaven's sake. That's no big deal."

"The sandwich itself isn't. The way you pamper Andy is."

"He didn't *ask* me to fix his sandwich. It was simply easier to do. What you forget is that Andy's learning problems have left some emotional residue. Maybe if I'm more understanding, more helpful, he won't wind up with the kinds of problems John has."

"Barbara, doing things for him only makes him feel more helpless!"

"Well, your screaming at me—and Andy—isn't the answer!"

"What the hell is the answer? Do we bring John back into a family that operates in the same screwed-up way it always has?"

"What you mean," I replied, in a flat voice, "is a family where Mother has screwed up."

Bill didn't answer. He turned off the light and climbed into bed, while the silence between us stretched out. That night, we lay far apart from one another in our king-size bed.

CHAPTER TWENTY-ONE

I FORGOT OUR differences as Thanksgiving approached. John was coming home, not just for a few hours, but for the whole weekend. For the first time since that frantic day in July, he would sleep in his own bed.

"Just remember," Mrs. Tabor warned, when we picked him up on Wednesday afternoon, "if there's a return to the old manipulative behavior, John comes back early." She said this in front of John, her blue eyes stern. Then, like sunlight hitting a high mountain lake, a smile warmed her eyes. She gave him a hug. "Go home and have fun."

It was a gray overcast day as we sped down the road. The weatherman had forecast possible snow, but who cared about the weather? A tremulous joy bubbled within me as I watched John bounce exuberantly on the back seat. The early fights, the antagonisms, all would be set aside this weekend.

"Hey John, let's go shoot pool!" Andy shouted, as soon as we walked into the house.

"In a minute," John said. I marveled at how mature he seemed. He reached into his jeans pocket, pulled out a small leather change purse, and handed it to Allison.

"It's a present," he said shyly. "I made it in shop class. D'ya like it?"

"Of course," said Allison. "Thanks a lot, John." She hugged him tightly, and they both grinned.

The weekend seemed to go better and better. Although we weren't thrilled at the prospect, we let John spend Thursday morning with Curt, but at our house, not his. "You're home to visit family, not friends," I reminded him.

Very early that morning, before anyone else was up, I had found him in his underwear, wrapped in a blanket, Indian style, in the still darkened living room.

"What are you doing up?" I asked, surprised. "I thought you'd sleep in."

The vulnerability in his eyes made me catch my breath. "It feels so good to be home, I couldn't sleep." He pulled me down to the couch. His arms went around me in a hug. "I love you, Mom."

"Why, John. I love you, too." And I hugged him back.

The warmth of that exchange stayed with me all day, so that when we sat down to eat at four o'clock, I could truthfully say, "Thank you, Lord, for this happy family brought together again."

Bill had made his special oyster stuffing, and I had baked my holiday sweet potatoes, filled with walnuts and orange slices. While Allison set the table with our good china and sterling silver, the boys built a fire. As the brimming dishes were passed, John's blond curls caught the reflection of the firelight.

Who knows? I thought happily. Maybe he'll come home before eighteen months. Maybe he'll be home by spring.

Out came pumpkin pie and ice cream.

"Wow, what a great dinner," John said rubbing his stomach. "I'm stuffed."

"You and the turkey." Andy laughed.

"Cor-ny," Allison said.

I pushed back my chair. "Well, no free lunch—or free turkey dinner. Time to do the dishes."

"Aw, Mom, in a few minutes."

"Okay, ten minutes. Then, let's hit the kitchen."

Bill went into his den, where he was working on a business proposal. I walked to our front window. The promised snowfall had arrived, eight inches by morning, the weatherman said. Snowflakes swirled and danced in the yellow glow of the porch light. How nice to stand inside by a fire and look out, I thought. I was glad I didn't have to go into the gathering storm.

John and Andy were setting up the chess board in front of the fire while Allison sprawled on the couch, reading a book. The clock clicked forward.

"Okay," I said. "Ten minutes are up. John, you take charge of cleanup tonight."

He looked up from the chess board and scowled. "Why me? I'm only home for the weekend."

A familiar churning stirred in my stomach.

"It's no big deal," I said lightly. "your brother and sister will help. I thought you might like to be in charge."

"I don't wanna do the dishes. And I don't wanna be in charge."

180

"Oh, let's not fight about it," Allison said. She put down her book. "I'll take charge."

"No. I asked your brother."

"Why me? It's not fair. I don't even live here any more. You kicked me out."

"That's not so. We're getting help—"

"Some help. Do you know, they drug kids out there? And I'm with guys who have prison records? You just wanted to get rid of me. You never liked me."

"I do like you!" But my protest sounded weak. I loved John, that I knew, but like him? Guilt wrapped darkly around me. "Of course, I like you!" I said, more heartily.

Andy shoved the chess set aside. His blond bangs shadowed his eyes. "Boy, every time you come home, John, things turn creepy."

"Creepy? Thanks, toad. You really make me feel good."

"Oh, come on, let's just do the dishes. John, I'll help," Allison said. But John didn't budge, even when his sister stood up. Outside, the swirling snowstorm seemed to match the intensity building within.

"It's not fair!" John repeated stubbornly.

A heavy voice came down the hall. "You've got two choices, John. You can do the dishes willingly, or unwillingly. But you will do them. Now! Any more arguments and it's back to the Boys' Home. Understand?"

"You can't order me around. You're not my father."

"John, I won't—"

"Wait!" my voice rose. "Wait!" I tried to speak more normally. "Look," I said to John, "I'll go back to the den with Bill. Let things calm down a bit. You get going in the kitchen. I'll check back in twenty minutes."

I trailed Bill down the hall. Twenty minutes passed. When I peered into the kitchen, there sat the dishes, still gravy stained and cranberry splotched. I could hear the boys playing pool in the basement. The churning in my stomach worsened.

"John," I said, tromping down stairs. "what about the dishes?"

"In a few minutes." He hit a ball. It went into a pocket.

"Hey, one for me, Andy."

"John, now," I pleaded.

"I'll do them in a while, Mom. When I get ready—"

"Too late, John," came Bill's voice. "You lost your chance."

"Huh?"

"Get packed," he ordered from the step behind me. "We're going back to the Boys' Home."

"No!" John's pool cue clattered to the floor. He raced toward the basement steps and grabbed my hand.

"Mom, don't let him. I'll be good. I'll be good, I promise! Don't send me back there, please!" He was on his knees, grabbing my skirt, tears streaming. "Please, Mom. I'll do the dishes—I don't know why I messed around. Please, give me another chance."

I hesitated, but Bill stood firm. "You're going back, John."

John's face changed. The tears stopped instantly, as if a tap had turned off. His eyes turned cold. "You hate me. You've always hated me. I should have known I couldn't come home."

Pushing past us, he ran up the stairs and down the hall to his bedroom. In a minute he returned defiantly with a lit cigarette. He knew the rules; no smoking.

Bill jerked him forward. "Get your jacket."

"Don't touch me, you son of a bitch!"

Andy and Allison watched with frightened eyes as Bill half-shoved, half-dragged John out to the car. It was seven o'clock, and snow was coming down fast. The ground was white. I watched through the window as Bill shoved John into the car. The motor started, then stopped. Bill got out, opened the trunk, and pulled out a jack. A rear tire was flat.

Andy peered over my shoulder. "Bill's mean. John was going to do the dishes."

"He should get another chance," Allison agreed.

I dug my fingernails into my palms. Should he? Was I right or wrong to let him go? Why did I always feel so helpless, so unsure?

Bill stuck his head through the front door. "Goddam tire is flat. Where are my gloves?"

"Bill," I said quickly, as I brought him his gloves. "Can't we give John a second chance? Please?"

"No, Goddammit! You heard Mrs. Tabor!"

Heavy, wet snow covered the forms of the man and the boy as they bent over the car's rear wheel. John had forgotten his gloves.

The trunk lid closed and they climbed into the car. Headlights flashed on. As we watched, the car rolled slowly down the snowy street.

Thanksgiving's aftermath was a weekend of quarreling. "It's our fault," I said after Bill returned. "John was right. Why should he have to do the dishes? If only I had realized—"

"Wait a minute," Bill said. "Asking him to help in the kitchen was legitimate. John just wanted to ring your chimes, Barb. And you let him. As usual."

"What do *you* know?" I said, nearly shouting. "He's not your son. What do you care?"

"I care a hell of a lot, which is why I wouldn't let him get away with that behavior."

Tears rolled down my cheeks. "If it weren't for you, he'd be here now."

"If it weren't for me," Bill hollered, "he'd be more messed up than he is. You're not loving your son when you give into him. That's not love!"

"What do you know about love," I said bitterly.

"What do you?"

We stared at each other over a chasm of anger. For the first time, I wondered if our marriage could survive. I found no answer in Bill's eyes.

CHAPTER TWENTY-TWO

AFTER OUR stormy weekend I could hardly believe it when I appeared in Mrs. Tabor's office the next Tuesday and she ushered in a penitent John. "It's my fault," he said. "I'm sorry I gave you and Bill such a hard time."

"You're sorry?"

"John was testing you," Mrs. Tabor said, "and he's really quite glad you didn't give in."

"He is? I mean, you are?"

John grinned. "Next time, I'll do the dishes right away. I almost froze my fingers off, changing that damn tire."

I could only stare.

"You see?" Mrs. Tabor said as the door closed behind John. "Children really don't want to get away with murder. The key is to be tough when you need to be—without demeaning the child."

I swallowed. "I guess we both learned something."

Mrs. Tabor smiled, looking pleased. "I hope so."

How much more, I wondered, must John and I learn before he'll be home for good?

Some of the boys from the Home went to public school, but John stayed on campus that first year. The campus school was essentially a one-room schoolhouse, where studies were fitted to each boy's particular needs. Because the boys who stayed on campus were in the most severe throes of their emotional illnesses, classes were very individualized. In the beginning, John studied math at a sixth grade level and English at about fifth grade.

"John's willingness to work is sporadic," his teacher, Mrs. Major, wrote. "But every once in a while he lights up as if he has really learned something. His biggest problem is his constant attempt to run the class. He demands rather than requests. At his best, he can be a delight, full of information, very personable. At his worst, he is surly and hostile and becomes abusive even when asked to do something simple, such as put his feet on the floor."

Nonetheless, John was starting to learn again. His first-quarter grades were A's and B's.

"John is quite bright," Mrs. Tabor said as we sat in her office. A box of Christmas candy sat on the corner of her desk. "Want one?" she asked. I shook my head no.

"But he can be quite exhausting," she continued. "He manipulates people quite successfully. The dorm staff has a hard time keeping up with him."

"Really?" For the first time, something nudged me, a small voice that said, "if he's hard for a whole staff to handle, it's no wonder you found him difficult. Maybe it's not all your fault." But I could carry the thought no further. I was conditioned to feeling depressed, ashamed, and guilty.

"John plays on your guilt," Mrs. Tabor continued. "He goads you into a situation where the two of you become like two children, screaming at each other. He wounds you, then you wound him. It's become a vicious game that the two of you play."

I looked over her shoulder at the winter world outside. A snowman had been built a few yards from the window. As I watched, two boys trotted past. One pushed the snowman's head until it rolled from the body and fell, smashing into small chunks of white. Snapshot memories flashed through my mind. Bits of dialogue, like pieces of tape, scrambled together.

"I hate you! You're an awful mother!"
"Well, you're an awful kid!"

"You don't love us. If you loved us, you wouldn't go to work."
"Bart, just pick up the living room."

"You're always making us work. I wish I had another mother."

"Is that so? Maybe I wish I had another boy."

"I hate you! I'm going to run away to Mom and Granddaddy's!"

"They won't love a bad boy like you."

I squeezed my hands over my ears.

"You're right," I whispered. "I'd become so angry, but I never started out that way. It was just that he'd push and push and push until..." I swallowed. "But I'm grown up. If I felt hurt, how much more pain and helplessness John must have felt, as a child."

Mrs. Tabor tapped a finger briskly against the box of candy. "That's right, but that's why we're here, to help you and John both stop the destructive game-playing. And we'll do it. It just takes time."

Time was in a pre-holiday squeeze for me. We were into our busy season at the advertising agency, and at home there were Christmas cards to write, gifts to buy, and holiday invitations to pencil in our calendar.

A small, troubling incident occurred at one holiday party. Don Baker, a senior account executive at the ad agency, had invited us to an open house. Since his wife was a hospital administrator, a diverse assortment of people wandered through their spacious living room. I had just walked away from the punchbowl, when Ginger Baker appeared at my elbow. With her was Mrs. Tabor. I nearly dropped my cup of mulled wine.

"Barbara," Ginger said. "Meet one of my favorite people. Maxine Tabor."

Mrs. Tabor put out her hand, as if we'd never met. "I'm delighted."

I stared. Were they putting me on? Did Ginger know about John? What was Mrs. Tabor doing here?

"Mrs. Tabor is a therapist at the Boys' Home," Ginger bubbled. "We send her kids from the hospital. Whooops, here come George and Lucille Castleman. Will you excuse me?"

I was left alone with Mrs. Tabor. "It's nice to see you," she said.

I could barely force a smile. With relief, I saw a friend wave from the buffet table. It gave me an excuse to nod and move on. As I walked through the crowded living room, where voices and laughter rang like Christmas chimes, I felt small and vulnerable. It was as if an intruder had come in with the dark, shameful secret that I had failed in my most important role, that of mother. The fact that Mrs. Tabor had not acknowledged that we knew each other reinforced my sense of shame. It didn't occur to me that she was only trying to respect my own unwillingness to mention my association with the Boys' Home.

I found Bill and pulled him aside. "You want to leave?" he asked, astonished.

"I know it doesn't make sense. It's just how I feel. As if she's judging me. Please, can we leave?"

Reluctantly, he allowed me to say our goodbyes. As he brought me my coat, I saw Mrs. Tabor standing by the Bakers' Christmas tree. She nodded and smiled, but I pretended not to see her. She doesn't belong in this part of my world, I thought angrily. Why has she intruded?

Our drive home was silent. But as we pulled into the garage, Bill clasped my hand. "Barbara," he said softly, "getting help for a hurting family is *not* a mark of failure. It shows you're a parent who cares. When will you see that?"

Miserably, I shrugged. In restless dreams that night, I saw myself hiding behind masks while a huge crowd of people searched for me.

It was shortly after this that my parents telephoned to find out when we would arrive in California for the holidays. When I explained that John couldn't travel, my mother's voice rose in hurt disbelief. "You mean this *home* will not let John see his grandparents?"

Her disappointment seemed to float across the phone wires and curl up inside me. We had spent Christmas together every year since John died. "I'm sorry," I said unhappily. I knew my father's doctor had discouraged winter travel. I also knew how much it meant to my parents to spend Christmas with us.

"Maybe I should argue with Mrs. Tabor," I said to Bill. "Or just ignore her instructions. After all, he's *our* son."

Bill looked at me in silence for a moment. "We have to trust them," he said finally. "We have to believe they know what they're doing." He reached out and touched my hand lightly. "Holidays will come again, Barb. When John will be well and home with us for good. It's just one Christmas."

I thought of the joy with which John greeted his grandparents each year. This Christmas, Mrs. Tabor had said, he could come home only for Christmas Eve and Christmas Day. "Christmas will seem very different this year," my mother's next letter said sadly. The words brought scalding tears to my eyes. I was not at all certain we had made the right decision.

CHAPTER TWENTY-THREE

THE COLD months of winter marched forward into spring. Bill and I continued to meet separately with Mrs. Tabor. I met with her most often, about three meetings to every one of Bill's. It was my relationship with John that needed the most exploration. I struggled to understand how I had exacerbated John's problems. And how I felt about John, and about myself.

"Why do I feel so helpless as a parent?" I pondered, on a blustery February afternoon. It was a rhetorical question I had asked many times before. "I don't remember feeling so uncertain when the children were small, before John died."

"Your husband was with you then. You weren't juggling so many roles. The children hadn't lost a parent. For all of you, it was a different world."

I hardly heard her. I was thinking about the previous Friday. "Here's an example," I said, leaning forward. "Friday I told Allison and Andy to pick up their school books. Is that such a big deal? I said it nicely, too, but no one moved. So then, the usual happened. I started nagging, which, God knows, doesn't do any good either. I feel as if no one ever listens, no matter what I say or how I say it. I always wind up boxed into a corner, not knowing what to do next."

"Put cause and effect together," Mrs. Tabor said. "Say, 'I'll cook dinner after you pick up your belongings.' Something like that."

"But what if they still don't pick up?"

"Then you don't cook dinner."

"But I don't want my children to go hungry."

Mrs. Tabor looked exasperated. "You can't always rescue them. Your children want some control, Barbara. Kids don't want to get away with obnoxious behavior, but they have to believe you mean what you say. You're all talk and no follow-through."

"You sound like Bill. He says I can't stand to see my children unhappy."

"Children are unhappy when they feel no one is in charge."

"But that's where Bill comes in. I want Bill to take charge."

"He doesn't want to be the only one in charge. He's told you that. He wants a parenting partner."

I sighed. "Why am I so capable in other areas of my life and such a failure in this one?"

"You're not a failure, just as you're not the sole cause of John's disturbance. But you do need to learn new parenting

189

habits, just as John must learn new ways to relate to authority."

Relating to authority was a major stumbling block for John. He defied his teacher, his dorm counselor, the recreation leader, and the kitchen staff. He even tried to defy Mrs. Tabor.

After a home visit where there had been a big blowup, she asked John why he got so mad at Bill.

"Because he's a jerk. Always nitpicking about stupid stuff like cleaning the kitchen and mowing the lawn. And doing it 'correctly.' He likes to play the hard ass."

"You'd rather he didn't try to discipline you?"

"Well, why does he start so many fights over trivial stuff? He thinks he has to train me. I'm not some monkey to train."

"You don't think you might need some fatherly guidance since your real father abandoned you?"

"Don't say that! My real father loved us. He didn't abandon us! He'd be with us today if he hadn't been killed in that stupid war!"

"Whether or not he meant to, he left you with a feeling of abandonment."

"He didn't abandon me!" John cried. "What the hell do you know about it anyway? My real father didn't abandon me—and I won't let Bill take his place. I don't need him!"

"I see. What kind of stepdad do you need?"

"I told you. One who doesn't nitpick about stupid things. I want a stepdad who stays out of the way instead of messing up a guy's life."

"I don't think it's Bill who messed up your life."

"Oh yeah? Who, then?"

"How about your real father? He died and left you alone and left your mother alone. Isn't he the one who messed up—"

John jumped to his feet. "You shut up!" he screamed. "I don't want to hear that!" Tears began streaming down his face. "I'm not going to listen to you anymore. *You're* messing up my life now. Not my real father. You!" He stumbled towards the door.

"Don't leave, John. We need to talk about your anger. Let's talk about who you're really angry at."

"No," he mumbled, opening the door.

"I said, don't leave. We need to talk."

"I'm all through talking."

"Very well. Then you can spend time thinking. In your room. From now until dinner."

"Sit in my goddam room? That's not fair! I won't go."

"It's either your dorm room or the Time Out Room."

"No!" The Time Out Room—an isolation room where boys were sent when they got out of control—frightened him.

"Then report to your room. I'll call your dorm counselor to expect you. And John, I mean it. Do some thinking."

Angrily, John stalked out, slamming the office door behind him. Instead of walking directly to the dorm, he swung around behind the back of the tennis courts. It was a chilly March evening. Thunderheads were piling up in the northeast. He stopped where he was partially hidden by a wall and lit a forbidden cigarette. Around the corner, he could hear boys playing Frisbee. Overhead, an electrical box on the telephone pole hummed. He smoked slowly, pulling the smoke deeply into his lungs. He was taking a final drag of his cigarette when he heard the jingle of keys.

Schotte! Quickly, John dropped his butt, trying to blow the smoke out of his mouth before it was seen. He was too late.

"What are you doing back here?" Schotte demanded. "You're supposed to report to your room. I've been waiting."

"I was on my way."

"Yeah. After you smoke a butt. Okay, Bartocci, for that you got an extra hour's restriction."

"Aw, Schotte, can't I do pushups instead?"

"No."

"Your damn rules are full of bullshit."

"Why don't we make that an hour and a half for cussing."

"Cussing? You call that cussing? That ain't cussing, you mother fucker. This is cussing, and go ahead, make it two hours, you son of a bitch."

"Okay, then. Two hours." He grabbed John's arm and began marching him to the dorm.

"Asshole," John muttered.

"Two hours and thirty minutes," Schotte replied.

I looked up from my pad of graph paper. Bill was sitting at his desk in the den, his head in a pool of yellow lamp light. I sat across from him, at the long refectory table. The Brahms Second Symphony played softly on the stereo. The only other sound was the scratching of my pencil. It should have been a peaceful evening. It often was when we worked together. But tonight, all I felt was the nervous pulse of adrenalin as I tried to make my penciled figures add up differently. For the first few months, insurance had helped us pay for residential treatment. Now insurance had run out. Yet the inexorable cost of the Boys' Home continued: $55 a day, $1,650 a month, nearly $20,000 for the first twelve months. My salary was a good one for the 1970s, but there was no way I could stretch it to cover John's treatment and our living expenses, too.

Bill couldn't help either. His consulting fees still didn't cover much more than office overhead, child support, and alimony payments.

"I don't know what to do," I said, flinging the pencil against the table.

"How about state aid?"

"No!" I broke the pencil point in my nervousness. "You know what Doctor Kruepper said. State aid means signing away all parental rights to John. It would be like giving away my own son!"

"He said it was just a formality, Barb. Other parents have done it."

"No. There must be a better way." I went back to my figures, hoping I could somehow make them add up differently.

CHAPTER TWENTY-FOUR

AT THE Boys' Home, John's dorm counselor shook his head in frustration. It was his turn to give his report in Treatment Review.

Treatment Review for each boy was held quarterly. The therapeutic counselor, the dorm supervisor, the teacher, and Dr. Kruepper would gather in Dr. Kruepper's office to discuss their written reports and decide how best to proceed with each boy.

"Don't matter what you tell him, John's got to argue," said Schotte. "He'll get a fifteen-minute room restriction and next thing you know, he's cursing and threatening me so bad, the fifteen minutes is up to two hours. He pushes and pushes. But when it comes to friends, he's like a puppy dog, following anybody who's nice to him. His self image is very poor. He lets himself be bullied by the bigger boys. They're always telling him to run up and he gets caught every time."

"John doesn't see cause and effect," Mrs. Tabor said. "He lives for the moment, always wanting immediate reward. He cannot tolerate the least delay. It's an attitude his mother shares," she added.

"How does he respond to you?" Dr. Kruepper asked.

"Depends," she smiled. "John swings from one extreme to the other. When he's trying to deny a painful truth, he screams and calls me names. He hasn't yet been willing to face the anger he feels toward his father for dying. At other times, he's quite charming. But he's like Peter Pan. He doesn't want to grow up."

193

Her brow furrowed. "I can't seem to motivate him to change his behavior. He's never made it past Level One for more than a few days. Any suggestions?"

Dr. Kruepper sucked on his pipe thoughtfully. "We can help John overcome his depression, even his overriding anxiety, but for long-term recovery, he's got to change his self-destructive behavior. Somehow, we have to find that motivating key."

I picked up the mail from our credenza. Usually, I drove directly from work to the Boys' Home for my Tuesday meeting with Mrs. Tabor, but today, I'd been on a production shoot for a client's TV commercial. The nearly impossible had happened and we'd finished early. So here I was at home with the house quiet around me. Allison was probably at school, painting sets for the spring musical. All year, she'd tried out for parts in plays. She hadn't won one yet, but it didn't seem to discourage her. Each time she joined the stage crew instead.

"That's my kind of spunk," Bill had told her, giving her a hug. I admired her grit, too, although I couldn't imagine myself going through all those tryouts and never winning a role. As Mrs. Tabor had pointed out, impatience was my middle name. I wanted things to happen *now*.

I sifted through the envelopes, wincing at the bills, but when I saw my mother's familiar handwriting, the tenseness became a hard knot in my belly. I ran my fingers along the envelope, then shoved it into my purse. Later. I'd read it later.

My mother's letters had become sharper and more critical. Week after week they repeated the same worried message. *Bring John home. If you want to be a good mother, don't abandon your son to that home.*

"You know we haven't abandoned John," Bill always pointed out.

Maybe not, I thought, as I drove past new spring foliage, *but are we doing what is best?* My mother's urgent letters brought me weekly shivers of uncertainty. Bill complained that every time a letter from my mother came, I picked a fight with him.

I entered Mrs. Tabor's office. The sweet fragrance of lilacs drifted through her open window, along with the steady thwack-thwack of tennis balls.

She frowned at my question. "Are you doing what's best? Of course. Mrs. Bartocci, you and John have made a start in understanding your emotions. I'm hoping that John will verbalize his anger over the father who abandoned him—which is how his seven-year-old mind translated your husband's death—but meanwhile, he's still acting out inappropriately."

For a long moment, she looked not at me but at the grounds outside. Two boys ran past, laughing. "He argues constantly with authority," she continued. "He follows the wrong leaders. He's forever getting into hot water because he fails to think through the results of an action. And he refuses to take responsibility. It's always someone else's fault when things go wrong."

Her clear, concerned eyes met mine. "A person who carries this kind of behavior into adult life is doomed to an unhappy, unfulfilled existence. Until we can motivate John to change his self-destructive behavior, the best place for him is right here. He's a long way from going home."

"Well, not too long," I said. "Just eight more months."

"Why do you say that?"

"Doctor Kruepper said it. He said John will be here eighteen months."

Mrs. Tabor stared in startled amazement. "That was only an estimate, Mrs. Bartocci, based on John's making steady progress. But it will soon be a year, and he's still on Level One. I doubt very much if he'll be home eight months from now."

"But you promised—"

"Mrs. Bartocci, please! We're not a prison, keeping your

195

son until his term expires. We're a therapeutic treatment center, and we treat our boys as long as they need us." Her voice grew thoughtful. "Have you told John he'll be home in eighteen months?"

"Why, yes."

"Oh, my dear. Don't you see what is happening? John has decided to simply wait it out. It hurts to make changes, you know. He must figure, if he just sits tight long enough, his eighteen months will be up, and he can go home. And he'll still be Peter Pan. He won't have to grow up."

It had never occurred to me that treatment could last longer than a year and a half. The idea was devastating—for more than one reason. We were running out of money.

Money worries sharpened our family exchanges. "Bill," I complained after rushing in from work and finding him home but no dinner started, "I thought our marriage was supposed to be a partnership. Why didn't you start dinner?"

Bill looked at me over the evening paper. "Because, Barb, I think our kids are old enough to start dinner for both of us."

"They clean their rooms and do the dishes. I don't think dinner is their job."

"Why not?"

"It's asking too much."

"We need to ask more from the kids."

"Now you sound like my friend Polly. Why should the kids fix dinner while you just sit there?"

"Why should I fix dinner while they just sit there?"

"Because they're still kids!"

"Whose mother doesn't expect enough of them."

"Whose stepfather acts like Simon Legree!"

We glared at each other from opposite sides of the kitchen.

Bill related our exchange in parents group that week. "I'm swimming against the tide," he said, and his voice sounded weary. "I'm getting so damn tired of fighting Barb every time I want the kids to do anything."

"But you demand too much!" I protested, a familiar refrain.

"A family is created through mutual giving," he said, "not when parents give and kids take. You've done all the giving over the years, so no wonder it's hard for the kids to accept that I expect them to give, too. But in the long run, they'll feel good if you'll just support me."

"You make sense," I admitted, "when I hear you now, but—"

"But what?" Kruepper prompted.

I hesitated, not really knowing what did follow my "but." Somehow, theory and practice seemed so different. While I hesitated, Millie suddenly spoke. As usual, she started with a cough. One night on the way home Bill had joked, "She's like a Model-A Ford. Has to sputter to get going."

"I—well, I'd like to say—I think Howard demands too much."

"*Demands* too much?" A tremor ran across Howard's face. I almost felt sorry for him. He clenched his jaw tightly. "How can you say that, after what we learned this week?"

"What was that?" Kruepper asked.

For a moment I thought Howard wasn't going to reply. "Howard Junior has left college," he said bitterly. "He informs us he is not going to pursue law. He is going to be a musician. In a rock band!"

"I know you're disappointed," Millie said. "But you never asked Howie what he wanted to be. You *told* him. You want our boys to be the way you see them in your mind instead of the way they are."

I remembered the night Howard had been out of town and Millie had come alone to group. A dam seemed to burst that night. She talked as I had not heard her talk since. She said she thought Gene had a right to be less than outstanding and wanted to say so to Howard. She said she was starting to see things for herself but was afraid to change because it could destroy her marriage. And she said she loved Howard. He didn't show his best side to group, but he had one. Really, he did.

Silently, I urged her to keep going now, but her bravado was spent. Like a small bird that has flown too high, her wings suddenly drooped.

Cora spoke into the silence. "I know what you mean about pictures in the mind. Sometimes it's your own picture, ya know? Like me. I ain't never thought I was worth much, but the more I talk to you folks, the more I start to think maybe that ain't so."

"You do a better job of loving your children when you love yourself," Kruepper said. He winked at Cora. "When are you going to buy some teeth, Cora?"

She clapped her hands across her mouth like an embarrassed little girl. "Aw, Doctor K, don't you hassle me, now. I'm saving my money. Harry, here, he even told me he'd like to see me with teeth. I didn't never think he cared before."

I looked from her to Millie to Betty. We all lived so differently, yet how similar we were in many ways. It occurred to me that I no longer felt as if I didn't belong in this group. But was that good or bad, I wondered.

CHAPTER TWENTY-FIVE

FOR THE residents that summer at the Boy's Home brought something new. The staff decided to group the boys into dorms according to their caseworker. All the boys who counseled with Mrs. Tabor were to move into the southeast wing. It was a major shift for John. More than simply changing rooms, it pulled him away from the tougher juveniles like Ghetto, Diablo, and Diego, who stayed in the northwest wing. Only skinny Fuller moved with John.

Most of the boys in the new southeast wing were twelve and thirteen, and came from families with serious problems, but they were families rather than foster homes. The boys were emotionally troubled, not delinquent. At fourteen, John was one of the oldest and biggest, which made him a potential leader, but John was furious at the move.

In the boys' subculture, the northwest wing was the elite dorm. It held Ghetto and Ghetto was Head Honcho. Everyone looked up to—or steered clear of—the northwest boys. In intramural volleyball and baseball northwest was the wing to beat. John had won acceptance from the tough, street-wise leaders, and now they were moving him. It wasn't fair!

"Hey Bartocci," Ghetto called as John left his old room, carrying piles of underwear and jeans. "Who you gonna smoke with? You're moving in with a bunch of pussies."

Diego and Diablo laughed. John's face grew stony.

"I don't want to move to this dumb dorm," he stormed to Joe Connoli, his new dorm counselor. "They're all klutzes. These guys can't play volleyball or baseball worth shit. They can't do nothing!"

"Maybe you can coach them," Connoli suggested.

John looked at him swiftly. Was he joking? But Connoli's expression was serious.

"Shit. They can't learn. I've never seen a worse bunch of athletes."

John let his temper fly. Within a week, the smaller boys began complaining that John was a ball hog. In volleyball games, he shoved other boys out of the way and jumped over the heads of the shorter twelve-year-olds, swearing at them when they missed a ball. "Dummy!" he hollered at Fuller, who let a ball go by. "Can't you do anything right?"

"I-I-I-I tr-r-r-ried."

"Yeah? Your trying sucks."

"That's enough, Bartocci!" Connoli yelled from the sidelines. He pulled him aside. "You're making your team worse instead of better. Stop telling 'em how bad they are."

"Somebody has to do something. We're losing every game!"

"Is winning that important?"

"Sure. To me. You guys should have left me where I was. I belong in the northwest wing."

"You belong where we put you, John. And that's that. Now learn to get along."

"And if I don't?"

Connoli was short, broad, and swarthy, with a round face that liked to smile. His belly hung over his pants, but the hand that gripped John's arm was strong. "Don't push me, Bartocci. You could do these kids a good turn, you know, if you'd work with 'em, help develop a team, instead of being a bully."

"I ain't a bully!"

"No?"

A flicker of something moved across John's face. He spun away from Connoli and stomped out of the gym.

To John, the shift in dorms seemed one more way the world mistreated him. He had to fight back. His tantrums grew noisier and more frequent. Mrs. Tabor decided John's temper was out of control and placed him on a tranquilizing drug called Mellaril.

"No!" John screamed when the nurse came around for the first time. "You're not gonna drug me!"

Connoli marched in behind Miss O'Brien. "Come on, Bartocci. Fighting won't do you any good, and you'll feel better once you take it."

"Feel drugged out, you mean. Flat on my ass by seven o'clock at night. No!"

But he took the small cup of liquid medicine—he had no choice—and the violent bursts of temper calmed. However, a week later, John made a horrifying discovery. "Oh my god," he whispered, "they've sterilized me!"

He was unable to produce semen. Orgasm, yes, but no semen. For weeks, he lived with his horrifying, secret discovery. He could never father a baby. They had taken that from him!

Finally, he could stand it no longer. He went to the nurse, Miss O'Brien. She was young and pretty and he swallowed several times, an awkward fourteen-year-old, whose face blushed redder and redder as he stood in the doorway of her small office.

"Yes, John," she said kindly. "What is it? It's okay. Tell me."

"Miss O'Brien," he blurted, "you've sterilized me!"

"Oh!" She was taken aback. A puzzled look spread across her features, then, slowly, awareness. "Oh," she said again and drew him inside. "Temporary loss of sperm is sometimes a side effect with Mellaril, John, but it's not permanent. You'll see."

Initial relief yielded to outrage. "Then why don't you warn us?" he said, almost in tears. "Why do you scare guys like that?"

Miss O'Brien looked embarrassed. "I'm sorry, John." But she was talking to his back. He had already left her office, a frightened adolescent, having to deal with the changes of puberty in a way most boys never imagine.

I was nearly as uncomfortable as John when we learned he had been put on medication. Dark visions of news stories citing institutional drug abuse ran through my mind, increasing my own periodic anxieties about this road we were taking.

"Mrs. Bartocci, you must trust us," Mrs. Tabor urged. Ultimately, I did, but it was one aspect of treatment I never liked.

For John it was a summer of disappointment and turmoil, for us a summer that would end with a horrifying revelation. But in the middle came one brief, splendid weekend.

While John coped with his new dorm, Allison and Andy flew to California to see their grandparents. I pleaded with Mrs. Tabor to let John go, too—"just for a week. What can happen in a week?"—but she was adamant.

"John still thinks his problems will disappear in California. He must learn he has to make changes here."

She was calling the shots, but the week before the other

two were due home, Bill asked if we could take John camping. "A splendid idea," Mrs. Tabor agreed. "A weekend alone with his parents could be very good for John. And it may encourage him to try for a higher level."

When Bill suggested a return to the site of our disastrous "family honeymoon," I was against it, but he was persuasive, and John, when we picked him up, expressed nothing but boyish enthusiasm. All that mattered to him was the fact that we were going camping. Just the three of us.

"Isn't this terrific?" he exclaimed over and over, as we drove to the lake. He sat in the back seat but leaned forward, his hand resting casually on my shoulder, as if he needed to feel us touch.

We set up camp in the familiar clearing. This time, it was John who helped Bill put up the tent, laughing boisterously as the tent poles fell and he found himself buried in canvas.

We barbecued hamburgers and sat around the campfire that night, looking through the trees to the silvery lake, while cicadas made their summertime noise. Bill began describing what it was like to grow up on Lake Michigan.

"When I was your age," he told John, as a log sputtered in the fire and fell, "another kid and I took a ten-day canoe trip down a river so secluded that in three-hundred miles, we only saw two roads leading in or out."

"Yeah?" said John. In the darkness, I couldn't see his face, but I heard a new tone in his voice. I tried to put my finger on it. Respect? Friendliness? "What was it like? Out by yourselves, like that?"

Their voices wandered on in the darkness. *Man-talk*, I thought. And then, tentatively amended, maybe *father-son talk*.

The next morning Bill roused John early for fishing. They came striding up the path from the lake at midmorning with big grins and three small bass. In the afternoon, we rented a speedboat and went water skiing, and on Sunday morning John and Bill fished again.

"Bill showed me how to run the motor," John said proudly.

"This year, you're old enough," Bill answered.

"It's been a super weekend," John said with a happy sigh as we packed up to go home.

"Glad you enjoyed yourself," Bill said. "But remember the rule: we leave our campground cleaner than we found it."

"Sure thing," John said.

I watched in wonder as he scrupulously picked up small pieces of trash. Did he remember our earlier camping trip, and the angry red mark my slap had left on his face? *Surely*, I thought, *we are making progress.*

But not fast enough.

I lifted my head from my checkbook and looked across the den at Bill. "I've got fourteen dollars and twenty-one cents until the end of the month. That won't even pay my parking fees at work. We've got to do something."

He stared at me somberly. The thick, cloying heat of August left both our faces shiny with sweat, especially since we had turned off the air conditioner to save electricity. I glanced down again at my checkbook. So many bills. The plane fare to California. Allison's orthodontia. And last week our landlord had announced he was returning to the city. We would have to move from our rented house. It made sense to buy, but that would totally deplete our slim family savings. I felt like one of those chipmunks, running round and round on a wheel that went nowhere.

Somewhere I had read that arguments over money end more marriages than any other difficulty. I could believe it.

"What can we do?" I groaned. Bill's silence gave me the answer.

I opened our front door to Dora Meyer, a plump, dark-haired social worker carrying a briefcase. "I can't believe I'm talking to you," I said as she sat down beside me on the sofa. "We're not welfare types."

"You're also not the only suburban family I've visited," she said, pulling forms out of her briefcase. "I've already talked to Doctor Kruepper. Here's what will happen next."

Two weeks later Dora escorted us into the windowless judge's chambers. Dust motes danced in the indirect lighting and our feet sank into heavy carpeting. The air conditioner's hum seemed only to accentuate the hush.

A pert young woman in platform shoes and bulging maternity dress sat at one of the two tables facing the bench. "The court-appointed lawyer for John," Dora whispered. I stared. "It's a formality," she added quickly.

Everyone talked so blithely about formality, but I was worried about the reality of giving up my son.

"Most of our families need help from state welfare," Dr. Kruepper had said. "You're wise to apply. Don't get upset with nomenclature. It's just formality. John's treatment won't change when he's a ward of the state."

A ward of the state. My son. Once again, I had the sense of standing outside myself, as if this were surely someone else and not Barbara Bartocci, a well-brought-up young lady of loving middle class parents whose children had all been eagerly awaited babies. What was I doing here, asking the state to take temporary custody of my child? The reality of it—the courtroom's hush, the lawyer for John, as if we were on opposite sides—made me want to turn and run. Bill's hand gripped mine.

"If we believe in what we're doing for John, we won't bring him home too soon," he whispered. "Hang onto that, Barb. You're doing this *for* John. Not against him."

A small flurry of noise erupted at the front of the chamber, and in walked the black-robed judge. I took a deep breath. Bill and Dr. Kruepper were right. It was all just formality to obtain financial aid. I passed a sheaf of typewritten pages, our budgets, to Dora. She and the judge and the young pregnant attorney conferred.

But I wasn't prepared after all. The judge read the final court petition. "Now on this twenty-eighth day of August, the court has heard recommendations of those present and finds on behalf of minor child John Bartocci that he shall be declared a dependent and neglected child."

No one had warned me. They told me later, said again and again, "It's only a technical term, Barbara. A legal term they have to use." But I shall never forget the awful sound of those words as they fell into the silence of the courtroom. "A dependent and neglected child."

When we left, I felt as if we had signed over all rights to John forever. And I felt failure as I had never felt it before.

CHAPTER TWENTY-SIX

FOR SEVERAL weeks after the court hearing I struggled again with the fog of depression. My mother's entreaties to bring John home or send him to them left me sweating and anxious. Now, even if I wanted to, I couldn't send John to California. My parents would never understand, or perhaps forgive, what I had done, if they knew—but the thought of telling them brought me to the point of physical nausea. Over and over, I agonized. Why had I done it?

Then, at a party I didn't want to attend, I received an answer to my question. A business acquaintance had invited us for cocktails. Though I had no appetite for social affairs where I knew nobody, Bill persuaded me to go. "We won't stay long. We can leave in time for that movie you want to see, but it will do us both good to get out with other people."

The party itself was, as I expected, a loud, smoke-filled sea of unfamiliar faces. Too depressed to make the usual social rounds, I leaned instead on a doorjamb leading to the hall. That's where the auburn-haired woman found me.

"I know you," she said, weaving just a little.

It was Mary Hammond, my neighbor when we lived in the town house. I hadn't seen her in two years. Her son's name was Mike, I remembered and shivered, thinking of our many angry encounters. But nothing—no memory, no recent news story—prepared me for what she said next.

"Mike—remember Mike?"

I nodded.

Tears slipped out of her eyes. "Mike...is dead," she mumbled.

"Dead? Your son?"

Her expression was so naked, so filled with pain that I had to look away, but her next words snapped my head around again.

"He killed himself three months ago."

My whole body went cold. We stood in the center of that noisy party, people eddying around us like river water around a small projection, and the angry words of bygone years were forgotten. My hand reached out to hers, one mother reaching to another.

"I should have seen," she mourned. Her mouth made a motion as if to smile, but the effort brought only a grimace. "He threatened it, you know. But I was busy—didn't listen—just the jabber of a fourteen-year-old, I thought. Only fourteen, and we thought he was happy, never any trouble, never like—" she stopped.

"It's all right," I said. "We're getting help for John."

"Help. Why didn't we get help? Why didn't we see?"

Because it hurts to see, I thought. It's easier to say a child's behavior is just a phase, something to be outgrown, or to believe that teachers and other parents are picking on our child. It's easier to just hope that something will change. I shivered. What if we hadn't gotten help when we did? Suddenly, whatever we had to do seemed worthwhile, even if it meant temporarily losing custody of John.

One result of my encounter with Mary Hammond was my decision to tell Tina about the Boys' Home.

Because of our different lifestyles, our get-togethers usually involved lunch or dinner out. That night we were eating at Tina's favorite Chinese restaurant. The lighting was dim but I could still see her faintly hurt look.

"He's been there a year? And you're just now telling me? Why did you wait so long, Barb?"

"I don't know. I guess I wasn't sure you'd understand."

"You know, I may be single and childless, but I'm not blind and stupid. Don't you think I noticed some of the problems you and Bart—excuse me, John—were having?" She reached across the table and touched my hand. "I saw a mother who was trying hard and a kid who was hurting a lot and who was madder'n hell, to boot. I think it's wonderful that you're getting help. And I'm a little put out that you didn't trust me to understand."

I felt as if a small tight spring had uncoiled inside me. My smile was sheepish. "I guess I deserve that."

She smiled back. "Have an eggroll."

I planned to discuss my feelings about the court hearing in our parents group, but something overshadowed even that, something quite unexpected.

Bill and I had arrived late. The cookies were almost gone. But what immediately caught my eye was Cora. In all our months of meetings, I had never seen Cora wear anything but one of two cotton print housedresses, faded from many washings. Tonight, she wore a new dress, bright red, patterned gaily with yellow and white daisies.

Cora laughed delightedly as she saw my surprise. Now my surprise turned to astonishment. Cora had teeth!

"I'll be damned," Bill whistled. The whole table erupted into laughter.

"Isn't it wonderful?" Betty said leaning over and giving Cora a hug. "Doesn't she look pretty?"

Cora blushed like a little girl. "Awww, I ain't never been pretty."

Harry rubbed a hand across the back of his neck. "You was pretty when I met you. Before you got fat."

I saw Bill swallow hard to avoid laughing. Others in the group hid smiles. Yet in his own way, I realized, Harry was paying his wife a compliment.

207

Cora seemed to think so, too. She blushed again and ran her hands gently down the fabric of her dress. "This here is a birthday present," she said for Bill's and my benefit. "Harry gave me a Penney's gift certificate. He ain't never given me nothing before. I decided, well, with a new dress, I ought to have some teeth."

"Harry," Dr. Kruepper said, "why did you give Cora a birthday present this year?"

Now Harry grew red in the face. "You been pushing at me all year, doc. Telling me I got to pay more attention to Cora and Benjie. Let 'em know I, uh, I think they're okay."

"How do you feel about yourself?" Kruepper asked Cora. "Do you feel like an okay person?"

She beamed. "I sure do. I feel like an okay lady who's got the best set of choppers in town!"

We laughed again, happily, spontaneously. Even Howard seemed to sense the joy of Cora's teeth.

"Why," I asked Bill, as we drove home that night, "does a set of false teeth give me so much hope?"

He reached across the seat and squeezed my hand. "Because if those teeth could talk, they'd say, look how people can change."

I giggled, but as we sped through the dark countryside, I felt warmed and comforted.

Obtaining financial aid had not removed all our practical problems. We still had to find a house to buy. We looked for one in the same school district and miraculously, it seemed to us, discovered a four-bedroom split level for sale only a few blocks away. Before moving in, we decided to take a weekend and clean and paint and wallpaper. Mrs. Tabor said John could join us.

"Wow," John said, as Bill turned into the driveway of our new home, "this place is cool." He ran inside. Even in sneakers, his footsteps echoed in the empty rooms. Andy and Allison were already at work, scrubbing down bedroom walls. "You can paint your own bedrooms any color you want," Bill had said, "but you have to do the work yourself."

Andy was upstairs in the largest bedroom, while Allison worked in the medium size corner room. Like the story book bowls of porridge, that left one room, but it was very small.

"Hey," John complained. "I should have a bigger bedroom. I'm the oldest boy."

"Well, I said dibs first," Andy said.

"So what, toad? Mom, shouldn't I have the biggest room?"

Bill set a can of spackling compound down on the floor. "Once you're home again for good," he said, "we can rearrange the bedrooms. Right now, with you home only on occasional weekends, Andy might as well use the larger bedroom."

John's face tightened. It wasn't long before we heard heavy thumping from the top floor bedroom, then a muffled shout. Bill and I ran upstairs.

John and Andy were grappling with one another, their breaths coming out in heavy grunts. An open can of paint sat, forgotten, on the floor.

"What's going on?" Bill yelled, yanking the two boys apart.

"John started it," Andy gasped. "I was minding my own business—"

"Sure. Just making snide remarks about your big bedroom." He turned on Bill. "It's not fair, you know? You're never fair to me."

"That's enough," Bill said. "John, go downstairs. Andy, not another word about bedrooms. Get busy with that paint."

Bill followed John downstairs. "Look, John, it just makes good sense—"

John whirled. "Sense? Who cares about sense? I'm the oldest boy. I should have the biggest bedroom."

"But you don't live here. Right now, you're just a guest in this house."

John's face whitened. Two tears appeared at the corners of his eyes. With a little boy gesture, he scrabbled at his eyes with his fists.

The positive steps from our summer camping weekend seemed lost in that gesture.

Mrs. Tabor was angry. "Why did you say that?" she demanded of Bill when we met with her next. "You made him feel like an outsider, as if he no longer belongs in your family."

Bill perched miserably on the edge of his chair. "I didn't mean—I wasn't trying to push him out—I just—" his voice dropped. "I don't know what I meant."

His words caused another noisy quarrel between the two of us. We had been married less than three years and every one of those years had been marred by incredible emotional stress. Bill's business was not taking off as he had hoped, and this increased the strain between us, even though we now had help with the heavy weight of John's therapy expense.

"Maybe we should just call it quits," I said after an angry exchange.

Bill's face grew still. "That's not what I want."

I stared miserably at my hands. "Me neither. Not really. But all we seem to do is fight."

I felt the nubby weave of his shirt as he gathered me close. His breath blew softly in my hair. "No," he whispered. "That's not all we do. I love you, Barbara, and you love me, and that's what we have to hang onto. The fights are temporary."

I hugged him back, but I could not totally blot out a tiny voice inside. Could love pull us through? Was love, alone, ever enough?

CHAPTER TWENTY-SEVEN

A T THE Boys' Home, John was called into Mrs. Tabor's office after hours. It was his week for kitchen KP, and he was setting tables when Fuller ran up. "M-M-Mrs. Tabor w-w-wants—"

"Okay, okay, Fuller, I get it." John thrust silverware into Fuller's hands. "Take over, okay?"

He approached his caseworker's office warily, but Mrs. Tabor's greeting was warm. "Good news, John. I forgot to tell you earlier. You're going off grounds to school this fall."

"Off grounds? To Granville? Wahoo!"

Mrs. Tabor smiled at his exuberance. As soon as possible, boys were transferred to local schools, not only because the schools were better equipped to handle broad educational needs, but because it encouraged the boys to see themselves as normal, as part of the mainstream. As boys moved up in the Level System, they were allowed to participate in extracurricular school activities, even to date.

For John, it meant a return to the real world. He would be a ninth grader. Ninth graders, he remembered, were top bananas in junior high. He liked that. Eagerly, he took a seat in his assigned home room on the first day of school.

A boy leaned toward him.

"Hey, you from the Home?"

"Yeah."

"What's it like?"

John began describing it. At lunch, he saw the boy again. They ate together. Jud Morrison introduced him to his friend, Barry Feifer.

John walked to his next class with a jaunty step. "I already made two friends," he told Mrs. Tabor, that afternoon. "And they're townies."

In home room the next morning, Jud waved to John again. Within a couple of weeks, he, John, and Barry had become a threesome.

When the Boys' Home school bus pulled up before the school on a Friday in late September, John was the first one off. He looked around, then spotted Morrison and Feifer, lounging on the graffiti-speckled school steps.

Morrison grinned as John hurried over. The three boys slipped down the steps toward the parking lot. Sliding into one of the unlocked cars, Morrison pulled out a weed. John took a deep drag.

"Ummm. Good."

"Yeah, well, pay up, Bartocci."

John handed him a buck. "I'll get more this weekend. I'm going home."

"Don't they ever notice you're lifting money from your old lady's purse?"

"Haven't yet. Anyway, it's their fault I have to swipe a few bucks. The crappy Boys' Home only gives me fifty cents a week."

The morning bell rang. "You want to go?" Feifer asked.

Morrison shrugged. "Nah. There's a math test first hour, and I ain't studied. How about you, Bartocci?"

"If I skip, they'll report me to the Home for sure."

"So, one class. Come on, we'll borrow my old lady's car and take a ride."

"Yeah, well, okay."

Mrs. Tabor looked at John severely. "We're getting poor reports from school, John, and yesterday you cut class. You know we won't tolerate that. Do you want to return to on-grounds school?"

John sulked in his chair, saying nothing.

"Answer me, John."

"No! You know I don't want to come back on-grounds."

212

Silence fell. John scratched idly at a small blue cross he'd tattooed on his arm.

"You say you don't want to but you're acting in a way that will bring it about. Why, John?"

"Why, why? Why do you always want to know why?"

"I want you to know why."

Another silence. The shadows of a September evening were becoming visible through the window.

"We've talked before about the principle of—"

"I know." His tone was mimicking. "—of cause and effect. One thing causes another, and I should look ahead."

"It's part of growing up, John."

"I am grown up!"

"Why are you getting angry?"

"Because you always want me to change, that's why! I want you to leave me alone!"

"I can't change you."

"Oh shit, there you go again. Just like my Mom. Always quoting stuff."

"What do you mean?"

"'I can't change you.' I already know the next line. 'You have to change yourself.'"

"Well?"

"The only thing I want to change is this stinking Boys' Home. I want to move back to my home! Where case-workers don't get their jollies trying to change somebody all the fucking time!"

"You'll apologize for the language, John."

"Oh shit, I'm sorry, but why do you jump at me 'cause I made a couple of friends?"

We didn't know about John's new school friends, but it became apparent that at-home visits that fall were going to suffer. The reason was simple and unexpected. As John began ninth grade, Andy entered seventh. He, too, wanted to go out for Y football. He did and was picked to play fullback. I was thrilled for him. He wasn't tall or particularly strong, but his lean wiry body was made for running, at least at the seventh grade level. His snakes—Andy had acquired two baby boa constrictors after Hercules—had helped raise his self-esteem in sixth grade. Now, in seventh, there was football. But fullback was the position John had lost out on in seventh grade, and team sports had always been more important for John than for Andy.

John came home for one of Andy's games in early October. Andy was in the living room, wearing his football jersey, practicing hike positions.

"Wait'll you see me play, John! I'm a star! I am great!" He thumped his chest like Tarzan.

A pained look crossed John's face. He swallowed, but managed to smile. "I'm looking forward to it, Andy."

The YMCA Sports Complex was as crowded with parents and kids as it had been two years earlier. Football jerseys dotted the green fields in reds and purples and blacks and blues. Pennants and homemade signs fluttered. Cheerleaders practiced their yells, and coaches hollered instructions against the noisy rumble of the crowd.

Andy's team, The Buckeroos, ran onto the field in blue and black jerseys. Bill, with John beside him, watched from the fifty yard line. The Buckeroos were nine points behind at halftime. After a third quarter touchdown, they were only three points behind. In the final two minutes of play, the ball was handed off to Andy. He made a quick feint, scooted between two linebackers, and started up the field.

"Go! Go! Go, Bartocci, go!"

Tacklers grabbed and missed. Hands reached for, clutched, slipped. No one could touch him. Parents and kids screamed and cheered as Andy pulled away from the other players, sprinting for the goalposts with the ball in hand. "Go! Go!" And he did it! An amazing zigzag run for a touchdown. The winning touchdown!

Pandemonium broke out. Andy was lifted onto the shoulders of his cheering teammates, who carried him victoriously to the soft drink stand. But Bill spoke softly in my ear. "Take a look at John."

214

He stood alone on the sidelines, six inches taller than his younger brother, his open, boyish face so transparent, it hurt to look at him. I had to turn away.

John tried. "You were terrific, Andy," he said, as we climbed, finally, into the car.

Andy was still flying. Hero was a new role. He couldn't let it go. All the way home, he chortled, "I am great! Did you see how I ran? Did you, huh?"

"A few linebackers had to make the holes for you to run through," Bill pointed out.

But I didn't want to rob Andy of his moment of glory. He'd experienced enough failures over the years. "Yes, you were great," I agreed with a hug.

Two hours later, we heard a commotion in the back yard. Bill looked out. Andy and John were scuffling over the football.

"It's his fault!" John shouted as Bill ran to pull the boys apart. "Andy took my ball!"

"It's not your ball!"

"It is, too. I left it here!"

"You said I could use it!"

"Well, I'm taking it back. It's my ball!"

I watched from the patio. Somehow, I knew it wasn't the ball they were fighting over.

Andy's touchdown precipitated increasingly grim reports from Mrs. Tabor. "John's schoolwork doesn't reflect his true abilities," she said in November, "and I'm afraid he's fallen into his old habit of tagging after whoever is nice to him. In this case, two known troublemakers."

It sounds like Curt, all over again, I thought. After nearly eighteen months, where had we arrived? Nowhere.

A week before Thanksgiving, John was caught smoking in the boys' bathroom at school and suspended for three days. Now my anger and frustration turned toward Mrs. Tabor. "You're not doing one bit better than we were. Maybe we should bring John home."

215

Mrs. Tabor sat very still. Her skin had a wintry pallor. With her silvery hair, it gave her the look of a frozen sculpture. "Actually, Mrs. Bartocci, it's no longer a decision you can make."

I blanched and burst into tears. Suddenly, vividly, I was reminded of all we had signed over that day in the courthouse. And for what, I wondered, bitterly. For what?

CHAPTER TWENTY-EIGHT

MY SENSE of futility was exacerbated in our next parents group meeting when Betty Lehman took the floor. She wore a pleasant expression. "I talked to my mother last week."

"Yes?" Dr. Kruepper said.

Betty wrapped a strand of long hair around one finger. "I told her she couldn't see her granddaughter again until she started behaving better toward her grandson."

"Well!" Mrs. Tabor said. "How do you feel about the encounter?"

"I thought she was going to fall apart afterwards," Art smiled. "But she recovered pretty well. And her mother may come around."

"Before you know it, you'll be taking Jacob home," Cora said.

"We're not quite there," Art said, "but yes, we're getting closer."

A pang of pure jealousy ran through me. When would we be able to say we're getting closer?

"How about you, Howard?" Mrs. Tabor asked. "You're not talking much tonight." A few smiles appeared around the table. When did Howard ever say much?

"Howard's been very busy at work," Millie said quickly.

"What do you hear from your son?" Bill asked. "The musician?"

Howard's features seemed to shrivel. With a nervous sideways glance at her husband, Millie answered for him. "Howard isn't talking to Howard Junior right now, but I got a postcard, and his band is booked to play at a resort in California. A week's engagement. I—I think he's doing quite well, Howard."

"Really, my dear?" Howard's voice held a new tone for him, the pursed, sour sound of bitterness. His gaze fastened on the rest of us.

"I did my very best for both of my sons. What happened? Howard Junior leaves college and a respectable future to play in a rock band, and Eugene beats up his mother and winds up in a psychiatric home. I ask myself why. What did I do to deserve such punishment from God? My sons might as well be dead."

Millie looked helplessly from Howard to the rest of us. She opened her mouth to speak but no sound came. Instead, tears began to run slowly down her cheeks.

"Durn it all, Howard," Kruepper said, "your sons aren't dead. Gene's getting well."

"Well? Doctor Kruepper, I'm only grateful he can stay here until he's eighteen."

"Now wait just a cotton picking minute!" It was the first time I ever heard Dr. Kruepper sound angry. "This isn't some cold storage. Some place where parents can dump their kids. The boys we take are boys we believe we can help.

"Although," the psychiatrist added, "it may be, Howard, that the healthiest place for Gene till he can be on his own is right here."

Howard's jaw clenched, and he didn't reply, but to my surprise, Millie nodded. "I'd rather see Gene stay here than come home to a father who sees him as damaged goods. Because he's not. He'll make it, Gene will. And so will Howie. But they have to live their lives, not yours, Howard." Tears were pouring down now. Black mascara smudged beneath her eyes, and her nose was running. Millie didn't cry prettily, but for the first time, she seemed to me to be a real person.

"Don't you fret no more," Cora comforted.

Dr. Kruepper cleared his throat. "Let's continue this next week. Time to go home anyway." Chairs scraped. People stood. Everyone seemed relieved to leave.

"Poor Gene Boynton," I said to Bill as we drove home. "How awful to be written off as 'damaged goods.' I'll bet if Howard could return his son for a refund, he would."

"Howard is hurting," Bill said, turning from the country road onto the freeway. "He had a view of what his life was supposed to be like, and when reality didn't conform, he couldn't cope. He isn't able to see that change is always possible."

I sighed. My life hadn't conformed to what I had expected, either, but dammit, I thought, as Bill pulled into our driveway, I wouldn't consider my son "damaged goods."

Still, after eighteen months, where had we come?

It may have been a reflection of her own frustrations as well as ours that prompted Mrs. Tabor to agree to our Christmas ski trip.

Against the uncertainties of Bill's business and our continuing money worries, the idea of a holiday ski trip seemed preposterous, but Janie and Jack Duggan assured us it would hardly cost more than our lift tickets. "It's my folks' condo," said Jack, who, like Bill, had divorced and remarried. The two men had met in their early single days. "We can cook our own meals and share the drive to the Rockies. Cheapest offer you'll ever have to take your family skiing."

"It's still not cheap," I pointed out. "And Mrs. Tabor will never let John go away with us at Christmas."

But to our surprise, Mrs. Tabor thought the trip was a good idea. "It might motivate John," she said.

"You mean—he can go?"

"Why not?"

"But last Christmas when we asked about California—"

"That was different. John still thinks all his problems could magically disappear if he could only return to California. He has to see that here is where problems are solved and changes must be made. A family ski trip may be the right carrot for that stubborn donkey of yours. Encourage him to move beyond Level One. He stopped even trying this fall. When do you plan to leave?"

"The day after Christmas."

"Good. I'll tell John he can go if he makes Level Three."

"I'd like to invite Linda too," Bill said. He was always looking for ways to remind his youngest daughter that she was still an important part of his life.

John was overjoyed at the idea of skiing. So were Andy and Allison.

"I will be a great skier!" Andy postured, beating on his chest.

"It's a wonderful way to spend a family Christmas," Allison said.

Linda said she'd like to come, too. I bought waterproofing for jeans and checked our old supply of ski gloves and mittens, but the week before the trip, the telephone rang. It was Bill's ex-wife.

I watched Bill's face change from a pleasant noncommittal expression to obvious anger. "That's ridiculous!" he sputtered at one point. "You don't know what you're talking about." He began to pace the floor. "Look," he said finally, "call Doctor Kruepper. Ask him. You're totally off base. I'll talk to you tomorrow."

The telephone slammed down. Bill turned to me. "Sally doesn't want Linda to go skiing with us because we're taking John."

My body reacted before my mind did. A buzzing crept into my ears and my skin prickled. I felt a moistness in my palms, and deep in my belly, a fluttery queasiness. "I don't believe it!"

"Don't take it personally, Barb. She's scared to death of anything that smacks of psychology. Hell, I couldn't even persuade her to try marriage counseling."

I knew, in my head, that Bill was right. The views of Bill's ex-wife reflected the ignorance of mental health that is still prevalent in our society, but wasn't that what I had been afraid of all along? An indefinable sense of shame crept over me, as if our family were somehow unclean, as if we deserved her condemnation.

Bill shook his head in disbelief. "Barbara, it's not Sally's prejudice you have to fight. It's your own."

Linda did go with us on the ski trip. Dr. Kruepper convinced her mother there was no reason she shouldn't. The Duggans had a boy and girl Allison and John's ages and a high school senior who brought along a friend. Altogether, twelve of us piled out of two cars in Breckenridge, Colorado on the day after Christmas.

Our first day on the slopes was one of those incredible Colorado days when the sky is brilliant blue and sunlight dazzles the eye. John and the Duggans' son, Kevin, trailed by Andy, headed for the ski lift with the big boys, Randy Duggan and his friend Tod. We didn't see them again until nightfall. They stomped into the condo, clumps of snow clinging to their jeans, cheeks red, eyes alight.

"Wow, what a day! Did you see me take those moguls on Little Johnny?"

"How about North Star? I thought I was a goner when that crazy lady ran into me."

"Listen, I want to tackle Mach One tomorrow. I should have skied it better than I did."

Skiers' talk, replaying the mountain. Bill and Jack Duggan built a fire, while Janie and I fixed mulled wine and hot cider. Kids wandered around in their long johns, draping sweaters and jeans over chairs to dry. I was on my way to one of the bedrooms, when I overheard Kevin Duggan say, "What's that place you're in, John?"

"A boys' home."

"What the devil's that?" Randy asked.

"Oh, we're all supposed to be messed up in the head.

Some of the guys there are real creeps. There's one kid who killed his old man, you know?"

"You're kidding!"

"Nope. 'S truth."

My scalp tingled. I had been careful to say nothing to Janie and Jack. At my insistence, Bill promised to keep quiet, too. Now here was John, blabbing about the Boys' Home as if it were, as if it were okay.

Shamefacedly, I realized Bill was right. I was the one with the prejudice.

"Don't worry about John's behavior," Mrs. Tabor had said before we left. "He knows what a privilege this is. He'll probably be the best-behaved boy in the bunch."

Her prediction proved correct. We had four beautiful days of skiing and nights filled with laughter and warm camaraderie. I never found out if the Duggans learned that John was in residential treatment, but he was a model of boyish decorum.

But the long-range effects of the ski trip were minimal. John had worked up to Level 3 so he could go, but like a dieter who promptly reverts to overeating, he quickly returned to Level 1 once the ski trip was over.

CHAPTER TWENTY-NINE

IT WAS time again for midwinter Treatment Reviews. Carrying steaming cups of coffee along with thick collections of files and records, members of the staff gathered in Dr. Kruepper's office. As usual, the process would be lengthy. Kruepper told the switchboard to hold all calls.

By late afternoon, the staff had reached Bartocci. Kruepper stood, stretched, and re-slanted the venetian blinds behind his desk. Outside, a car rolled up the snow-covered drive, noisily chased by Dog.

"Well?" the psychiatrist said settling back in his chair.

Mrs. Tabor glanced at her notes. "John still feels all his problems are the fault of other people."

"I've never met a more likable boy—when he chooses to be," Connoli said. "And I feel for the kid. Every so often we talk. He's told me about some of his dreams, where he wanders, alone and lost, in a dark forest. John doesn't like to be alone. You'll always find him in a crowd of kids, but either he lets himself be bullied or he loses his temper and bullies the younger kids."

"He goes along with whoever is nice to him, like a lovable puppy," Mrs. Tabor added. "And then accepts no responsibility for the inevitable consequences."

"He's been suspended twice for smoking in the school bathroom," Mrs. Weissman, the school liaison, reported.

"He's still acting out his anger," Mrs. Tabor said. "He continually castigates his mother and stepfather for sending him here. But I haven't succeeded in making John face the root cause of his anger, his father's death."

"Where is he in the Level System?" Kruepper asked.

The caseworker sighed. "Back to Level One."

"Looks like we're still searching for the key to this young man," Kruepper said. "Something that will motivate John."

Out of that staff review came two changes in treatment. First, John was permitted to try out for the Y swimming team. Next, Mrs. Tabor instituted family therapy.

John had asked to try out for the swimming team in the fall and had been turned down because of his smoking. Now, the staff decided the opportunity might motivate him. He was elated at Mrs. Tabor's new decision. So were we—here was a way for John to cope with Andy's football success.

"You make the team and we'll come to your meets," Bill promised. He had been a swimming instructor in college, so he understood the sport and liked it. So did I, much more than baseball and football. I was a good swimmer myself.

"You watch," John promised. "I'm going to be a champ."

Bill hid a smile. I knew he was thinking about Andy's line: "I am great."

John had shot up, overnight, it seemed, until he'd reached six feet. He had a rangy physique that bore little resemblance to the pudgy boy of thirteen. With his wide blue eyes, dimpled chin, and blond curls, he had the ingenuous good looks of the All American boy. He looked like a swimming champ.

And in his first meet he swam like one. Andy had come with us, and the three of us cheered loudly when John grabbed the lead in the breaststroke. Outside the school gym, the February day was frosted with snow. Inside, there was moist chlorinated warmth and the echo of voices peculiar to indoor pools. A field of thirty swimmers waited their turn to swim. John came away with a blue ribbon that day. He was exuberant. "Didn't I tell you? Huh? Didn't I tell you?"

"You're pretty good," Andy admitted.

"We're proud of you, son," Bill said clapping John on the shoulder.

I had now accepted that John's recovery would take longer than eighteen months. Mrs. Tabor and I spent many stormy sessions in her office. "But when? When?" I railed.

"When John decides to leave Peter Pan behind and start the difficult task of growing up. And when his family is ready," she replied with infuriating calm.

Therapy for the entire family, in Mrs. Tabor's opinion, might speed up this readiness, so, beginning on the first Tuesday in February, all five of us settled ourselves with Mrs. Tabor in Dr. Kruepper's empty office. While Allison looked around curiously, Andy hunkered down sulkily in one of the cracked leather chairs. He had loudly resisted the idea of family therapy.

"I don't wanna talk to that ol' gray-haired witch," he insisted.

John greeted family therapy with a grin. "This is great," he said happily, straddling a straightback wooden chair. "All of us together at last." Now I'm no longer the outsider, his posture seemed to say.

Mrs. Tabor began. "How is it at home?"

Allison hesitated. "We still fight a lot."

"Who fights with whom?"

"Oh"—she picked at a thread in her jeans. "Mom gets mad because we don't pick up the house. And Bill gets mad at us because no one listens to Mom. Then he gets mad at Mom because she doesn't make us listen."

"Why don't you listen?"

Andy sank deeper into his chair. His eyes were veiled.

"I'd do more around the house if Andy would," Allison said. "He waits for me to do it all."

"Boy!" John said. "Andy gives Mom a harder time than I ever did. She babies him. She always has. If you ask me, he belongs out here, too."

"Don't say that!" Andy screamed in genuine terror.

"Take it easy," Mrs. Tabor said. "You're not coming here, Andy. But why doesn't anyone listen to your mother?"

"Aw, she's always nagging. She goes on and on and on."

"Andy's right," Bill sighed. "Barbara does run on, but she seldom follows through, so the kids have learned to turn her off."

"Thanks," I said. "What everyone forgets is that Bill is always out of town on business these days, and I come home tired at night. My job has a lot of stress, you know. I'm too beat to follow through. Why can't you kids just be nice guys?"

"Because they're kids," Bill said. "They're going to test you, Barb. That's part of being a kid. You've got to stand up to them. Be firm. That's part of being a parent."

To hell with being a parent, then. But I didn't say it out loud.

Every Tuesday, we thrashed out issues that kept our family in an uproar.

"The first thing I see when I walk in at night is clutter."

"Mom nags."

"Bill gets mad too quick."

"I'm tired of Andy treating me like dirt."

"Bill's always ordering us around. He's no fun."

"John tries to lord it over me."

"It all sounds so trivial," I burst out one evening. "What does all this have to do with John coming home?"

"Don't you see?" Mrs. Tabor said. "Your family is like water that simmers on a perpetual rolling boil. It doesn't matter what the fights are about—how trivial the topic—what matters is the constant rolling turbulence. John can't come home to that."

The television incident seemed to epitomize our rolling boil. Bill was reading the paper in the family room one evening while Allison watched TV. I was in the den, my briefcase open beside me, when Andy wandered out from his bedroom and plopped down beside Allison on the family room sofa. He glanced at the TV screen, then jumped up. "Channel Five has a better show, Allison. Let's watch that."

"Hey!" Allison said as he switched channels, "I liked the show I was watching."

"But this one's better. Come on." His voice grew cajoling. "Come on."

"Oh," with a disgusted shrug, she stood up. "watch your show, then. I'll go read a book."

She had started toward her bedroom when Bill spoke. "Wait a minute! Allison, you don't have to give in to Andy. Andy, your sister was watching TV first. Now turn it back to her program."

"Why yell at me?" Andy said. "Allison didn't have to leave."

"It's okay," Allison said. "I'd just as soon read my book."

"No, it's not okay," Bill insisted. "Andy, members of this family cooperate with each other. It's time you showed

Allison some consideration."

"Gee, it's only a TV show."

Their voices had brought me in from the den. I listened, dumbfounded. "Bill, aren't you the one who says children should solve their own problems?"

"Of course, Barb, but within a framework of fair play. The rules around here are stacked against Allison. All her life, she's given in to Andy. Now, Allison, do you want to watch TV?"

She shook her head. "Its too much hassle. I'd rather read."

With a small sigh, Bill watched her retreat. Andy settled down to watch his program. I argued with Bill until bedtime. "You're making a mountain of a molehill. Andy's a nice kid. Why do you treat him as if he's not?"

Bill sounded exasperated. "Of course, he's a nice kid. He's also very spoiled. I'd like to see that change."

"I don't understand Bill," I complained in our next family therapy session.

"It appears your husband wants to put some limits on your children's behavior."

"*My* behavior, you mean," Andy sulked. "Bill picks on me."

"Andy does get his own way a lot," Allison acknowledged.

"Andy gets his own way because Mom lets him," John said. "When I was home, I could do exactly the same thing as Andy, and I'd get into trouble and he'd be home scotfree."

"I don't play favorites," I insisted.

"Mom," Allison said with infinite patience, "You don't realize that you do, but you do. You've always babied Andy."

It was on the tip of my tongue to say that he had learning problems, but I stopped. Andy had outgrown his learning problems.

Another night we discussed combs.

"I take care of my tools, large and small," Bill said.

"That's true," I giggled. "Bill still has the nail clippers he got as a high school graduation gift over twenty years ago. I lose about five ball-point pens a week."

Bill's smile was brief. "You also—and the kids, too—fail to respect the property of others in the family. Like my comb."

He turned toward Mrs. Tabor. "Barbara and the kids are always losing their combs. So they borrow mine because they know I take care of my things. For months, I've had to buy a package of new combs every month. I put one in my shaving kit, hide two, and sure enough, the first comb will disappear. Still, no one knows anything. By the end of the month, I'll need to buy another package of combs."

We all started laughing. Combs! "Bill, I didn't realize," I said through bursts of laughter. "We'll try to be better, won't we, kids?"

"I don't think your husband considers it a laughing matter," Mrs. Tabor said drily.

"I sure don't. I'm a generous man with my belongings, but I like them returned. I used to loan my tools to the boys, until the boys never put them back. Andy left a good saw out to rust in the rain. Now, I tell them hands off. But I'd much rather share and have the members of my family show respect for my things."

"But *combs*," I protested. "I mean, that's so small."

"Yeah," Andy said. "You make too big a deal out of things."

Allison spoke more slowly. "I understand what Bill is talking about. I don't like it when the boys take something of mine without asking, then don't return it. And it happens a lot."

Again, I protested. "Isn't this too trivial to talk about?"

"Not at all," Mrs. Tabor said. "Daily family life is made up of small incidents. Remember my telling you that most boys who come here come from families that have clogged? Become nonfunctional? That happens because a lot of small incidents build up."

"Combs on top of combs," I said.

Andy and John hid smiles, but Bill's voice was firm. "That's right, Barbara. Combs on top of combs."

Daffodils began splashing spots of yellow in our neighbors' yards. The colds wind of winter mellowed into early spring breezes. Family therapy began to make some differences, especially in the parents-as-partners approach Bill wanted. We began to resolve more of our differences privately so we could present a united front to the kids.

Andy still complained about attending therapy sessions, and many evenings sat with his jacket hood pulled up and his eyes hidden, as withdrawn as he could make himself in our small circle, but John, conversely, seemed to blossom in the warm light of sharing with his family.

As Mrs. Tabor observed later, "Family therapy has been very beneficial for John. It's allowed him to verbalize to his family his feelings about being 'kicked out' and sent here. It's also helped him feel that he's more than the problem child in an otherwise okay family. He's one member of a family that is seeking a better way."

At the ad agency, meanwhile, I had been called in to George Castleman's office. I went nervously. Sunlight from the corner window made a small rainbow in the paperweight prism on George's desk.

"Barbara," he said in his rapid fire manner, "you're a copy writer for the McSparren Company, the coal people. They like what you're doing."

I relaxed slightly. "I'm glad."

"Yes. Well—" he picked up the paperweight, shattering the prism's rainbow. "Our problem is, they don't like Don."

Don was the account executive. I tried to look non-committal.

"I think," said George, "I'll give you a chance to manage the account. Are you up to it?"

I smiled in delight. In the mid-1970s, midwestern advertising agencies were conservative. Our agency had no women account executives. I had let George know I'd like a crack at it, but I hadn't expected to get my chance so soon.

"I'm definitely up to it," I said with real fervor.

Bill, too, had new responsibilities. A former employer had asked him to tackle the job of revamping the management at a production facility. The factory was located four hours away, and he often had to spend several days each week on site, but the project offered a major consulting fee.

Suddenly, it seemed as if everything was falling into place, at work, and in the family. I began to envision John coming home before school started in the fall.

CHAPTER THIRTY

I WAS overly optimistic. Although John participated eagerly in family therapy, his behavior in other areas didn't change. In April he was dropped from the swimming team. The coach said the reason was his refusal to follow instructions. He argued continually. She had warned him, but he wouldn't listen. She warned him again. He still argued. After the third confrontation, she tossed him off the team.

Mrs. Tabor called John into the office. He came in reluctantly and slouched in his chair with a sulky expression.

"What happened, John?"

"Aw, her rules were stupid. She was always hassling me. It's not my fault. She nitpicked little stuff that didn't matter."

"You don't think a coach has the right to 'nitpick'? Isn't that what a coach's job is all about? To help you improve?"

"I don't need her to tell me how to swim."

"This happens every time you come up against authority—coaches, teachers, parents. Do you feel you don't need anyone? Is that it?"

He was silent.

"Or is it because, when you did need someone—your father—he wasn't there? He had left you, abandoned you."

John sat up straight. His fists were clenched, but his lower lip trembled. "Don't say that! You're always talking like that and it's not so. My father loved me!"

"But you felt he abandoned you."

"No!"

"You're still angry at your father, John. He had no right to abandon you! How could he do that if he loved you?"

John jumped to his feet. "Shut up!" He began to cry. "I won't listen to that crap. Stop pulling it on me. I won't listen."

"I want you to listen, John. It's time for you to."

"No!" His chair fell back with a clatter. "My father loved me! He loved me!" He jerked open her office door.

"John, sit down. You know better than to leave therapy."

"No! I won't listen to your fucking lies!"

"If you leave my office, John, you'll be in big trouble."

"Fuck you."

"I mean it. Come back here."

But he was already running down the hall. Still sobbing, he flung open the outside door. Dog saw him and jumped, ready for a chase, but John ignored him. He ran toward the field behind the tennis courts. When he reached it, he flung himself down on the ground, his chest heaving. Defiantly, he lit a cigarette and took a long drag.

"Fuck you, Mrs. Tabor, you and your lies. My father loved me!"

He was taking another drag when he saw the four staff members striding toward him across the field. John jumped up. Four! That meant—but she wouldn't. Not the Time-Out room. Time Out was for the boys who'd run away, or gone bonkers or—but he could see it in their faces as they drew closer.

"Come with us quietly, John," Connoli said.

"No fucking way!" John shouted and took off running. He ran blindly, cursing and screaming. He could hear the footsteps pounding behind him. He reached the barn, ducked inside, scooted out again, and headed through the old pasture. Across the pasture was the river. He heard a shout. They'd spotted him. His sides ached but he didn't stop. At the river, he began to wade across. Now he was off the property of the Boys' Home. He'd be safe for a while.

As he climbed up the river bank, he heard a motor. Connoli in the jeep! He had driven around to cut him off. Frantically, John ducked sideways, but it was too late. Hands clutched him from all sides. He clawed and bit and yelled, but the counselors didn't let go. They dragged him into the jeep. Connoli headed back to the dorm.

Curious stares from the other boys followed John as the counselors dragged him into the Time Out room.

"Take off your clothes," Connoli ordered.

"No way! I want my clothes."

You know the rules. Either you take them off or we do."

"Try, you faggot."

Percy stepped up, his huge black frame looming over John. "You take them clothes off, punk, or I'll sit on you."

Somehow, the image of Percy sitting on him struck John funny. He didn't want to, but he laughed. "All right, all right. Anything but that!" As the four staff members watched, he pulled off his clothes, down to his underwear.

"I can't believe Tabor sent me here. For how long?"

"Until she lets you out," Connoli said, and shut the door.

John stared at the closed door. It had no handle. He felt around the edges. Nothing. The window was barred, too. There was no furniture, just the dingy white tile floor. The walls were a grimy tan, covered with little bits of dried spit, obviously, a time passer. The room had a sick, stale smell that grabbed the throat. He knew what it was. It was the smell of old piss, stronger in places like the corner of the vacant closet. Shit.

He began to pace the empty room. There was nothing to do, nothing to do but think, and he didn't want to think. He decided to exercise. Situps. Fifty situps. One. Two. Crappy old witch. Four. Five. Crappy old bitch.

He finished fifty situps, paced the room again, and looked

out the window. Nothing to see. Damn. Why the hell did she put him in here?

An hour passed. *Why am I here?* He banged on the door. "Connoli! Hey, Connoli!" No one came. He banged again. "Connoli, come here, please!"

Someone appeared outside the door. John peered through the small window in the door, a window designed for staff members to look in. A boy stood outside, a new kid he didn't know.

"Listen, shut up, will you? I'm trying to take a nap."

"Fuck you. Go get Connoli for me."

The boy left. Ten minutes passed. Connoli appeared.

"What do you want, John?"

"I've got to piss. Can I go to the bathroom?"

"All right." The door opened. "But make it quick."

"Okay, okay." He lingered in the bathroom as long as he dared, until Connoli stuck his head in. "Come on, Bartocci."

Reluctantly, John followed him back to the time out room. "How long do I have to stay in here?"

"Mrs. Tabor decides that, not me."

"Yeah? Well, tell her I want out." He looked at the empty room and shuddered. His eyes filled with tears. "I don't like this place. Ask her to let me out, Mr. Connoli. Please."

The rotund counselor patted John awkwardly on one shoulder. "Come on, you'll be out before you know it." The door slammed shut again.

Like a prison, John thought. He began to bang on the door again. "Connoli, let me out! You tell Mrs. Tabor I'm really going to raise hell if you don't let me out. You hear me, Connoli? You hear?"

A voice came through the door. "Goddam it, shut up. I'm trying to sleep!" It was the new boy.

"Fuck you," John said. "I'll make all the noise I want."

"Shut up or I'm going to kick your ass when you get out."

"Yeah, punk? Go ahead and try." He pounded on the door again, kept pounding, just to make the kid mad. "Connoli. Let me out! You hear me, Connoli?" But no one came.

Even the kid went away. John stopped his pounding and slumped against the door.

Where was the old witch? He'd been in here for hours. Seemed like hours, anyway. Why did she put him here? She was the one who abandoned him. Shit. That word again. Abandoned...father...why did his father die?

He stared at the wall, at a piece of dried spit that made a path like a plane's contrail, like his father's plane, high in the air, coming down to the carrier, like pictures he'd seen and the ship's deck coming up coming up, and now, now, the plane crashing, and flames bursting skyward and noise, men yelling and the plane, the part with his Daddy in it, skidding across the deck, falling into the ocean, and the waves rolling over it, covering it, covering his Daddy forever. Tears poured down his cheeks. *Why, Daddy? Why did you die? Why did you leave me?* He fell sobbing to the cold tile floor. *Why did you leave me, your Barty Boy?*

When Mrs. Tabor opened the door a half hour later, John was slumped against one wall, his eyes and cheeks swollen. She looked at him silently for a moment. He didn't look at her. When she spoke, her voice was gentle. "Are you ready to talk now, John?"

For another long moment he didn't say anything, then, slowly, he nodded. She handed him his jeans and shirt. When he emerged, dressed, a few minutes later, her arm went, briefly, around his shoulders. Together, they walked back to her office.

"Why were you crying?" Mrs. Tabor asked when they were seated again.

John's voice was a monotone, so soft she had to ask him to speak up. "I said, I was crying because I started thinking about my Daddy."

"What did you think?"

"About how he died. His plane crashing and burning and him going into the ocean. I never believed them, you know. They said he was dead but I never saw any dead body. My Daddy"—he choked up again—"my Daddy told me he'd

233

come home. And I waited and waited and waited. I didn't believe Mommy when she said he was dead. I knew he'd come home. He was hiding on an island somewhere, like I saw in a TV movie one time, and he'd come back to me. I'd say my prayers every night—Daddy, hurry up and come back to your Barty Boy—but he never did. He never ever did. Why didn't he come back? I needed my Daddy. I needed you, Daddy." His voice rose to a wail and his six-foot-tall body shook with great gulping sobs. "Why did you leave me?"

Mrs. Tabor sat quietly as his sobs poured out, a great gushing flood, seven years in the making. At last, they began to subside, and turned into small gulps and hiccups. He stared at the wad of tissues in his hand, as if surprised to find it there.

Mrs. Tabor smiled. Her voice remained gentle, but brisk. "It's awfully disappointing when someone you love fails you. You were a little boy who believed your Daddy. He told you he would come back to you and he didn't. If your Daddy—the most important person in your world, besides your mother—could lie to you, could let you down, who could you trust? No wonder you were angry!"

"I guess I have been angry." John's voice expressed the same puzzled surprise that showed in his eyes. "I remember, Doctor Brusheski tried to talk to me about that, but I wouldn't listen. I couldn't be angry at my dead father! That—that's terrible!"

"No, it's not. Most people feel angry when someone dies. It's a natural part of grieving. What creates problems is when a person fails to recognize the anger and move beyond it. That's what happened to you."

"I'm not weird? Or awful?"

"Not in the least, John." She glanced at the darkening sky out the window. Familiar dinner noises were coming from the dining room. "Why don't you go put some cold water on your face and join the others for dinner. We'll talk more tomorrow."

As he rose, so did she. "Feel better?"

"Yeah. A lot." He suddenly wiped one hand on his jeans and stuck it out toward the therapist. "Thanks."

Gravely, she shook it. "You're welcome."

He walked down the hall as if a great weight had lifted.

CHAPTER THIRTY-ONE

JOHN'S EXPERIENCE in the Time Out Room opened an important hidden door to his emotions. Family therapy had encouraged him to express his anger toward Bill and me. Now, for the first time, he faced his deeply buried grief and anger over losing his father. But John had to do more than recognize his emotions; he had to see why he should change his behavior.

"Unfortunately," Mrs. Tabor said in a private aside as Bill and I left family therapy one night, "John still doesn't see a need to change himself. I'm afraid he is fantasizing that he will simply move home when school starts next fall."

"Well?" I asked, "isn't that possible?"

"Not unless more changes occur."

"Change, always change. You want John to be perfect."

"No, I want John to achieve emotional health so he can live a full life. Taking responsibilities for your own actions is the essence of mental health. And Mrs. Bartocci, if I may say so, you still appear to share your son's fantasy that he will simply come home at some point."

"Why is it a fantasy?" I asked. "I understand so much now. How I failed to see John's hidden grief; how we got into those awful battles because I let John hook the child inside me until we were like two kids fighting; how I felt responsible for him but didn't know how to help him, so wound up resenting him. I understand all that, Mrs. Tabor. And I love my son! I know we can make things work if you'll just send him home!"

My plea was so impassioned that I failed to notice that Bill did not second it.

What neither Bill nor I foresaw that night was the crisis that loomed in all our futures, a crisis that threatened to pull our family apart forever, a crisis that was precipitated by a small, innocuous pair of pliers.

Bill's consulting job had grown until it required him to be on site nearly five days a week. Neither one of us felt he could afford to drop it, but after he had missed three family therapy sessions in a row, it became apparent that something had to give. Without every family member present, Mrs. Tabor said, the group dynamics weren't the same. Reluctantly, we agreed to stop family therapy. Mrs. Tabor and I began meeting one on one again. And for a time, I attended my parents group without Bill.

The muggy heat of a Midwest summer arrived. Allison and Andy were not going to California this year. Allison had a chance to be a junior counselor at Y camp, and Andy wanted to attend the same camp as a camper. Instead of the kids' flying to California, my mother decided to visit us for a few days. I was happy—and scared. She was still urging me weekly to bring John home, and no matter how often I told myself that she didn't understand, I felt anguished uncertainty after every letter. Oh please, I prayed, once she sees for herself, let her agree that we are doing what is best for John.

Mom arrived on Friday, and on Saturday we drove out together to pick up John. As usual, Dog chased the car noisily up the drive. My mother's eyes widened slightly as she saw the broad expanse of lawn and the well-kept brick buildings.

I remembered Andy's surprised first impression: "It doesn't look like a prison." My mother said nothing.

236

At the administration building Mrs. Tabor greeted us with a firm handshake and a warm smile. "John is beginning to talk about his feelings at the time of his father's death," she said. "His anger caused him to act out inappropriately and led to a breakdown of the family. It's a slow process, but your grandson is getting well. He'll be able to live a full life after he leaves here."

John came striding through the doorway. He wore tennis shorts and looked tan and healthy. My mother, who at five foot four, had always been called the family shrimp, stared up at John's six feet. "Good heavens," she said as he wrapped her in a giant hug, "what happened to my little Barty Boy?"

John's face broke into a wide smile. "He's still here, Mom, just waiting to hug his grandmother."

"Go home and enjoy yourself," Mrs. Tabor said. "And please call me," she said to my mother, "if I can answer any questions about our program."

During John's two day visit, my mother never alluded to the Boys' Home. John had made her a key chain in wood shop. He talked enthusiastically about his tennis game and how he hoped to ride horseback if he reached Level Three. I could tell that his casual referral to "levels" and "case-workers" startled her, but she asked John no questions. After he went back to the Boys' Home, she deflected every attempt I made to discuss the program.

"Look, Barbara," Bill said, "you couldn't talk about the place for a year, even to your best friend. Why are you so surprised that your mother can't discuss it? It's a shock to her, probably more of a shock because she sees that John hasn't been thrown to the wolves."

So we never talked about it, but after she returned to California, the criticism in her letters stopped. For the first time in two years, I was able to pick up an envelope in my mother's handwriting and not feel my stomach twist.

John had made a new friend at the Boys' Home. Leo was sixteen, a tall, darkly handsome foil to John's blond good looks. The two became inseparable that summer. Leo was a high school junior. His family lived in another state, so his parents never visited him. Leo was smart, and he saw the advantages of the Level System. Quickly, he began to climb it. Within a few months of his arrival, he had climbed to Level 3.

"Maybe he'll encourage John," I said.

Mrs. Tabor tapped a pencil against her teeth. "Maybe," she said. Leo wasn't her patient; he was seeing a different therapist. "We aren't perfect here," she remarked, almost to herself. "A therapist can occasionally be conned."

I met Leo one Sunday. He was polite, with an engaging smile. His father, I learned, was a small town banker. "He seems like a nice boy," I told John.

But oddly, John soon began to get into more trouble.

I wasn't happy at the ad agency. Though I had pushed to become an account executive, I found I missed copywriting. I wanted something more in my career but I wasn't sure what. Meanwhile, the demands on my time were heavy. Summer is usually a slow time in advertising, but that summer was an exception. I came home drained, frequently exhausted.

With Bill out of town most of each week, I was back in the role of single parent again, though it should have been easier by now. Allison was seventeen, Andy thirteen.

Andy returned from camp before Allison. Too old to need a babysitter, he stayed home alone. Once again, I walked in at night to a cluttered house and messy kitchen, but I didn't want to fight with Andy. The two of us had a good time together as long as I didn't "get on his case," as he put it, about a "lot of dumb chores." It was easier to ignore the house. This worked fine until Bill arrived home each weekend.

"Barbara," he insisted, "there's no reason why Andy can't be more responsible. He can vacuum, mop the kitchen floor. Hell, he can have dinner waiting for you instead of your running around to cook dinner for him."

It was an echo of many past conversations.

"I don't want any more battles in this family."

"I agree. No battles. But that doesn't mean you give up. The kid *needs* responsibilities."

We were sitting in our bedroom, Bill's suitcase sitting on the floor. "Look," I said, "you're home for two days. Let's not argue. Andy and I get along fine during the week when you're not here. Let's leave it at that, okay?"

Bill started to say something, but I stopped him with a kiss. He smiled, a rueful smile, I realized later, and put his arms around me.

"Let's just think about us," I whispered. "To heck with being parents for a night."

"*Us* is a powerful word," said Bill. "I like us. I love us."

So, that night, we paid attention to each other.

But an undercurrent was there, the kind of heavy current that flows beneath the deceptively calm surface of a lake. The current caught us two weeks later when John came home for the weekend. Ironically, it was a birthday weekend. On Sunday, we planned to celebrate the July birthdays of Allison, who was now home from camp, Andy, and Bill's son, Marc.

I picked John up at the Boys' Home on Saturday morning. I had errands to run and so did Bill. The boys were left alone. In our basement, John's bicycle—the bike he had so carefully purchased with his paper route wages— was stored for his use on visits home. He and Andy had decided to bicycle to the nearby swimming pool, but when John went to fetch his bike, the chain was loose and needed to be adjusted. Andy said he'd help fix it.

It was a little past six, dinner time, when I heard Bill come in the house. I was in the kitchen, marinating some chicken for Sunday's birthday barbecue.

"Barbara," Bill called. His voice sounded tired, defeated. My first thought was he was having a heart attack. He sounded so unlike himself. Before I could reach the living room, Bill appeared in the kitchen doorway, still wearing his Saturday blue jeans. He held up a pair of pliers and a crescent wrench.

"Look what I found in the dirt beside the driveway."

"Ohhh, honey. I'm sorry. The boys?"

A funny expression crossed his face. No, not funny, sad. It was gone so fast, I almost didn't see it.

"You know, Barbara, I told the boys very specifically—you heard me, you were there—that they were never to touch my tools again. Remember? After Andy left my saw outside and John scattered my tools all over the garage and never picked them up?"

I remembered. I nodded. "But kids forget," I said.

"No. They don't forget. They simply ignore. Because their mother ignores. For three years, Barb, I've wanted to help create a family where we respect each others' personal belongings, where the kids as well as the parents contribute to the family welfare, where we cooperate with each other so you're listened to and I don't have to be the heavy all the time. And it's not working."

I put the top back on the marinade bottle and wiped my hands on the tea towel. Why did Bill sound so tired?

"Look, I know you're irritated, and I'll back you up with the boys, but it's just a pair of pliers, Bill."

The pliers hit the floor with such force, the sound was like a gunshot. I jumped and knocked a glass into the sink. It shattered.

"No!" Bill shouted. "It is not *just* a pair of pliers. That's the whole problem. You don't see it as any more than that. Those pliers belong to me, Barbara. If I can't live where I can count on my belongings being safe from misuse, safe from simply being taken, then I'm not living in a family, just a collection of adults and children. And I want more than that."

"I don't understand you."

"I know you don't. That's why I feel there's no use."

I stared at him, confused. They were only pliers! What

240

did he mean he wanted more?

The heavy crash of metal and the noisy shattering of glass had brought the kids running.

"What happened?" Allison asked.

John and Andy appeared behind her. Bill bent over and picked up the pliers, holding them aloft. "Who took these?"

The boys looked at each other. On each face, I saw red-faced guilt. "Cripes," Andy muttered.

"Boys," I said sternly. "You were told Bill's tool box was out of bounds. Why did you take his pliers?"

"Bill wasn't here to ask," Andy said in a sulky voice. "You said we could go to the pool, but John's bike was broken."

"I should have made sure we put the pliers back," John said.

Good for John! He *was* learning. I turned toward Bill, proud of John's response, but Bill's face wore the same peculiar expression I had seen before. It unnerved me. I felt myself tremble and didn't know why. He looked from one boy to the other, then toward me, and shook his head sadly. What was going on?

"Sit down," Bill said. His voice held a heaviness, that tired note I had heard before. The kids sensed it, too. The boys glanced at each other, then at Allison. Slowly, the three of them took their places around the kitchen table. Bill laid the pliers in the middle.

"I wanted very much to bring something to this family that it seemed to lack," he said slowly in that same strange, defeated tone. "I knew we'd have problems. I knew that before your mother and I ever married. But I thought I could effect change. Bring stability. Be like a magnet to pull this group together, so we'd start living as a family, as a team, with everyone contributing. That's my definition of family. A family is not where parents give and kids take."

He sighed, a strangely mournful release of breath. "But it isn't working. I hoped—with family therapy—but it's like running in soft sand. I used to do that along Lake Michigan to build my legs for high school football. No matter how hard I ran in the oozing, shifting sand, I never really got anywhere. That's how I feel with this family."

The summer sun had shaded into dusk while we talked. A purplish shadow fell across the group at the table. It went through my mind that they looked like a painting by some Dutch master. How still everyone was sitting. I felt odd. My ears were ringing and my skin prickled and felt sensitive to the air. I seemed to be standing outside myself, watching the unfolding of a play. I had felt this way before. Then I remembered when and my mouth became dry. It was hard to speak.

"What are you saying, Bill?"

That you're driving me away. All of you. I failed to make you understand what *family* means. We're not talking the same language, and I don't know what else to say. The effort is exhausting me."

If there had been one constant in our marriage, it was the knowledge that Bill said what he meant. And meant what he said. I might grow angry or upset and rattle on with words that I couldn't even remember after I calmed down, but not Bill. The children knew this, too. I saw in their faces a dawning knowledge, and fear.

Allison's eyes had grown dark and wide. "You mean you want to leave us?"

"No. I don't *want* to. I love you all. But I may have no choice."

Andy stared at the tablecloth and made random designs on it with the fingers of one hand. His eyes were veiled, but I saw his lip tremble.

John made a gasping sort of sound. "What's going on here?" His voice rose. He looked over at me. "I said I was sorry, Bill. I should have put the pliers back. It won't happen again."

"John," Bill said and his voice held an infinite patience I found more upsetting than any loud shout. "I told you and Andy not to touch my tools again. I didn't say you could use them if you put them back. It hasn't dawned on either

242

one of you that it's not the fact that you didn't put the pliers back, it's the fact that you took them in the first place. My words have no weight with you. If it's not pliers, it's something else."

"Wait a minute!" The panic I heard in John's voice echoed the panic I felt building in me, a strange, suffocating panic— as if I might start screaming. I seemed to see the face of my dead husband and then Bill's superimposed.

John was crying. The tears rolled down his cheeks, but the big, strapping boy didn't appear to notice. "I thought you loved us. If you love a family, you don't leave it. You hang on and work things out. Isn't that what the Boys' Home is all about? You don't leave your family!"

"I'm not saying I'll leave this minute. Tonight," Bill said. "I'm saying, unless things change, your actions will drive me away. I'll feel there's no choice but to go."

I didn't hear the last. The panic had swelled inside me like some balloon until I felt like I might burst with it, and fly into pieces, scattered about the floor, little bits of me too small to put back together again. Tears rolled down my cheeks, and I didn't notice any more than John had until I heard Allison say, in a shocked voice, "Look how Mom is crying."

Andy suddenly began pounding Bill with his fists, yelling, "Don't you make our mother cry!"

John was shouting, "I can't believe you'd leave us. I thought you loved us!"

But I wasn't there to hear any more. I was running to the bedroom, to my bedside table. It took three tries before my fingers could keep the telephone book open to the right page. The telephone rang a half-dozen times. I was about to hang up when I heard the familiar voice.

"Oh! Thank God! Mrs. Tabor." Now I was blubbering, the words and sobs all mixed together. "It's Barbara Bartocci. Bill's going to leave us. You know he doesn't make idle threats. He's going to leave us. I'm losing my husband all over again and the children, their father—" I had completely lost control. Someone pulled the telephone from my fingers. I heard Bill's voice say shakily, "Yes. Yes, all right. We'll meet you there. Thirty minutes. All right."

We gathered in Dr. Kruepper's office at eight o'clock. The summer sky had still not totally darkened. I smelled a stale remnant of pipe tobacco. Mrs. Tabor, her rawboned frame looking taller and more commanding in a navy blue pantsuit, gazed with severity at our huddled group.

"Now," she said, her voice brisk with authority, "one at a time. Tell me what the devil is going on. Mr. Shirley, you may begin."

Words tumbled out of Bill, me, the boys, Allison. Our words fell across each other, stumbled, careened, grew wet with sobs, hot with anger. For three hours, our voices rose and fell, and the words piled one on top of each other. Combs on top of combs. Words on top of words. Finally Mrs. Tabor stopped us.

"Enough!" She sat in silence looking at us, bedraggled, forlorn, a family in disintegration.

But during those heated hours when our words piled on top of each other, like leaves for a bonfire, something had stirred within me. What was Bill saying? He wanted a family that contributed to each others' well being, a family based on mutual respect, where parents work together consistently and believably.

But that was what I wanted, too. Why were we fighting? Why did he say, over and over, "It's not that I want to leave, it's that you'll drive me away if we don't make some changes"?

Change. That was John's problem. "He's got to change before he can come home," Mrs. Tabor had said. "He fantasizes that he'll come home without making changes, but that's not possible. The key to mental health is taking responsibility for your own actions. Changing your actions when it's necessary."

We were alike in more ways than I'd thought, John and I! How had I missed that before? We were both running

244

from responsibility, avoiding the tough, grit-your-teeth reality of personal change.

With sudden insight, I realized that just as I had struggled to grow up as a woman after my first husband died, I now had to grow up as a parent, so our home was no longer, "water on a perpetual rolling boil," as Mrs. Tabor called it, so that Bill wouldn't, in despair, feel himself driven away. It was up to me to take the lead with Allison, Andy and John. Maybe then John would see that he had to make changes himself. That he couldn't go through life blaming his father's death or big bad authority or mean stepfather or anyone else for his own behavior.

I was so caught up in my burst of revelation that I missed what Mrs. Tabor was saying. "I'm sorry. What?"

"I said," she repeated, "that since your husband believes he may be driven away if some changes don't occur, perhaps you need a new family contract."

"We don't have an old family contract," I pointed out.

"Of course, you do. All families do. It's just not written out. Why not write a new one, all of you?"

"What would it say?" Andy asked. He looked suspicious.

"That's up to you. Do you ever do contracts in school with your teachers?" Allison nodded. "It's the same principle. Perhaps a family contract that's up for renewal in a month or two will give Bill the feeling that the rest of you are serious, that you want to change. Do you?"

Heads nodded.

I looked at Bill. He looked miserable. His eyes, behind his glasses, were red rimmed. His hands, I noticed suddenly, were trembling. I reached over and touched one hand gently. He grasped mine tightly, as if he needed the support. We both need each other, I thought. This family needs one another.

"I think a family contract is a very good idea, I said in a firm voice. I want you guys to know, I *heard* Bill tonight, and I'm willing to make the changes necessary to make our family work. To turn our family into—into what I always dreamed a family should be."

Bill's fingers tightened around mine.

Our family crisis was such that Bill arranged to take Monday morning off for the next three weeks. I took the mornings off, too, and all five of us met with Mrs. Tabor to hammer out the tenets of a family contract.

The contract that finally emerged from our talks, that I typed out on yellow paper, was based on a simple premise of consideration and cooperation. It read, in part: "Our family values are summed up in this question: Have I done my part to show my love and concern for my family by keeping my things out of our home's common rooms; by respecting others' privacy and possessions; and by actively looking for little ways to help other family members?"

On July 25, almost exactly two years after we brought John to the Boys' Home, all five of us signed it. We agreed to reexamine it in two months. Since John was not living at home, one sentence read, "John agrees to work individually on these values so he can carry them back into the family home."

But I didn't need the written contract. I understood, on that anguished summer night in Dr. Kruepper's office, that I couldn't expect some magical fix to make us happy-ever-after. We make our own happiness when we accept responsibilities for ourselves and our lives. That, Mrs. Tabor had once said, is the essence of mental health.

I had finally heard. Now, I only hoped John would hear, too.

CHAPTER THIRTY-TWO

IN AUGUST, one month after we signed our family contract, and twenty-five months after we took a screaming, crying, cursing boy to the Boys' Home, I wrote John a difficult letter.

> Dear John,
>
> You know how much I hoped you would come home with us this fall, but life is not a fairy tale where wishes come true simply because they are wished for. The reality is that I can't bring you home. I can want it, I can ache for it, but only when you decide you want to come home badly enough, when you work on the problems that are keeping you away, can it happen. The reality is that I will not bring you home until Dr. Kruepper and Mrs. Tabor tell me you're ready, and that won't happen until you show them you're ready. It's up to you, John. You control the ticket home. We'll all be waiting.
>
> With much love, Mom.

For me, the letter represented a great step forward. For the first time I truly accepted the reality that I could not guarantee my children's happiness. It was not my responsibility to make their lives trouble free. I could not rescue them from the consequences of their own actions. The mark of growing up is becoming responsible for ourselves.

I could change myself. I could establish an environment that would encourage change in John and support the changes he made, but I could not make the changes for him. And I would not be a loving parent if I "rescued" him so he didn't have to go through the pain of becoming responsible.

I knew that if he didn't grow up now, his pain would be immeasurably worse later on.

I wrote the letter with a calm sense of certainty.

For John my letter was a capstone to the deep feelings that had been stirred up by Bill's threat to leave. He was in Mrs. Tabor's office, the week after our family crisis. "If Bill leaves, it's all my fault," he said miserably.

"Why do you say that?" Mrs. Tabor asked.

" 'Cause I'm the messed up kid. If it weren't for me, our family would be like other families. I'm responsible for all the fuckups."

"After all this time, John—and those weeks of family therapy—do you really believe that? Haven't you seen otherwise?" Mrs. Tabor placed her steepled fingers beneath her chin. "You're not responsible for your family's problems, but you are responsible for... whom do you think?"

John's gaze swerved to Mrs. Tabor's latest poster. "Change starts with the letter I" it read. For a few minutes, he was quiet. When he spoke, his voice was very low. "I've always worried about my Mom, you know? We've had a lot of fights and stuff, but I love her a lot. I don't want her to be alone. And lonely. If Bill leaves, it will ruin her life, and she'll hate me."

"Do you feel guilty? Is that it?"

He considered the question. "No, not guilty. I feel scared. Really scared that because I screwed up, my Mom will be left alone. Bill is good for my Mom. He's good for all of us. I'll feel awful bad if he leaves. Is that what you mean by cause and effect?"

"Yes, except you aren't the only one responsible for Bill's staying or leaving. Who are you responsible for, John?"

For the first time since he'd entered her office, a gleam of humor appeared in his blue eyes. "Shoot, I know the answer you want. 'I, John Bartocci, am responsible for *me!*' "

"Do you believe that?"

He shrugged. "I dunno, but I do know that I'd better do my part to keep our family together."

"And also do your part for you, John."

But to that, he didn't reply.

For John, as for me, the family confrontation, the sudden possibility of something he had never considered—Bill's leaving—brought a heightened awareness that a lot more was up to him than he had been willing to recognize. Years later, he acknowledged that truth. "Yeah, after that night, I knew some things had to change—in me."

But real life is never tidy. People make resolves and break them. Change either happens too fast, or not fast enough. In any relationship, people seldom move at the same pace.

That summer John continued his friendship with Leo. Leo was the only son of parents who had given up hopes of ever having a baby. His mother doted on him. Her darling Leo could do no wrong. His father expected him to "do us proud, son." Leo did. He also learned early how to manipulate the adults in his world to gain his own ends.

In the small town where his parents were leading citizens, he was used to getting his own way and not having to accept consequences. In high school, the kids he ran around with, the "good kids," sampled pot and speed and alcohol. What else could you do for thrills in a town of 6,000? Leo collected a few speeding tickets and was picked up once or twice for driving while drunk, but, as the son of the town's leading banker, he got off with fines. Hit and run was a different story. One cold winter's night, Leo hit an old man and drove away. Fortunately the man recovered, which saved Leo from a manslaughter charge, but Leo's parents were told they must either send their son to a psychiatric treatment center or he'd be tried on criminal charges.

"It's ridiculous that I'm here," Leo told John as they shared lawn duty. "I don't need this shit. My old man told me to keep my nose clean, follow the rules, and get the hell out, and that's what I'm going to do. You with me?"

"What do you mean?" John asked, spearing a piece of trash.

"I mean, we work our way up the Level System and get out." Leo smiled. "Stick with me, John-boy, and you'll go far."

John grinned. "Right on!" Following Leo's example, he moved up to Level Three. In the summertime, that meant horseback riding privileges and an occasional off-grounds baseball game.

What amazed John was Leo's ability to talk to the staff. "How can you keep a straight face?" he demanded after Leo had responded respectfully to Connoli's suspicious question about cigarettes.

Leo grinned. He and John had smoked a forbidden cigarette fifteen minutes earlier in the bathroom. "You got to ask yourself what you want. If I want staff to leave me alone, then I got to treat 'em nice so they don't hassle me."

"Kiss ass, you mean."

"That's the way you get ahead, John-boy. The trick is knowing what ass you got to kiss." He laughed and put a sudden hammer lock on John. "I don't have to kiss yours. How about getting us some smokes?"

"You mean run up?"

"Sure."

"If I get caught, they'll bust me a level."

"So? Don't get caught."

"You come with me."

"Not me, John-boy. But I'll make you a deal. I'll buy the stash. How's that?"

"Deal."

As summer wore on, Leo began ordering John around more and more. Since it happened gradually, John didn't notice at first. Then one morning John saw it. "Hey John-Boy," Leo said, "how about making my bed?"

"Shit, no," John answered, and Leo suddenly slugged him hard in the belly.

John doubled over. "Hey! What the fuck—"

Leo smiled. "A simple request from a friend and you turn me down. I don't think that's nice. Now make my bed."

His face wore its usual pleasant expression, but there was something in his voice. John made the bed. After that, Leo's demands accelerated.

One morning Connoli pulled John aside after gym. "Bartocci, why don't you tell Bromley to shove it?"

"What do you mean?"

"I mean I'm not blind, and I wasn't born yesterday. I see what's happening between you two. He's making you his fall guy."

"Leo's my friend, Mr. Connoli."

"Yeah? Some friend. You got busted last week for trying to run up. Now who was behind that? You or Bromley?"

"I'm no narc."

"Give it some thought, Bartocci. Leo's no good for you."

The truth was, John didn't know how to get away from Leo. Besides, just when he'd feel like he'd really had it with Leo's bullying, Leo would turn on the charm.

School began. John was a sophomore, Leo a junior at Granville High. The best thing about high school, most of the guys agreed, were the girls.

"Hey, John-boy, I've got a great idea," Leo said a few weeks into school. "You know Judy? The foxy redhead in my chemistry class? She's got a friend and she and her friend are willing to sneak out and see us. Judy's friend thinks you're cute." He grinned and imitated a girlish smirk.

"Wow," John said. "Sneak off grounds to meet girls?" The idea had never occurred to him, but talk about exciting! It was more thrilling than running up. "What if we get caught?"

"We won't. We'll do it on Friday when we get free recreation after dinner. You know the pasture behind the stables? There's a road with a bunch of trees for cover."

John thought about it. Girls! Off grounds! A little necking. Wow!

On Friday he and Leo met in the pasture. Evening birdcalls blended with the soft hum of distant traffic from the highway. A branch cracked. A squirrel scooted up a tree.

251

John wondered if the girls would really show. Suddenly, he heard a little giggle and the tall field grass near the road swayed.

The girls came forward tentatively. One, with light hair and a scattering of freckles, kept looking over her shoulder. Judy urged her on.

"Over here," Leo called softly.

John swallowed hard. He hadn't believed they would really come. For a few minutes the four of them stood around awkwardly. "This is Kim," Judy said. Leo murmured something in Judy's ear. She giggled and nodded. The two of them walked toward the grove of trees. John and Kim sat down. He put his arm around her. After awhile they kissed.

Twenty minutes later John heard running footsteps. Fuller, his face red and his chest heaving, appeared around the corner of the barn. He gasped and pointed back toward the dorm.

"Connoli?" John asked. "He's looking for me?" Fuller wheezed and nodded. John jerked his arm from Kim's shoulder. "Sorry. I gotta split."

At the dorm, he tried to play it cool, but Connoli knew something was going on. "You were out of bounds, John. I'm putting you on room restriction tonight and all day tomorrow."

"On Saturday? Aw, Mr. Connoli—"

"Where's your friend Leo?"

"How would I know?"

Connoli looked hard at Fuller, still red faced from his run, then at John. "I'll find out what's going on, Bartocci."

He did. They caught Leo and Judy, and Leo was busted a level. He was convinced John had narked.

"I didn't," John protested, but Leo's eyes held a cold, angry gleam. "I don't appreciate getting busted a level, John-boy. And you're going to pay for it. That's a promise."

By noon, the word was out among the boys. John was a narc. That night, John lay in bed tense and awake. No one showed up. Maybe, he thought, Leo's decided to drop it.

But the next afternoon, as John sat in a bathroom stall, Leo strolled casually into the bathroom, acting, at first, as if John weren't there. John began pulling up his pants, and that's when Leo jumped him. "Narc!" he hissed and slammed his fist into John's face. John's head smashed backwards, into the stainless steel fixture behind the toilet. Leo kneed him in the chest. John groaned and fell across the toilet.

The bathroom door opened. Fuller walked in. He took in the scene: John, sprawled in the stall, his pants down, his lip bleeding, Leo standing over him.

"Wh-wh-wh-what's g-g-g-g-oing on?"

"Get outta here, Fuller," Leo said. "This doesn't concern you."

Fuller looked scared and began backing away, but then, with another glance at John, he suddenly sprang forward. "N-n-no f-f-fair," he stuttered and started to pound Leo. Caught by surprise, Leo fell against the wall. Fuller pursued him, gasping, hitting, shoving, crying, while John stumbled to his feet and grappled with his zipper. Leo was twenty-five pounds heavier than skinny Fuller. In a minute, he was on top of the smaller boy, but by now, John had his pants up. He grabbed Leo. Leo kicked John. John gasped, then punched Leo hard. The bathroom door slammed open again.

"What's going on in here?" Connoli yelled. Two other counselors appeared behind him.

All three boys were put on room restriction. Both John and Leo were busted a level. This brought John down to Level One, Leo to Level Three.

But the next day, as John walked from the dorm to the dining room for dinner, Connoli passed him. The dorm counselor's round face didn't crack a smile as he spoke. "Glad you stood up for yourself, Bartocci."

Leo tried once to rekindle the friendship. John looked him in the eye. "Sure, I'll play pool, Leo, but you're not going to order me around anymore." Something in John's expression apparently convinced Leo that he meant it. Leo soon found another friend, someone else he could dominate. In a few weeks, he had moved back to Level Four.

"Why did Fuller stick up for me?" John asked Mrs. Tabor.
"Why do you think?"
John looked genuinely puzzled. "Because he likes me?"
"You're a very likable boy when you want to be, John. You don't have to be friends with someone just because he's nice to you. You have a lot to offer. You can choose your own friends."
John smiled. "Ol' Fuller . . . he sure came at Leo. He was risking a lot, you know?" Without realizing it, John sat up straighter in his chair. "You really think I have a lot to offer?"
"I really do," Mrs. Tabor said.

CHAPTER THIRTY-THREE

BILL'S CONSULTING project ended that fall, and he came home for good. We were both relieved that there were no more four-hour drives every weekend. So was Allison, who had begun her senior year and liked to have Dad around, she said with a hug. Only Andy pouted, mostly because he knew Bill's presence meant firmer rules, but I was trying to do my part, too.

The five of us had reconvened with Mrs. Tabor two months after the signing of our family contract. "Well?" she said. "Is it working?"

We all looked at Bill. The silent deference to him was so obvious that it made us all laugh, including Bill.

"I think so," he replied. "Barbara says the kids seem more conscious of keeping their belongings in their own rooms,

254

so the house is staying neater. That means her temper is less frayed."

"It's only a few steps farther to drop my books in my bedroom instead of the family room," Allison admitted.

"How about cooperation with each other?" Mrs. Tabor asked.

"Andy has started baking cakes," I reported.

"That's 'cause he likes to eat them," John scoffed.

Andy grinned and licked his lips. Again, group laughter. It was good to hear.

"You're right," I said. "But so do the rest of us. The point is, Andy's doing something in the kitchen that benefits us all. And he cleans up afterward. Also," I added, "everyone now does his or her own laundry."

"What about looking for little ways to help other family members?" Mrs. Tabor persisted.

We glanced at one another. I shrugged. "We have a way to go. But I'm trying to be more consistent in my follow-through," I continued. "Last Friday I told Andy if he wasn't home by five-thirty he couldn't spend the night with his friend Danny. And he wasn't, so he didn't."

My statement turned Andy's smile into a scowl, but Mrs. Tabor looked pleased.

We ended the meeting with an agreement to meet again in two months. "Work on the little ways of helping one another," Mrs. Tabor suggested. We all said we'd try.

In November, a new couple joined our parents group. That same night Betty and Art Lehman came in late. Betty looked as if candles had been lit behind her eyes. She glowed.

"We're here to say goodbye," she said in her gentle voice. "Jacob is coming home. For good."

"No foolin'!" Cora whooped. "That's terrific. Ain't it terrific, Harry?"

"Yeah."

"Congratulations," Bill said. "I don't know Jacob, but I've seen big changes in you, Betty."

"I'm happy for you." Millie sounded wistful.

"We know there's no happy-ever-after," Art said, "but now that Jacob has learned to deal openly with his anger—"

"Me, too," Betty added.

"Don't we know it!" Cora shouted, and everyone laughed, remembering our stormy group meetings when Betty began to let out all the anger she had buried for years.

"What about the grandparents?" Bill asked.

"Visits will be strictly monitored," Art said. "But now that Jacob—and Betty—feel so much better about themselves, they think they can handle Betty's parents."

"We're getting there too, ain't we, Harry?" Cora said and smiled.

The new couple, Jim and Amorline Anderson, glanced at each other. "It's hard, isn't it? Coming here?," I said impulsively. "I had a dreadful time accepting it."

Betty Lehman laughed. "That's for sure."

"You were so defensive," Art added, "that I didn't like you very much. You looked at the rest of us as if we were bugs."

"But you were hardest on yourself," Betty said. "You're so much more accepting now. And we like you so much."

Her words touched me. I could see the changes in her. How wonderful that she saw changes in me, too.

"How do you feel about yourself as a parent?" Dr. Kruepper asked me.

I looked at the new couple, then at Bill. "Well, when we first got married, I think Bill and I made an unconscious contract: he was the perfect parent, I was the failure parent. Now"—I smiled and reached for my husband's hand—"I feel as if Bill is still a great parent, but not perfect. And I've made mistakes, but I'm not a total failure."

"In other words," Mrs. Tabor said, "you can say to Bill: 'You're okay and I'm okay.'"

I laughed. "Sounds like a good title for a book. But yes, I guess that's where we are now."

"Feeling okay about yourself is the first step to feeling

okay about your child," Kruepper said with a meaningful glance at Cora.

It seemed as if, for all of us, there was real movement that fall. Progress at last. Then Christmas came, and with it, disaster.

Our friends, the Duggans, had suggested we share another holiday ski vacation. The kids were overjoyed. So were Bill and I. For all of us, last year's trip had left shining memories. Bill's daughter had other plans for Christmas this year, but John could definitely go along, Mrs. Tabor said.

"Wahooo! Skiing is absolutely my favorite thing to do!" he shouted.

"Remember, John," Mrs. Tabor cautioned, "you'll have to reach Level Three and stay there."

"I will! You bet I will! Skiing's like flying. You feel so free when you ski. Oh, gee, Mom, Bill, I can hardly wait!" His eyes held a light that made me reach over and hug him.

It was three weeks before Christmas. Our plan was to leave Christmas afternoon for the Rockies. At the Home, John could talk of little else. On the bus going to school, at meals, when he played pick-up pool or bounced a basketball around the court, he talked about the ski trip.

"John," Connoli said finally, "will you shut up about skiing? You're getting on the other kids' nerves."

"I'm sorry, Mr. Connoli." John's grin was infectious. "I'm just so darn happy. I'm doing good in school, I'm getting my shit together, I really am, and with the ski trip—it's like flying, Mr. Connoli. You gotta try it some day. It's the most wonderful feeling in the world!"

"Okay, okay," Connoli laughed. "Just cool it a little bit with the other boys, all right?"

"Yes, sir." John's grin widened. "But I'm so excited!"

He could hardly wait, he felt so full of exuberant energy. Three weeks seemed forever. Would the days never pass? At school, he could scarcely sit through classes. He stared

257

out windows, watching the sky for snow, thinking about the snowy mountains and what it was like to swoop down the face of a wide mountain bowl. Beneath his desk, his feet tapped to a hidden rhythm. Students replied with smiles to his wide grin as he walked through the school halls.

Two weeks to go. He asked for passes. Please, could he go to the bathroom? He began smoking again. After three suspensions last year, John had dropped his cigarette habit during school, but smoking killed time, seven minutes a cigarette. He had clocked it once.

Ten days to go. John asked for a pass out of study hall to go to the bathroom. And that's where the vice-principal discovered him.

"Mr. Dougherty!" John gasped.

Dougherty, a thin man with a large adam's apple, plucked the cigarette from John's limp fingers. "Might have known it would be one of you Boys' Home boys. Come with me."

John's skin grew cold. He heard a buzzing in his ears. He felt as if someone had hit him in the belly.

"God almighty," Connoli said when he arrived with the Boys' Home van. "Why the devil did you mess up, Bartocci? You had so much going for you!"

"Go to hell," John muttered slumping against the door. "I'm not the first guy who snuck into their damned johns to smoke. Shit, why am I always the one to get caught? It's not fair."

Mrs. Tabor marched into his dorm room, her high heels clicking against the tiled floor. Her face held an expression he'd never seen before. She looked angry, but something else as well, something he couldn't fathom.

"Why, John? Why?"

"A lot of guys smoke in the john," he sulked. "They don't get suspended."

"I don't care about the other guys. You will be on full room restriction as well as work detail. I've also talked with your parents and we agree. You'll have to wait until next year to go skiing."

"What?" He grabbed her hands so hard, she winced.

"No, please, Mrs. Tabor. I'm sorry. I'm so sorry, but don't make me miss the ski trip. Please, please. I'll work seven hours a day, serve a month's room restriction, anything. Only, please, let me go skiing." Tears poured down his cheeks, ran in rivulets into his shirt collar.

Her voice was stiff. "You'll see your family on Christmas morning and return here in the afternoon." She turned to leave, then abruptly spun around. "Other people care, too, John. It's not just yourself you've hurt!" With that, she was gone.

He stood transfixed. His trips had mattered to her, too. That was it. It was a victory for her. And now he had failed her, not just himself. No, he wouldn't think that. He had to hold on to his anger. It wasn't fair. The world was treating him like shit again.

He flung himself back on his bed, but something was wrong. He couldn't hold on to his anger at Dougherty, or Mrs. Tabor, or Connoli. He kept hearing a whisper. "You dummy. You did it to yourself. How could you blow a ski trip for a lousy cigarette? You dummy."

He tried, every day until Christmas, to change Mrs. Tabor's mind. "Why can't I go skiing? Please. Please let me go."

To every entreaty she simply shook her head. "You break rules. You lose privileges. That's the name of the game. You've been here long enough to know that, John. In fact, it's because you've been here so long that I'm being so tough. You knew better."

"Yeah," he said bitterly. "I knew I shouldn't get caught."

"If you're still thinking like that, you're in worse shape than I thought."

"Well, what if I am? I told you when I first came here, you'd never change me."

For the first time, she smiled briefly. "Oh, but you have changed, John. More than you know."

He wasn't sure how to reply so he fell into a sulky silence.

* * *

Christmas morning dawned cold, with grey skies and a hint of snow. I picked John up at seven.

Bill and I had spent hours, days, talking about John and the ski trip. I had wept. "But I want him to go!" And Bill and Mrs. Tabor had insisted that it was not in his best interests to go. He had to be made to see cause and effect.

"Like our first Thanksgiving visit," Bill reminded me.

"Remember your letter," Mrs. Tabor said.

I knew they were right. And yet...

I opened the car door and John slid in beside me. My tires spun against the gravel. For the first few minutes of the drive home, we were both silent. I spoke first.

"I was heartbroken when Mrs. Tabor called. We'll miss you on the ski trip, John. We thought it would be such a special family Christmas." I felt my throat constrict with the effort to hold back tears.

"You don't really care. Not as long as Allison and Andy are along. You've never cared about me."

For an instant, just an instant, he hooked the little child in me. Words came rushing up, angry words, the kind of words I would have used in years past, hurtful words that would have pulled us both into a no-win confrontation. I gripped the steering wheel hard. And then, suddenly, the angry words were gone. I was not a defensive, hurt child. I was an adult, with a responsibility to be a loving but firm parent. How wonderful to recognize that in myself.

"John," I said, "let's try to have a nice time opening presents and eating dinner. There will be another chance for you to go skiing with us, and it won't be that far in the future."

From the sudden relaxation in his body and the shift in his expression, I could tell I had said the right thing. He'd gotten my message. "You're an okay person. You made a mistake and you've got to pay for it, but you're still okay, and we love you." Although we didn't say much the rest of the way home, it was a peaceful, friendly silence.

The minute we walked inside, Allison ran up to John, threw her arms around him, and give him a big hug and kiss. "I'm so glad to see you, John!"

"I can't believe that old witch won't let you go skiing," Andy said.

Bill emerged from the kitchen, wearing his red apron and holding a wooden spoon. "Merry Christmas, son!"

John sniffed the rich aroma of roasting turkey and grinned. "I smell Christmas!" He heard Christmas too. Carols played on the stereo. Bill had even started a fire while I was gone.

"I can't wait for tomorrow," Andy said as we gathered around the tree. "I'm going to ski the whole mountain!"

"Hey," I said quickly, "I thought we agreed not to talk about the ski trip."

But John surprised me. "It's okay, Mom. If I can't go, well, at least I can talk about it. I love to talk about skiing. Anyway," he added, as Bill handed out the first gift, "it's my own fault I'm not going. I was the one who blew it."

There was a long moment of silence. Then Bill spoke. "Did I hear you right?" he asked, and without waiting for an answer, he wrapped John in a sudden, exuberant hug. "I'm proud of you, son."

At that moment, despite his disappointment, John looked proud of himself.

CHAPTER THIRTY-FOUR

I SAT IN the crowded restaurant and tried to decide between the chocolate derby pie — a house specialty — or my diet. "Oh, go ahead," Tina urged. "It's your birthday." For four years, we had taken each other out for lunch on our birthdays. I debated for another few seconds, then ordered the pie. Why not? I was celebrating more than my February birthday.

At our last meeting, Mrs. Tabor had given me good news.

"I've seen a remarkable change in John since Christmas. He's put in a new request for Level Three, and he's asked me to help him develop a list of goals." Her blue eyes had twinkled. "We started with authority figures. Learning how to deal with them."

She had another piece of good news. "Staff has agreed. Starting next week, we're going to send John home every weekend. It's on a trial basis, mind you, but we think it might be the right move."

"Whoopee!" John had shouted. "I'm going to be a real member of my family again!"

The waiter brought us two pieces of pie. Tina reached for her fork. "So, you think you've reached a real turning point?"

I held up crossed fingers. "It's starting to look that way." I no longer felt awkward discussing the Boys' Home with Tina. "It's as if John and I—and our whole family—finally understand how each one of us has contributed to our problems. Now that we do, we can make changes. Sounds simple, doesn't it? I wonder why it took so long?"

"Simple isn't the same as easy."

I laughed, thinking of the hours I sometimes spent to come up with a headline for an ad. The best headlines always seemed wonderfully simple—after they were created.

"You're right." I lifted my last forkful of pie. "Hold the thought that John will soon come home for good."

Connoli smiled in satisfaction. The gym echoed with boys' shouts and the thumping sound of sneakers and balls hitting the court, but Connoli's attention was on the volleyball game that was ending. The Southeast Dorm had lost again, but damn if Bartocci wasn't holding his temper. He'd even helped a couple of the younger boys instead of yelling at them.

The dorm counselor hitched up his pants and strolled toward the players as they came off the court. When he reached Bartocci, he clapped him on the back. "What's getting in to you, John? You're acting like a goddam member of a team."

John grinned and wiped sweat off his forehead with the back of his hand.

On a blustery day in early March, the staff gathered in Dr. Kruepper's office for spring Treatment Reviews. When Bartocci's name came up, Dr. Kruepper handed around copies of a report from their testing psychologist.

"The last psychological evaluations on John were administered shortly after he entered the Boys' Home. He's shown so much improvement in the last quarter, I requested a follow up evaluation from Dr. Gorsuch.

"As you recall, in the earlier test, John exhibited strong feelings of loss and image impairment. His picture of a butterfly with broken wings, for instance. Now," he tapped the one-page report—"Gorsuch says when John was asked to make up stories based on pictures of boys, he described boys who feel motivated, want to achieve, are inner directed, and show some amount of internalized ego ideal."

"The tests still show some conflict regarding his parents," Mrs. Tabor observed.

"Yes, some anger remains, but John also sees more nurturing in the mother figure. And the abandonment theme doesn't appear as it did earlier."

Joe Connoli spoke with force. "For two years I've watched John either bully the younger boys or let himself be bullied by kids like Leo, but in the last couple of months, there's been none of it. He's impatient and he still loses his temper, but his explosions don't come as often or last as long. No question in my mind that his relationship with staff and peers is radically improved."

Mrs. Tabor nodded. "I can say the same for John and his family, especially his mother. The family has begun to function again."

"Sounds like we finally found the key," Kruepper said with a thoughtful puff on his pipe.

Around the table, heads nodded.

* * *

In late March, the boys elected John president of his dorm. It was a high honor and it seemed to give him a new presence.

He continued to spend weekends at home, and so integrated had our family become, that, for all of us, it began to seem as if John simply resided at a boys' school instead of a psychiatric treatment center.

One Sunday afternoon I asked John if he'd like to go downtown with me. I had to pick up a television script in my office, and John could use his learner's permit to practice driving. He jumped at the chance.

While I retrieved the script, John waited in the wide-windowed lobby. When I came out, I found him standing at the window, watching a small plane take off from the nearby executive airport.

"You know," he said softly, as I went and stood beside him, and we watched the yellow plane climb, "I guess I'll always feel a little empty space. I wanted my Daddy to come home so bad."

"So did I, John. But do you know what happened to my empty space?"

"What?"

"It turned into a small golden hoop—that's how I see it, anyway—a bright golden circle of love for your father that's always going to be there in my heart, but the circle is complete. Now that it's closed I can go on. I'll never lose it, but it doesn't ache any more."

He had grown so tall, he had to look down at me. "Are you making that up?"

"No, not a bit. That's how I picture it in my mind."

The little plane had almost disappeared. John flung one arm around my shoulders. "A golden circle, huh?" He bent down and squeezed me in a sudden hug. "You're a neat mom."

I hugged him back, my big, tall strapping young son that I loved, and liked so very much. "You're a neat son."

* * *

In May, Mrs. Tabor asked if both Bill and I could meet with her on the following Tuesday. Her window was open to the warm spring air as we settled ourselves in our familiar chairs.

A fluttery sensation rippled in my belly. I had been tempted, many times that spring, to ask if John could come home, but had forced myself to stay quiet. Hadn't I said in my letter last August that John controlled the ticket home? When Dr. Kruepper and Mrs. Tabor believed the time was right, we'd get the word. Now I wondered if the time was right.

Mrs. Tabor played with a fountain pen. An old poster was back on her wall. "Today Is the First Day of the Rest of Your Life."

After what seemed an interminable silence, she smiled and spoke. "I think we've turned the corner with John. We'll want to continue outpatient treatment but..." She leaned back in her chair, this tall, commanding woman who had been such a fixture in our lives for three years. "I think, when school gets out, your son is ready to go home."

Bill was the one who blinked back tears. "What d'ya know," he whispered. "We made it."

Summer sounds were evident as we walked into the dining room for our final parents group. Howard Boynton sat with his arms folded across his chest. Millie appeared different though, something about her posture. She sat straighter. Cora was reaching for a cookie. Beside her, Harry fidgeted with a piece of paper.

As soon as we were all seated, Harry grinned and held up the paper. "Thought I'd show you folks something. Benjie drew it of me. It ain't half bad."

He passed the paper to Millie on his left. "Why, it's quite good," she said.

She passed it to me. It was a charcoal drawing, and Millie was right. Young Benjie had captured very well the hearty lines of his father's face.

"I thought it was good," Harry said as the drawing re-

265

turned to him. He nodded in satisfaction and tucked the paper carefully into a large envelope to protect it.

Bill leaned forward. "I have an announcement. This is our last night."

"Well, ain't that something!" Cora said. "You taking your boy home?"

I nodded, feeling oddly shy, and a little detached, as if we had already separated from the group.

Millie's smile was tremulous, and her cough more noticeable. "Imagine! You haven't been here as long as we have."

"That ain't what counts," Cora said comfortingly. "Shoot, Harry and me, we been here forever. But we'll be leaving one day, won't we, Harry?"

"Gawd, I hope so!"

Everyone but Howard laughed. He stood and extended a hand to Bill. "You're luckier than some of us."

"You're luckier than you realize," Bill replied. "I hope you'll see that some day."

Dr. Kruepper tapped his pipe. "You're still going to have problems, remember. After all, so called normal families have problems and fights and disagreements. But now you're to a place where your family can stand on its own two feet. You've learned new ways to resolve your problems. And John got rid of the emotional baggage that was holding him back.

"There's no perfect way to raise kids," he continued. "Shoot, kids are different. Parents are different. What makes a good parent is the ability to recognize if you and your child need help. No need to be ashamed of that, is there, Barbara?"

It had taken a long time, but I could finally say, and mean it, "No. There's no reason to be ashamed."

We made our final trip to the Boys' Home on a Friday in early June. Dog raced our car, as usual, up the graveled road, while shouts of boys at play echoed through new-leafed trees.

Our shoes clicked against the tile floor of John's dorm. He didn't see us. He was standing near the door of a new boy's room.

"Listen," we heard him say. "You talk it out with Mrs. Tabor. She's a tough old lady but she knows what she's doing. She sure helped me."

Helped us all, I thought. Helped us when love, alone, was simply not enough.

AFTERWORD

by Bill Shirley

JOHN INTRODUCED you to our family's story. Barbara told it, warts and all. It's been seven years since John came home. I hope you will re-read his foreword. The maturity of this man should remove any doubt about what is possible when struggling parents have the courage to seek professional help and a child has the desire and ability to accept it.

John's despair was real and our remorse over our inability to provide for his needs was immense. For nearly four years, it seemed as if whatever we did only made matters worse. In hindsight, I can point to only one fundamental thing we did correctly: we did not give up. We did not quit.

Before Barbara and I decided to marry, I had to decide if I could make the same commitment to raise John and his brother and sister as I had made to raise my own three children. We considered marriage because we wanted to build a strong, loving family. It was not that I thought of myself as a replacement for their natural father, John Bartocci; but I knew I would have to accept the responsibility of succeeding him if we were going to be more than five people sharing a residence.

Barbara and I were naive regarding the complexities of creating a new family. We did our best to anticipate every conceivable problem and we discussed at length how we could handle these problems if they arose. We thought we knew exactly what we were doing. Each of us was shaken, disillusioned and, yes, angry with each other when things did not go as we had expected. It was only our commitment to each other that held us together.

I do not think it is possible to predict what life will be like in forging a new family. There are too many subtle

268

factors involved to make it possible to anticipate the results. Both partners must be willing to accept the pain of growth as natural and inevitable.

Our story shows how Barbara and I had to grow and change, along with our children, to build our family. The growing did not end when John came home. He finished high school and graduated from college with a BA degree in English and Theatre. During those years, our family experienced the usual difficulties common to any family with three teenagers moving through high school and college to become self-sustaining adults.

Today, John is working hard to become a writer. In addition to assisting his mother in writing this book, he is polishing his first novel. Allison completed a BA degree in psychology and then specialized in graphic arts. She and her husband will soon become parents. Andy is a junior at a major university, studying bio-engineering.

Our family today is more than a family; we are all good friends who greatly enjoy one another's company.

Barbara and John came to the decision to write this book only after much soul-searching. It is not easy to be so open, to be so exposed to public view. Once they decided to write it, Allison, Andy and I did everything we could to help.

We pray that our family's story gives hope and courage to all parents and step-parents who make the commitment to raise the children God places in their care.